BOOK
OF BIBLICAL
QUOTATIONS

BOOK
OF BIBLICAL
QUOTATIONS

Edited by
ANTHONY J. CASTAGNO
with
Faye C. Allen
Joseph M. Castagno

under the direction of
Lawrence Urdang

Pickering & Inglis
LONDON GLASGOW

BOOK
OF BIBLICAL
QUOTATIONS

Edited by
ANTHONY J. CASTAGNO
with
Faye C. Allen
Joseph M. Castagno

under the direction of
Lawrence Urdang

Pickering & Inglis
LONDON · GLASGOW

PREFACE

Book of Biblical Quotations is a topical anthology of better-known verses designed for use by Bible students, pastors and Bible teachers, professional speakers and writers, and laypersons who are interested in the Word of God. Its primary value is as a concise and easy-to-use reference to the most familiar or most interesting verses relating to topics ranging from biblical events and doctrines to important subjects in contemporary Christian life.

The editors have made every effort to include those verses most frequently cited for each topic and to examine closely the contexts of these quotes to avoid misinterpretations. Because of the limited size of this volume, it is suggested that the serious user treat this book as a guide to further study, searching the Scriptures in the area of a particular verse for additional information and insight.

The quotations under each topic are drawn from the Authorized King James Version and are arranged in the same order as their appearance in the Bible, from the Book of Genesis in the Old Testament through the Book of Revelation in the New Testament. Many of the topic headings are synonyms, referring the user to one or more other topics where appropriate quotations can be found. For example, **BRAVERY** See **COURAGE** indicates that the verses relating to **BRAVERY** are located under the topic **COURAGE.** Many other topics, in addition to their own quotations, include cross references that suggest other topics where further information may be found. For example, **REFUGE** cites nine verses, but also refers the user to **GOD, HELP OF; HELP;** and **PROTECTION,** three topics which include an additional twenty-nine quotations.

Containing more than 4,300 quotations arranged under almost 1,200 topics, *Book of Biblical Quotations* provides a guide for private prayer and reflection, is a ready source of scriptural references to enhance one's spoken or written presentations, and serves as a valuable aid for use in exploring the Bible.

June, 1979   *Anthony J. Castagno*

ABBREVIATIONS
Old Testament

Gen. Genesis	*Eccl.* Ecclesiastes
Exod. Exodus	*Song of Sol.* Song of Solomon
Lev. Leviticus	*Isa.* Isaiah
Num. Numbers	*Jer.* Jeremiah
Deut. Deuteronomy	*Lam.* Lamentations
Josh. Joshua	*Ezek.* Ezekiel
Judg. Judges	*Dan.* Daniel
Ruth Ruth	*Hos.* Hosea
1 Sam. 1 Samuel	*Joel* Joel
2 Sam. 2 Samuel	*Amos* Amos
1 Kings 1 Kings	*Obad.* Obadiah
2 Kings 2 Kings	*Jonah* Jonah
1 Chron. 1 Chronicles	*Mic.* Micah
2 Chron. 2 Chronicles	*Nah.* Nahum
Ezra Ezra	*Hab.* Habakkuk
Neh. Nehemiah	*Zeph.* Zephaniah
Esth. Esther	*Hag.* Haggai
Job Job	*Zech.* Zechariah
Ps. Psalms	*Mal.* Malachi
Prov. Proverbs	

ABBREVIATIONS
New Testament

Matt.	Matthew	*1 Tim.*	1 Timothy
Mark	Mark	*2 Tim.*	2 Timothy
Luke	Luke	*Titus*	Titus
John	John	*Philem.*	Philemon
Acts	Acts of the Apostles	*Heb.*	Hebrews
Rom.	Romans	*James*	James
1 Cor.	1 Corinthians	*1 Peter*	1 Peter
2 Cor.	2 Corinthians	*2 Peter*	2 Peter
Gal.	Galatians	*1 John*	1 John
Eph.	Ephesians	*2 John*	2 John
Phil.	Philippians	*3 John*	3 John
Col.	Colossians	*Jude*	Jude
1 Thess.	1 Thessalonians	*Rev.*	Revelation
2 Thess.	2 Thessalonians		

ABANDONMENT   See Desertion.
ABDUCTION   See Kidnapping.
ABOMINATION   See Decadence; Evil; Sin.
ABSENCE   See Departure.
ABSOLUTION   See Forgiveness.
ABSTINENCE   See Celibacy; Fasting; Sobriety; Virginity.
ABUNDANCE   (See also Fertility.)

1. The Lord thy God will make thee plenteous in every work of thine hand, in the fruit of thy body. *Deut. 30:9*

2. A place where there is no want of any thing that is in the earth. *Judg. 18:10*

3. My cup runneth over. *Ps. 23:5*

4. So shall thy barns be filled with plenty, and thy presses shall burst out with new wine. *Prov. 3:10*

5. I will cure them, and will reveal unto them the abundance of peace and truth. *Jer. 33:6*

6. Whosoever hath, to him shall be given, and he shall have more abundance. *Matt. 13:12*

7. As ye abound in every thing, in faith, and utterance, and knowledge, and in all diligence, and in your love to us, see that ye abound in this grace also. *2 Cor. 8:7*

8. My God shall supply all your need according to his riches in glory by Christ Jesus. *Phil. 4:19*

ABUSE   See Child Abuse; Drug Abuse; Rape.
ACCEPTANCE   (See also Approval; Belief.)

1. The Lord thy God accept thee. *2 Sam. 24:23*

2. Naked came I out of my mother's womb, and naked shall I return thither: the Lord gave, and the Lord hath taken away. *Job 1:21*

3. I will say to them which were not my people, Thou art my people; and they shall say, Thou art my God. *Hos. 2:23*

4. Whosoever shall not receive you, nor hear your words, when ye depart out of that house or city, shake off the dust of your feet. *Matt. 10:14*

5. Blessed are your eyes, for they see: and your ears, for they hear. *Matt. 13:16*

6. He that received seed into the good ground is he that heareth the word, and understandeth it. *Matt. 13:23*

7. They received the word with all readiness of mind. *Acts 17:11*

8. When ye do well, and suffer for it, ye take it patiently, this is acceptable with God. *1 Peter 2:20*

9. If any man hear my voice, and open the door, I will come in to him, and will sup with him, and he with me. *Rev. 3:20*

ACCOMPLISHMENT   (See also Fulfillment; Performance; Success.)

1. God saw every thing that he had made, and, behold, it was very good. *Gen. 1:31*

2. The house of the Lord was perfected. *2 Chron. 8:16*

3. The desire accomplished is sweet to the soul. *Prov. 13:19*

4. When they had performed all things according to the law of the Lord, they returned into Galilee. *Luke 2:39*

5. I have finished the work which thou gavest me to do. *John 17:4*

6. After this, Jesus knowing that all things were now accomplished, that the scripture might be fulfilled. *John 19:28*

7. I have fought a good fight, I have finished my course, I have kept the faith. *2 Tim. 4:7*

8. There came a great voice out of the temple of heaven, from the throne, saying, It is done. *Rev. 16:17*

ACCUSATION   (See also Blame; Slander.)

1. Thou chargest me today with a fault concerning this woman. *2 Sam. 3:8*

2. Accuse not a servant unto his master. *Prov. 30:10*

3. The chief priests accused him of many things: but he answered nothing. *Mark 15:3*

4. Woman, where are those thine accusers? hath no man condemned thee? *John 8:10*

5. What accusation bring ye against this man? *John 18:29*

6. Against an elder receive not an accusation. *1 Tim. 5:19*

ACHIEVEMENT   See Accomplishment.

ACTION   See Performance.

ADDICTION   See Drug Abuse.

ADOLESCENCE   See Youth.

ADOPTION   (See also Family; God, Family of; Orphan; Stranger.)

1. The stranger that dwelleth with you shall be unto you as one born among you, and thou shalt love him as thyself. *Lev. 19:34*

2. I will be his father, and he shall be my son. *2 Sam. 7:14*

3. As many as received him, to them gave he power to become the sons of God, even to them that believe on his name: Which were born, not of blood, nor of the will of the flesh, nor of the will of man, but of God. *John 1:12,13*

4. As many as are led by the Spirit of God, they are the sons of God . . . ye have received the Spirit of adoption, whereby we cry, Abba, Father. *Rom. 8:14,15*

5. I will call them my people, which were not my people; and her beloved, which was not beloved. *Rom. 9:25*

6. I will receive you, and will be a Father unto you, and ye shall be my sons and daughters. *2 Cor. 6:17-18*

7. Having predestinated us unto the adoption of children by Jesus Christ to himself. *Eph. 1:5*

ADORATION   See Worship.

ADULTERY   (See also Lust; Promiscuity.)

1. Behold, thou art but a dead man, for the woman which thou hast taken; for she is a man's wife. *Gen. 20:3*

2. Thou shalt not commit adultery. *Exod. 20:14*

3. The eye also of the adulterer waiteth for the twilight, saying, No eye shall see me: and disguiseth his face. *Job 24:15*

4. Whosoever looketh on a woman to lust after her hath committed adultery with her already in his heart. *Matt. 5:28*

5. Out of the heart proceed evil thoughts, murders, adulteries, fornications, thefts, false witness, blasphemies. *Matt. 15:19*

6. The works of the flesh are manifest, which are these; adultery, fornication, uncleanness, lasciviousness. *Gal. 5:19*

ADVANCEMENT   See Improvement; Self-Improvement.

ADVERSARY   See Enemy.

ADVICE   See Counsel.

ADVOCATE   See Mediation.

AFFECTION   (See also Brotherhood; Friendship; Love.)

1. A band of men, whose hearts God had touched. *1 Sam. 10:26*

2. Thy love to me was wonderful, passing the love of women. *2 Sam. 1:26*

3. How excellent is thy loving-kindness, O God! *Ps. 36:7*

4. Because thy loving-kindness is better than life, my lips shall praise thee. *Ps. 63:3*

5. Be kindly affectioned one to another with brotherly love. *Rom. 12:10*

6. Set your affection on things above, not on things on the earth. *Col. 3:2*

AFFLICTION   See Burden; Distress; Handicap; Illness; Suffering; Trouble.

AFFLUENCE   See Wealth.

AGED

1. As thy days, so shall thy strength be. *Deut. 33:25*

2. With the ancient is wisdom; and in length of days understanding. *Job 12:12*

3. I have been young, and now am old; yet have I not seen the righteous forsaken, nor his seed begging bread. *Ps. 37:25*

4. Thou hast made my days as a hand-breadth; and mine age is as nothing before thee. *Ps. 39:5*

5. Cast me not off in the time of old age; forsake me not when my strength faileth. *Ps. 71:9*

6. They shall still bring forth fruit in old age. *Ps. 92:14*

7. The hoary head is a crown of glory. *Prov. 16:31*

8. Despise not thy mother when she is old. *Prov. 23:22*

9. We all do fade as a leaf. *Isa. 64:6*

10. When thou wast young, thou girdedst thyself, and walkedst whither thou wouldest: but when thou shalt be old, thou shalt stretch forth thy hands, and another shall gird thee, and carry thee whither thou wouldest not. *John 21:18*

AGGRESSIVENESS   (See also Ambition.)

1. Frowardness is in his heart, he deviseth mischief continually; he soweth discord. *Prov. 6:14*

2. The wicked flee when no man pursueth: but the righteous are bold as a lion. *Prov. 28:1*

3. What is a man profited, if he shall gain the whole world, and lose his own soul? *Matt. 16:26*

4. Every man that striveth for the mastery is temperate in all things. Now they do it to obtain a corruptible crown. *1 Cor. 9:25*

5. Whereinsoever any is bold . . . I am bold also. *2 Cor. 11:21*

6. The servant of the Lord must not strive. *2 Tim. 2:24*

AGNOSTICISM   (See also Atheism; Faithlessness.)

1. They are a very froward generation, children in whom is no faith. *Deut. 32:20*

2. They believed not in God, and trusted not in his salvation. *Ps. 78:22*

3. He marvelled because of their unbelief. *Mark 6:6*

4. He that believeth not shall be damned. *Mark 16:16*

5. Art thou the Christ? tell us. And he said unto them, If I tell you, ye will not believe. *Luke 22:67*

6. What if some did not believe? shall their unbelief make the faith of God without effect? *Rom. 3:3*

7. Unto them that are defiled and unbelieving is nothing pure; but even their mind and conscience is defiled. *Titus 1:15*

AGONY   See Suffering.

AGREEMENT   See Covenant; Unity.

AGRICULTURE   See Farming.

AID   See God, Help Of; Help; Relief.

AIMLESSNESS

1. Your children shall wander in the wilderness forty years. *Num. 14:33.*

2. They grope in the dark without light, and he maketh them to stagger like a drunken man. *Job 12:25*

3. Let me not wander from thy commandments. *Ps. 119:10*

4. My people hath been lost sheep: their shepherds have caused them to go astray . . . they have forgotten their restingplace. *Jer. 50:6*

5. They have wandered as blind men. *Lam. 4:14*

6. They shall be as the morning cloud, and as the early dew that passeth away, as the chaff that is driven with the whirlwind out of the floor, and as the smoke out of the chimney. *Hos. 13:3*

7. Wandering stars, to whom is reserved the blackness of darkness for ever. *Jude 1:13*

ALCOHOLISM   See Drug Abuse; Drunkenness.

ALERTNESS   See Vigilance.

ALIEN   See Stranger.

ALLEGATION   See Accusation.

ALLEGIANCE   See Faithfulness; Loyalty.

ALMIGHTY   See God, The Almighty.

ALMSGIVING   See Charity; Giving.

ALTERNATIVE   See Choice.

ALTRUISM   See Generosity; Unselfishness.

AMAZEMENT   See Wonder.

AMBASSADOR   See Angel; Forerunner.

AMBITION   (See also Aggressiveness.)

1. Let us build us a city and a tower, whose top may reach unto heaven. *Gen. 11:4*

2. That I were made judge in the land, that every man which hath any suit or cause might come unto me. *2 Sam. 15:4*

3. Their inward thought is, that their houses shall continue for ever, and their dwelling places to all generations. *Ps. 49:11*

4. Grant that these my two sons may sit, the one on thy right hand, and the other on the left, in thy kingdom. *Matt. 20:21*

5. I will pull down my barns, and build greater. *Luke 12:18*

6. Seek that ye may excel to the edifying of the church. *1 Cor. 14:12*

7. I press toward the mark for the prize of the high calling of God in Christ Jesus. *Phil. 3:14*

8. Having therefore, brethren, boldness to enter into the holiest by the blood of Jesus. *Heb. 10:19*

AMENDS   See Restitution.

AMNESTY   See Forgiveness.

AMUSEMENT   (See also Dancing; Pleasure; Sports.)

1. The people sat down to eat and to drink, and rose up to play. *Exod. 32:6*

2. All the people went their way to eat, and to drink, and to send portions, and to make great mirth. *Neh. 8:12*

3. Our mouth filled with laughter, and our tongue with singing. *Ps. 126:2*

4. A merry heart maketh a cheerful countenance. *Prov. 15:13*

5. Let thy heart cheer thee in the days of thy youth. *Eccl. 11:9*

6. The city shall be full of boys and girls playing in the streets. *Zech. 8:5*

7. The earth shall rejoice over them, and make merry, and shall send gifts one to another. *Rev. 11:10*

ANARCHY   See Chaos.

ANATHEMA   See Excommunication.

ANCESTRY   See Genealogy.

ANGEL   (See also Demons; Forerunner.)

1. He shall send his angel before thee. *Gen. 24:7*

2. A ladder set up on the earth, and the top of it reached to heaven: and behold the angels of God ascending and descending on it. *Gen. 28:12*

3. He [God] shall give his angels charge over thee, to keep thee in all thy ways. *Ps. 91:11*

4. Angels came and ministered unto him. *Matt. 4:11*

5. There was with the angel a multitude of the heavenly host praising God. *Luke 2:13*

6. Be not forgetful to entertain strangers: for thereby some have entertained angels unawares. *Heb. 13:2*

7. Four angels standing on the four corners of the earth, holding the four winds of the earth. *Rev. 7:1*

ANGER   (See also God, Wrath of; Resentment.)

1. Thou sentest forth thy wrath, which consumed them as stubble. *Exod. 15:7*

2. Wrath killeth the foolish man. *Job 5:2*

3. O Lord, rebuke me not in thine anger, neither chasten me in thy hot displeasure. *Ps. 6:1*

4. His [the Lord's] anger endureth but a moment. *Ps. 30:5*

5. A soft answer turneth away wrath: but grievous words stir up anger. *Prov. 15:1*

6. He that is slow to anger is better than the mighty; and he that ruleth his spirit than he that taketh a city. *Prov. 16:32*

7. The discretion of a man deferreth his anger; and it is his glory to pass over a transgression. *Prov. 19:11*

8. Whosoever is angry with his brother without a cause shall be in danger of the judgment. *Matt. 5:22*

9. Let not the sun go down upon your wrath. *Eph. 4:26*

10. Provoke not your children to anger. *Col. 3:21*

11. Let every man be . . . slow to wrath: For the wrath of man worketh not the righteousness of God. *James 1:19,20*

ANGUISH   See Heartbreak; Sorrow.

ANIMAL   (See also Natural Religion.)

1. God created great whales, and every living creature that moveth. *Gen. 1:21*

2. God made the beast of the earth after his kind, and cattle after their kind, and every thing that creepeth upon the earth after his kind: and God saw that it was good. *Gen. 1:25*

3. The beasts of the field shall be at peace with thee. *Job 5:23*

4. Every beast of the forest is mine, and the cattle upon a thousand hills. *Ps. 50:10*

5. A righteous man regardeth the life of his beast. *Prov. 12:10*

6. Every creature of God is good. *1 Tim. 4:4*

ANIMOSITY   See Hatred; Hostility; Malice.

ANSWER   (See also Fulfillment; Prayer.)

1. My righteousness [shall] answer for me in time to come. *Gen. 30:33*

2. The Lord hath given me my petition which I asked of him. *1 Sam. 1:27*

3. God is departed from me, and answereth me no more, neither by prophets, nor by dreams. *1 Sam. 28:15*

4. Every man shall kiss his lips that giveth a right answer. *Prov. 24:26*

5. Answer not a fool according to his folly. *Prov. 26:4*

6. Give an answer to every man that asketh you a reason of the hope that is in you with meekness and fear. *1 Peter 3:15*

ANTAGONISM   See Hostility.

ANTICHRIST   See Cults, Religious; False Prophet.

ANTICIPATION   See Expectation; Hope.

ANXIETY   See Distress; Worry.

APATHY   (See also Indifference.)

1. Whoso stoppeth his ears at the cry of the poor, he also shall cry himself, but shall not be heard. *Prov. 21:13*

2. They regard not the work of the Lord, neither consider the operation of his hands. *Isa. 5:12*

3. Rise up, ye women that are at ease; hear my voice, ye careless daughters. *Isa. 32:9*

4. They hear thy words, but they do them not. *Ezek. 33:32*

5. Gallio cared for none of these things. *Acts 18:17*

6. Because thou art lukewarm, and neither cold nor hot, I will spue thee out of my mouth. *Rev. 3:16*

APOSTASY   See Backsliding, Heresy.

APOSTLE   (See also Bishop; Disciple; Follower.)

1. They straightway left their nets, and followed him. *Matt. 4:20*

2. They foresook all, and followed him. *Luke 5:11*

3. He [Jesus] chose twelve, whom also he named apostles; Simon, (whom he also named Peter,) and Andrew his brother, James and John, Philip and Bartholomew, Matthew and Thomas, James . . . and Simon called Zelotes, and Judas the brother of James, and Judas Iscariot, which also was the traitor. *Luke 6:13–16*

4. If ye continue in my word, then are ye my disciples indeed. *John 8:31*

5. I am the least of the apostles, that am not meet to be called an apostle, because I persecuted the church of God. *1 Cor. 15:9*

6. Paul, an apostle of Jesus Christ by the will of God. *2 Cor. 1:1*

7. He gave some, apostles; and some, prophets; and some, evangelists. *Eph. 4:11*

APPAREL   See Dress.

APPARITION   See Appearance.

APPEARANCE   (See also Beauty; Dream; Hypocrisy; Transfiguration.)

1. The angel of the Lord appeared unto him [Moses] in a flame of fire out of the midst of a bush . . . the bush burned with fire, and the bush was not consumed. *Exod. 3:2*

2. Look not on his countenance, or on the height of his stature . . . for the Lord seeth not as a man seeth; for man looketh on the outward appearance, but the Lord looketh on the heart. *1 Sam. 16:7*

3. When ye fast, be not, as the hypocrites, of a sad countenance: for they disfigure their faces, that they may appear unto men to fast. . . . But thou, when thou fastest . . . appear not unto men to fast, but unto thy Father which is in secret. *Matt. 6:16–18*

4. Judge not according to the appearance. *John 7:24*

5. When he shall appear, we shall be like him; for we shall see him as he is. *1 John 3:2*

APPRECIATION   (See also Praise; Thanksgiving.)

1. Thou art worth ten thousand of us. *2 Sam. 18:3*

2. I will call on the Lord, who is worthy to be praised. *2 Sam. 22:4*

3. It [wisdom] cannot be valued with the gold of Ophir, with the precious onyx, or the sapphire. *Job 28:16*

4. She [wisdom] is more precious than rubies. *Prov. 3:15*

5. The workman is worthy of his meat. *Matt. 10:10*

6. Ye are of more value than many sparrows. *Matt. 10:31*

7. Let each esteem other better than themselves. *Phil. 2:3*

APPROVAL   (See also Blessing.)

1. This is my beloved Son, in whom I am well pleased. *Matt. 3:17*

2. Well done, thou good and faithful servant. *Matt. 25:21*

3. Study to show thyself approved unto God. *2 Tim. 2:15*

4. With such sacrifices God is well pleased. *Heb. 13:16*

5. We keep his commandments, and do those things that are pleasing in his sight. *1 John 3:22*

ARDOR See Zeal.

ARGUMENT (See also Protest.)

1. What doth your arguing reprove? *Job 6:25*

2. I would order my cause before him, and fill my mouth with arguments. *Job 23:4*

3. Debate thy cause with thy neighbor himself; and discover not a secret to another. *Prov. 25:9*

4. The Lord hath a controversy with the nations. *Jer. 25:31*

5. They had disputed among themselves, who should be the greatest. *Mark 9:34*

6. There arose no small stir about that way. *Acts 19:23*

7. Lest there be debates, envyings, wraths, strifes, backbitings, whisperings, swellings, tumults. *2 Cor. 12:20*

8. Do all things without murmurings and disputings. *Phil. 2:14*

9. If any man have a quarrel against any; even as Christ forgave you, so also do ye. *Col. 3:13*

ARMY See Army, Christian; Draft, Military; War.

ARMY, CHRISTIAN (See also Disciple; Fighting; War.)

1. We wrestle not against flesh and blood, but against principalities, against powers, against the rulers of the darkness of this world, against spiritual wickedness in high places. *Eph. 6:12*

2. Take unto you the whole armor of God. . . . having your loins girt about with truth, and having on the breastplate of righteousness; And your feet shod with the preparation of the gospel of peace . . . taking the shield of faith, . . . the helmet of salvation, and the sword of the Spirit, which is the word of God. *Eph. 6:13-17*

3. Endure hardness, as a good soldier of Jesus Christ. *2 Tim. 2:3*

ARROGANCE See Boasting; Pride; Vanity.

ARSON (See also Fire.)

1. He that kindled the fire shall surely make restitution. *Exod. 22:6*

2. He had set the brands of fire, . . . and burnt up . . . the vineyards and olives. *Judg. 15:5*

3. He [Absalom] said unto his servants, See, Joab's field is near mine, and he hath barley there; go and set it on fire. And Absalom's servants set the field on fire. *2 Sam. 14:30*

4. Zimri . . . went into the palace of the king's house, and burnt the king's house over him with fire. *1 Kings 16:18*

5. They have cast fire into thy sanctuary, they have defiled by casting down the dwelling place of thy name to the ground. *Ps. 74:7*

ASSASSINATION   (See also Murder.)

1. Cursed be he that smiteth his neighbour secretly. *Deut. 27:24*

2. Ehud put forth his left hand, and took the dagger from his right thigh, and thrust it into his [Eglon's] belly. *Judg. 3:21*

3. Joab took him [Abner] aside . . . and smote him there under the fifth rib, that he died. *2 Sam. 3:27*

4. How much more, when wicked men have slain a righteous person in his own house upon his bed? shall I not therefore now require his blood of your hand, and take you away from the earth? *2 Sam. 4:11*

ASSISTANCE   See God, Help of; Help; Relief.

ASTROLOGY   (See also Fortunetelling; Occult; Paganism.)

1. [Take good heed] lest thou lift up thine eyes unto heaven, and when thou seest the sun, and the moon, and the stars, even all the host of heaven, shouldest be driven to worship them, and serve them. *Deut: 4:19*

2. Let now the astrologers, the stargazers, the monthly prognosticators, stand up, and save thee from these things that shall come upon thee. . . . The fire shall burn them; they shall not deliver themselves from the power of the flame. *Isa. 47:13–14*

3. Learn not the way of the heathen, and be not dismayed at the signs of heaven; for the heathen are dismayed at them. *Jer. 10:2*

4. In all matters of wisdom and understanding . . . he found them [four holy children] ten times better than all the magicians and astrologers that were in all his realm. *Dan. 1:20*

5. The secret which the king hath demanded cannot the wise men, the astrologers, the magicians, the soothsayers, show unto the king; But there is a God in heaven that revealeth secrets. *Dan. 2:27–28*

ASYLUM   See Refuge.

ATHEISM   (See also Agnosticism; Faithlessness.)

1. Curse God, and die. *Job 2:9*

2. The wicked, through the pride of his countenance, will not seek after God: God is not in all his thoughts. *Ps. 10:4*

3. The fool hath said in his heart, There is no God. *Ps. 14:1*
4. She [Samaria] hath rebelled against her God. *Hos. 13:16*
5. If any man love not the Lord Jesus Christ, let him be Anathema Maranatha. *1 Cor. 16:22*
6. [False prophets] denying the Lord that bought them, and bring upon themselves swift destruction. *2 Peter 2:1*
7. Ungodly men, turning the grace of our God into lasciviousness, and denying the only Lord God, and our Lord Jesus Christ. *Jude 1:4*

ATONEMENT   (See also Christ, Crucifixion of; Forgiveness; Mediation; Remission of Sins; Reunion; Salvation.)
1. He was wounded for our transgressions, he was bruised for our iniquities: the chastisement of our peace was upon him; and with his stripes we are healed. *Isa. 53:5*
2. This is my blood of the new testament, which is shed for many for the remission of sins. *Matt. 26:28*
3. Behold the Lamb of God, which taketh away the sin of the world. *John 1:29*
4. We were reconciled to God by the death of his Son, much more, being reconciled, we shall be saved by his life. And not only so, but we also joy in God through our Lord Jesus Christ, by whom we have now received the atonement. *Rom. 5:10,11*
5. He [Christ] is the mediator of the new testament, that by means of death, for the redemption of the transgressions that were under the first testament, they which are called might receive the promise of eternal inheritance. . . . all things are by the law purged with blood; and without shedding of blood is no remission. *Heb. 9:15,22*
6. Christ also hath once suffered for sins, the just for the unjust, that he might bring us to God, being put to death in the flesh, but quickened by the Spirit. *1 Peter 3:18*
7. The blood of Jesus Christ his Son cleanseth us from all sin. *1 John 1:7*

ATTORNEY   See Lawyer.
AUTHORITY   (See also God, Power of; Influence; Power.)
1. When the righteous are in authority, the people rejoice. *Prov. 29:2*
2. For he taught them as one having authority, and not as the scribes. *Matt. 7:29*

3. They [princes of the Gentiles] that are great exercise authority. *Matt. 20:25*

4. Jesus came . . . saying, All power is given unto me in heaven and in earth. *Matt. 28:18*

5. With authority commandeth he even the unclean spirits, and they do obey him. *Mark 1:27*

6. He . . . gave them [the disciples] power and authority over all devils, and to cure diseases. *Luke 9:1*

7. Servants, obey in all things your masters according to the flesh. *Col. 3:22*

8. [Jesus Christ] is on the right hand of God; angels and authorities and powers being made subject unto him. *1 Peter 3:22*

9. He that overcometh, and keepeth my works unto the end, to him will I give power over the nations. *Rev. 2:26*

AUTONOMY   See Independence.

AVARICE   See Greed.

AWARENESS   See Realization; Understanding.

AWE   See Fear of the Lord; Wonder.

B

BABY (See also Birth; Children.)
1. Out of the mouth of babes and sucklings hast thou ordained strength. *Ps. 8:2*
2. I will give children to be their princes, and babes shall rule over them. *Isa. 3:4*
3. Can a woman forget her sucking child, that she should not have compassion on the son of her womb? *Isa. 49:15*
4. When Elisabeth heard the salutation of Mary, the babe leaped in her womb. *Luke 1:41*
5. Ye shall find the babe wrapped in swaddling clothes, lying in a manger. *Luke 2:12*
6. They brought unto him also infants, that he would touch them. *Luke 18:15*
7. I . . . could not speak unto you as unto spiritual, but as unto carnal, even as unto babes in Christ. *1 Cor. 3:1*

BACKBITING See Slander.

BACKSLIDING (See also Reform.)
1. Return, ye backsliding children, and I will heal your backslidings. *Jer. 3:22*
2. Thou has forsaken me, saith the Lord, thou art gone backward: therefore will I stretch out my hand against thee, and destroy thee. *Jer. 15:6*
3. No man, having put his hand to the plough, and looking back, is fit for the kingdom of God. *Luke 9:62*
4. Then said Jesus unto the twelve, will ye also go away? *John 6:67*
5. After that ye have known God, . . . how turn ye again to the weak and beggarly elements, whereunto ye desire again to be in bondage? *Gal. 4:9*

6. If after they have escaped the pollutions of the world through the knowledge of the Lord and Savior Jesus Christ, they are again entangled therein, and overcome, the latter end is worse with them than the beginning. *2 Peter 2:20*

7. I have somewhat against thee, because thou hast left thy first love. *Rev. 2:4*

BANISHMENT   See Excommunication; Exile; Exorcism.

BAPTISM   (See also Born Again; Revival.)

1. Wash me thoroughly from mine iniquity, and cleanse me from my sin . . . I shall be whiter than snow. *Ps. 51:2,7*

2. Then will I sprinkle clean water upon you, and ye shall be clean: from all your filthiness, and from all your idols, will I cleanse you. *Ezek. 36:25*

3. I indeed baptize you with water unto repentance: but he that cometh after me is mightier than I, whose shoes I am not worthy to bear: he shall baptize you with the Holy Ghost, and with fire. *Matt. 3:11*

4. Jesus, when he was baptized, went up straightway out of the water: and, lo, the heavens were opened unto him, and he saw the Spirit of God descending like a dove, and lighting upon him: And lo a voice from heaven, saying, This is my beloved Son, in whom I am well pleased. *Matt. 3:16,17*

5. Go ye therefore, and teach all nations, baptizing them in the name of the Father, and of the Son, and of the Holy Ghost. *Matt. 28:19*

6. He that believeth and is baptized shall be saved; but he that believeth not shall be damned. *Mark 16:16*

7. Except a man be born of water and of the Spirit, he cannot enter into the kingdom of God. *John 3:5*

8. Repent, and be baptized every one of you in the name of Jesus Christ for the remission of sins, and ye shall receive the gift of the Holy Ghost. *Acts 2:38*

9. Why tarriest thou? arise, and be baptized, and wash away thy sins, calling on the name of the Lord. *Acts 22:16*

10. Know ye not, that so many of us as were baptized into Jesus Christ were baptized into his death. Therefore we are buried with him by baptism into death: that like as Christ was raised up from the dead by the glory of the Father, even so we also should walk in newness of life . . . in the likeness of his resurrection. *Rom. 6:3–5*

11. By one spirit are we all baptized into one body, whether we be Jews or Gentiles, whether we be bond or free . . . For the body is not one member, but many. *1 Cor. 12:13,14*

12. As many of you as have been baptized into Christ have put on Christ. *Gal. 3:27*

13. One Lord, one faith, one baptism. *Eph. 4:5*

14. Not by works of righteousness which we have done, but according to his mercy he saved us, by the washing of regeneration, and renewing of the Holy Ghost. *Titus 3:5*

BARRENNESS   See Sterility.

BEAST   See Animal.

BEATITUDES   (See also Blessing.)

1. Blessed are the poor in spirit: for theirs is the kingdom of heaven. *Matt. 5:3*

2. Blessed are they that mourn: for they shall be comforted. *Matt. 5:4*

3. Blessed are the meek: for they shall inherit the earth. *Matt. 5:5*

4. Blessed are they which do hunger and thirst after righteousness: for they shall be filled. *Matt. 5:6*

5. Blessed are the merciful: for they shall obtain mercy. *Matt. 5:7*

6. Blessed are the pure in heart: for they shall see God. *Matt. 5:8*

7. Blessed are the peacemakers: for they shall be called the children of God. *Matt. 5:9*

8. Blessed are they which are persecuted for righteousness' sake: for theirs is the kingdom of heaven. *Matt. 5:10*

9. Blessed are ye, when men shall revile you, and persecute you, and shall say all manner of evil against you falsely, for my sake. . . . for great is your reward in heaven. *Matt. 5:11,12*

BEAUTY   (See also Appearance; Transfiguration.)

1. The sons of God saw the daughters of men that they were fair. *Gen. 6:2*

2. Worship the Lord in the beauty of holiness. *1 Chron. 16:29*

3. Deck thyself now with majesty and excellency; and array thyself with glory and beauty. *Job 40:10*

4. Behold the beauty of the Lord. *Ps. 27:4*

5. Out of Zion, the perfection of beauty, God hath shined. *Ps. 50:2*

6. Beauty is vain. *Prov. 31:30*

7. Thine heart was lifted up because of thy beauty, thou hast corrupted thy wisdom by reason of thy brightness. *Ezek. 28:17*

BEGGAR   (See also Poverty.)
1. [The Lord] raiseth up the poor out of the dust, and lifteth up the beggar from the dunghill, to set them among princes, and to make them inherit the throne of glory. *1 Sam. 2:8*
2. I [have] not seen the righteous forsaken, nor his seed begging bread. *Ps. 37:25*
3. The sluggard will not plow by reason of the cold; therefore shall he beg in harvest, and have nothing. *Prov. 20:4*
4. To beg I am ashamed. *Luke 16:3*
5. The beggar died, and was carried by the angels into Abraham's bosom. *Luke 16:22*

BEGINNING   (See also Creation; Ending.)
1. In the beginning God created the heaven and the earth. *Gen. 1:1*
2. When I begin, I will also make an end. *1 Sam. 3:12*
3. The fear of the Lord is the beginning of wisdom. *Ps. 111:10*
4. The beginning of the gospel of Jesus Christ, the Son of God. *Mark 1:1*
5. In the beginning was the Word, and the Word was with God, and the Word was God. *John 1:1*
6. He is the head of the body, the church: who is the beginning, the firstborn from the dead. *Col. 1:18*
7. I am Alpha and Omega, the beginning and the ending. *Rev. 1:8*

BEHAVIOR   (See also Christian Obligation; Courtesy; Performance.)
1. Be strong, and quit yourselves like men. *1 Sam. 4:9*
2. Be of good courage, and let us behave ourselves valiantly. *1 Chron. 19:13*
3. Depart from evil, and do good; seek peace, and pursue it. *Ps. 34:14*
4. I will behave myself wisely in a perfect way. *Ps. 101:2*
5. They have behaved themselves ill in their doings. *Mic. 3:4*
6. All things whatsoever ye would that men should do to you, do ye even so to them. *Matt. 7:12*
7. Whatsoever ye do, do all to the glory of God. *1 Cor. 10:31*

BELIEF   (See also Christ, Belief In; Faith; Natural Religion; Trust.)
1. Believe in the Lord your God, so shall ye be established; believe his prophets, so shall ye prosper. *2 Chron. 20:20*

2. Daniel was taken up out of the den, and no manner of hurt was found upon him, because he believed in his God. *Dan. 6:23*

3. All things are possible to him that believeth. *Mark 9:23*

4. He that believeth and is baptized shall be saved; but he that believeth not shall be damned. *Mark 16:16*

5. Through his name whosoever believeth in him shall receive remission of sins. *Acts 10:43*

6. Let every man be fully persuaded in his own mind. *Rom. 14:5*

BELLIGERENCE   See Aggressiveness.

BENEDICTION   See Blessing.

BENEVOLENCE   (See also Generosity; God, Mercy of; Goodness; Kindness; Mercy; Unselfishness.)

1. Thou wilt not deal falsely with me, nor with my son, nor with my son's son: but according to the kindness that I have done unto thee. *Gen. 21:23*

2. The Lord God, merciful and gracious, long-suffering, and abundant in goodness and truth. *Exod. 34:6*

3. Thou art a God ready to pardon, gracious and merciful, slow to anger, and of great kindness. *Neh. 9:17*

4. Blessed be the Lord: for he hath showed me his marvellous kindness. *Ps. 31:21*

5. If thine enemy be hungry, give him bread to eat; and if he be thirsty, give him water to drink. *Prov. 25:21*

6. If thou draw out thy soul to the hungry, and satisfy the afflicted soul; then shall thy light rise in obscurity. *Isa. 58:10*

7. Inasmuch as ye have done it unto one of the least of these my brethren, ye have done it unto me. *Matt. 25:40*

8. Let the husband render unto the wife due benevolence: and likewise also the wife unto the husband. *1 Cor. 7:3*

BESTIALITY   See Sexual Perversion.

BETRAYAL   (See also Conspiracy; Deceit; Traitor.)

1. Why have ye conspired against me . . . that he should rise against me, to lie in wait? *1 Sam. 22:13*

2. He [Judas] sought opportunity to betray him. *Matt. 26:16*

3. Woe unto that man by whom the Son of man is betrayed! it had been good for that man if he had not been born. *Matt. 26:24*

4. The brother shall betray the brother to death, and the father the son; and children shall rise up against their parents, and shall cause them to be put to death. *Mark 13:12*

5. One of you which eateth with me shall betray me. *Mark 14:18*

6. Behold, the hand of him that betrayeth me is with me on the table. *Luke 22:21*

7. Jesus said unto him, Judas, betrayest thou the Son of man with a kiss? *Luke 22:48*

BETROTHAL   (See also Marriage.)

1. If he have betrothed her unto his son, he shall deal with her after the manner of daughters. *Exod. 21:9*

2. What man is there that hath betrothed a wife, and hath not taken her? let him go and return unto his house. *Deut. 20:7*

3. I will betroth thee unto me for ever; yea, I will betroth thee unto me in righteousness, and in judgment, and in loving-kindness, and in mercies. I will even betroth thee unto me in faithfulness. *Hos. 2:19,20*

4. I am jealous over you with godly jealousy: for I have espoused you to one husband, that I may present you as a chaste virgin to Christ. *2 Cor. 11:2*

BETTING   See Gambling.

BIAS   See Favoritism; Prejudice.

BIBLE   See Scripture.

BIGOTRY   See Prejudice.

BIRTH   (See also Baby; Fertility.)

1. The Lord God formed man of the dust of the ground, and breathed into his nostrils the breath of life; and man became a living soul. *Gen. 2:7*

2. In sorrow thou shalt bring forth children. *Gen. 3:16*

3. A hidden untimely birth I had not been. *Job 3:16*

4. A time to be born, and a time to die. *Eccl. 3:2*

5. A virgin shall conceive, and bear a son, and shall call his name Immanuel. *Isa. 7:14*

6. Unto us a child is born, unto us a son is given . . . and his name shall be called Wonderful, Counselor, The mighty God, The everlasting Father, The Prince of Peace. *Isa. 9:6*

7. She brought forth her firstborn son, and wrapped him in swaddling clothes, and laid him in a manger. *Luke 2:7*

8. Unto you is born this day in the city of David a Savior, which is Christ the Lord. *Luke 2:11*

9. A woman when she is in travail hath sorrow, because her hour is come: but as soon as she is delivered of the child, she remembereth no more the anguish, for joy that a man is born into the world. *John 16:21*

10. She brought forth a man child, who was to rule all nations with a rod of iron. *Rev. 12:5*

BIRTHRIGHT See Inheritance.

BISHOP (See also Apostle; Church; Deacon; Elder; Leadership; Ministry; Shepherd.)

1. Let his habitation be desolate, and let no man dwell therein: and his bishopric let another take. *Acts 1:20*

2. If a man desire the office of a bishop, he desireth a good work. A bishop then must be blameless, the husband of one wife, vigilant, sober, of good behavior, given to hospitality, apt to teach; Not given to wine, no striker, not greedy of filthy lucre; but patient, not a brawler, not covetous; One that ruleth well his own house, having his children in subjection with all gravity; (For if a man know not how to rule his own house, how shall he take care of the church of God?) Not a novice, lest being lifted up with pride he fall into the condemnation of the devil. Moreover he must have a good report of them which are without; lest he fall into reproach and the snare of the devil. *1 Tim. 3:1–7*

4. A bishop must be blameless, as the steward of God; not self-willed, not soon angry, not given to wine, no striker, not given to filthy lucre; But a lover of hospitality, a lover of good men, sober, just, holy, temperate; Holding fast the faithful word as he hath been taught, that he may be able by sound doctrine both to exhort and to convince the gainsayers. *Titus 1:7–9*

5. Ye were as sheep going astray; but are now returned unto the Shepherd and Bishop of your souls. *1 Peter 2:25*

BITTERNESS (See also Hatred; Malice.)

1. Their vine is of the vine of Sodom, and of the fields of Gomorrah: their grapes are grapes of gall, their clusters are bitter. *Deut. 32:32*

2. Shall the sword devour forever? knowest thou not that it will be bitterness in the latter end? *2 Sam. 2:26*

3. The heart knoweth his own bitterness. *Prov. 14:10*

4. I shall go softly all my years in the bitterness of my soul. *Isa. 38:15*

5. He hath filled me with bitterness, he hath made me drunken with wormwood. *Lam. 3:15*

6. Thou art in the gall of bitterness, and in the bond of iniquity. *Acts 8:23*

7. Let all bitterness, and wrath, and anger, and clamour, and evil speaking, be put away from you. *Eph. 4:31*

8. If ye have bitter envying and strife in your hearts, glory not, and lie not against the truth. *James 3:14*

BLAME   (See also Accusation; Guilt; Responsibility; Sin.)

1. Be it indeed that I have erred, mine error remaineth with myself. *Job 19:4*

2. A reproof entereth more into a wise man than a hundred stripes into a fool. *Prov. 17:10*

3. He, that being often reproved hardeneth his neck, shall suddenly be destroyed. *Prov. 29:1*

4. Their heart is divided; now shall they be found faulty. *Hos. 10:2*

5. I withstood him to the face, because he was to be blamed. *Gal. 2:11*

6. If ye be reproached for the name of Christ, happy are ye. *1 Peter 4:14*

BLASPHEMY   (See also Profanity.)

1. Thou shalt not take the name of the Lord thy God in vain. *Exod. 20:7*

2. He that blasphemeth the name of the Lord, he shall surely be put to death. *Lev. 24:16*

3. Curse God, and die. *Job 2:9*

4. They speak against thee wickedly, and thine enemies take thy name in vain. *Ps. 139:20*

5. My name continually every day is blasphemed. *Isa. 52:5*

6. Blasphemy against the Holy Ghost shall not be forgiven unto men. *Matt. 12:31*

7. Put off . . . blasphemy, filthy communication out of your mouth. *Col. 3:8*

8. Out of the same mouth proceedeth blessing and cursing. *James 3:10*

BLESSING   (See also Beatitudes; Gift; Grace.)

1. I will bless thee, and make thy name great and thou shalt be a blessing. *Gen. 12:2*

2. The blessing of the Lord was upon all that he had in the house, and in the field. *Gen. 39:5*

3. The Almighty, who shall bless thee with blessings of heaven above, blessings of the deep that lieth under, blessings of the breasts, and of the womb. *Gen. 49:25*

4. The Lord bless thee, and keep thee. *Num. 6:24*

5. I have also given thee that which thou hast not asked, both riches, and honor. *1 Kings 3:13*

6. Blessed be he that cometh in the name of the Lord. *Ps. 118:26*

7. Every man also to whom God hath given riches and wealth, and hath given him power to eat thereof, and to take his portion, and to rejoice in his labor; this is the gift of God. *Eccl. 5:19*

8. Blessed art thou among women. *Luke 1:28*

9. Bless them which persecute you: bless, and curse not. *Rom. 12:14*

10. God shall supply all your needs according to his riches in glory by Christ Jesus. *Phil. 4:19*

BLINDNESS   See Darkness; Handicap.

BLOOD   (See also Body; Eucharist; Wine.)

1. The voice of thy brother's blood crieth unto me from the ground. *Gen. 4:10*

2. Moses took the blood, and sprinkled it on the people, and said, Behold the blood of the covenant. *Exod. 24:8*

3. The life of the flesh is in the blood . . . for it is the blood that maketh an atonement for the soul. *Lev. 17:11*

4. This is my blood of the new testament, which is shed for many for the remission of sins. *Matt. 26:28*

5. Except ye eat the flesh of the Son of man, and drink his blood, ye have no life in you. *John 6:53*

6. [God] hath made of one blood all nations of men. *Acts 17:26*

7. We have redemption through his blood, even the forgiveness of sins. *Col. 1:14*

8. How much more shall the blood of Christ, who through the eternal Spirit offered himself without spot to God, purge your conscience from dead works to serve the living God? *Heb. 9:14*

9. The blood of Jesus Christ his Son cleanseth us from all sin. *1 John 1:7*

10. They have shed the blood of saints and prophets, and thou hast given them blood to drink; for they are worthy. *Rev. 16:6*

BOASTING   (See also Pride; Vanity.)

1. The wicked boasteth of his heart's desire. *Ps. 10:3*

2. The Lord shall cut off all flattering lips, and the tongue that speaketh proud things. *Ps. 12:3*

3. My soul shall make her boast in the Lord. *Ps. 34:2*

4. They that . . . boast themselves in the multitude of their riches; None of them can by any means redeem his brother, nor give to God a ransom for him. *Ps. 49:6,7*

5. Boast not thyself of tomorrow; for thou knowest not what a day may bring forth. *Prov. 27:1*

6. Though thou [Edom] exalt thyself as the eagle, and though thou set thy nest among the stars, thence will I bring thee down, saith the Lord. *Obad. 1:4*

7. Whosoever exalteth himself shall be abased. *Luke 14:11*

8. The truth of Christ is in me, no man shall stop me of this boasting. *2 Cor. 11:10*

9. By grace are ye saved through faith; and that not of yourselves: it is the gift of God: Not of works, lest any man should boast. *Eph. 2:8,9*

10. The tongue is a little member, and boasteth great things. *James 3:5*

BODY   (See also Blood; Drug Abuse; Eucharist; Soul.)

1. Fear not them which kill the body, but are not able to kill the soul. *Matt. 10:28*

2. The spirit indeed is willing, but the flesh is weak. *Matt. 26:41*

3. He [Jesus] took bread . . . and brake it . . . saying, This is my body which is given for you. *Luke 22:19*

4. Know ye not that your bodies are the members of Christ? *1 Cor. 6:15*

5. Your body is the temple of the Holy Ghost. *1 Cor. 6:19*

6. By one Spirit are we all baptized into one body. . . . For the body is not one member, but many. *1 Cor. 12:13,14*

7. I bear in my body the marks of the Lord Jesus. *Gal. 6:17*

8. We are members of his body, of his flesh, and of his bones. *Eph. 5:30*

9. The body without the spirit is dead. *James 2:26*

BONDAGE   See Captivity; Imprisonment.

BOOK (See also Gospel; Reading; Scripture; Writing.)

1. Whosoever hath sinned against me, him will I blot out of my book. *Exod. 32:33*

2. It was written in the book. *Esth. 9:32*

3. Oh that my words were now . . . printed in a book! *Job 19:23*

4. Of making many books there is no end. *Eccl. 12:12*

5. Fellow laborers, whose names are in the book of life. *Phil. 4:3*

6. Who is worthy to open the book, and to loose the seals thereof? *Rev. 5:2*

7. Another book was opened, which is the book of life: and the dead were judged out of those things which were written in the books, according to their works. . . . And whosoever was not found written in the book of life was cast into the lake of fire. *Rev. 20:12,15*

BOREDOM (See also Weariness.)

1. I am weary of my life. *Gen. 27:46*

2. Withdraw thy foot from thy neighbor's house; lest he be weary of thee, and so hate thee. *Prov. 25:17*

3. Much study is a weariness of the flesh. *Eccl. 12:12*

4. Lest by her continued coming she weary me. *Luke 18:5*

5. I be not further tedious unto thee. *Acts 24:4*

BORN AGAIN (See also Baptism; Revival.)

1. Except a man be born again, he cannot see the kingdom of God . . . That which is born of the flesh is flesh; and that which is born of the Spirit is spirit. *John 3:3,6*

2. Ye must be born again. *John 3:7*

3. He that heareth my word, and believeth on him that sent me . . . is passed from death unto life. *John 5:24*

4. Being born again, not of corruptible seed, but of incorruptible, by the word of God, which liveth and abideth for ever. *1 Peter 1:23*

5. Every one that loveth is born of God. *1 John 4:7*

6. Whatsoever is born of God overcometh the world. *1 John 5:4*

BORROWING AND LENDING (See also Consumerism.)

1. He that is surety for a stranger shall smart for it. *Prov. 11:15*

2. The borrower is servant to the lender. *Prov. 22:7*

3. Forgive us our debts, as we forgive our debtors. *Matt. 6:12*

4. I will repay it: albeit I do not say to thee how thou owest unto me even thine own self besides. *Philem. 1:19*

BOY   See Children; Man; Youth.

BRAGGING   See Boasting.

BRAVERY   See Courage.

BREAD   See Body; Eucharist; Food.

BRIBERY   (See also Judgment; Trial.)

1. Thou shalt take no gift: for the gift blindeth the wise, and perverteth the words of the righteous. *Exod. 23:8*

2. Cursed be he that taketh reward to slay an innocent person. *Deut. 27:25*

3. His sons walked not in his ways but turned aside after lucre, and took bribes, and perverted judgment. *1 Sam. 8:3*

4. Fire shall consume the tabernacles of bribery. *Job 15:34*

5. A wicked man taketh a gift out of the bosom to pervert the ways of judgment. *Prov. 17:23*

6. The king by judgment establisheth the land: but he that receiveth gifts overthroweth it. *Prov. 29:4*

7. [Woe unto them that] justify the wicked for reward, and take away the righteousness of the righteous from him! *Isa. 5:23*

8. [He] that shaketh his hands from holding of bribes . . . shall dwell on high. *Isa. 33:15,16*

9. [They] promised to give him [Judas Iscariot] money. And he sought how he might conveniently betray him. *Mark 14:11*

BROTHERHOOD   (See also Fellowship; Friendship; Love; Unity.)

1. Am I my brother's keeper? *Gen. 4:9*

2. Behold, how good and how pleasant it is for brethren to dwell together in unity! *Ps. 133:1*

3. Two are better than one. *Eccl. 4:9*

4. All ye are brethren. *Matt. 23:8*

5. Ye are brethren; why do ye wrong one to another? *Acts 7:26*

6. Be kindly affectioned one to another with brotherly love. *Rom. 12:10*

7. Bear ye one another's burdens. *Gal. 6:2*

8. We are members one of another. *Eph. 4:25*

9. Honor all men. Love the brotherhood. *1 Peter 2:17*

10. Be ye all of one mind, having compassion one of another, love as brethren. *1 Peter 3:8*

BULLY   See Ruffian.

BURDEN   (See also Trouble.)

1. They shall bear the burden of the people with thee, that thou bear it not thyself alone. *Num. 11:17*

2. Cast thy burden upon the Lord, and he shall sustain thee. *Ps. 55:22*

3. He hath borne our griefs, and carried our sorrows. *Isa. 53:4*

4. When this people, or the prophet, or a priest, shall ask thee, saying, What is the burden of the Lord? thou shalt then say unto them, What burden? *Jer. 23:33*

5. Ye that labor and are heavy laden . . . Take my yoke upon you . . . For my yoke is easy, and my burden is light. *Matt. 11:28*–30

6. They bind heavy burdens and grievous to be borne, and lay them on men's shoulders. *Matt. 23:4*

7. Bear ye one another's burdens. *Gal. 6:2*

8. Every man shall bear his own burden. *Gal. 6:5*

BURIAL   (See also Cremation; Death.)

1. I will lie with my fathers, and thou shalt carry me out of Egypt, and bury me in their burying place. *Gen. 47:30*

2. Where thou diest, will I die, and there will I be buried. *Ruth 1:17*

3. He [Jehoiakim] shall be buried with the burial of an ass. *Jer. 22:19*

4. I will open your graves, and cause you to come up out of your graves. *Ezek. 37:12*

5. She hath poured this ointment on my body, she did it for my burial. *Matt. 26:12*

6. [Joseph of Arimathea] took him [Jesus] down, and wrapped him in the linen, and laid him in a sepulcher. *Mark 15:46*

7. He [Jesus] was buried, and . . . rose again the third day. *1 Cor. 15:4*

8. Buried with him in baptism. *Col. 2:12*

BUSINESS   (See also Work.)

1. Seest thou a man diligent in his business? He shall stand before kings. *Prov. 22:29*

2. I must be about my Father's business. *Luke 2:49*

3. [Be] Not slothful in business. *Rom. 12:11*

4. Ye study to be quiet, and to do your own business, and to work with your own hands. *1 Thess. 4:11*

5. The merchants of the earth shall weep and mourn over her; for no man buyeth their merchandise any more. *Rev. 18:11*

BUSYBODY   See Gossip; Meddling.

CALLING   See Vocation.
CANDOR   See Sincerity.
CANNIBALISM
1. He will not give to any of them of the flesh of his children whom he shall eat. *Deut. 28:55*
2. Her eye shall be evil . . . toward her children . . . for she shall eat them. *Deut. 28:56,57*
3. So we boiled my son, and did eat him. *2 Kings 6:29*
4. [As punishment] I will cause them to eat the flesh of their sons and the flesh of their daughters, and they shall eat every one the flesh of his friend. *Jer. 19:9*
5. The hands of the pitiful women have sodden their own children: they were their meat in the destruction of the daughter of my people. *Lam. 4:10*
CAPITAL PUNISHMENT
1. Whoso sheddeth man's blood, by man shall his blood be shed. *Gen. 9:6*
2. He that stealeth a man, and selleth him, or if he be found in his hand, he shall surely be put to death. *Exod. 21:16*
3. Whoso killeth any person, the murderer shall be put to death. *Num. 35:30*
4. At the mouth of two witnesses, or three witnesses, shall he that is worthy of death be put to death; but at the mouth of one witness he shall not be put to death. *Deut. 17:6*
CAPTIVITY   (See also Imprisonment; Kidnapping; Liberty; Oppression.)
1. The Egyptians made the children of Israel to serve with rigor: And they made their lives bitter with hard bondage. *Exod. 1:13,14*

2. God hath not forsaken us in our bondage. *Ezra 9:9*

3. Will ye even sell your brethren? *Neh. 5:8*

4. My people are gone into captivity, because they have no knowledge. *Isa. 5:13*

5. I see another law in my members, warring against the law of my mind, and bringing me into captivity to the law of sin which is in my members. *Rom. 7:23*

6. Through the fear of death [they] were all their lifetime subject to bondage. *Heb. 2:15*

CARE See God, Help of; Protection.

CAREER See Vocation.

CAREFULNESS (See also Discretion; Vigilance.)

1. Thou hast been careful for us with all this care. *1 Kings 4:13*

2. Martha, Martha, thou art careful and troubled about many things. *Luke 10:41*

3. See then that ye walk circumspectly. *Eph 5:15*

CARNALITY See Lust; Promiscuity; Sex.

CAUTION (See also Discretion; Vigilance; Warning.)

1. The prudent man looketh well to his going. *Prov. 14:15*

2. A prudent man foreseeth the evil, and hideth himself. *Prov. 22:3*

3. Trust ye not in a friend, put ye not confidence in a guide: keep the doors of thy mouth from her that lieth in thy bosom. *Mic. 7:5*

4. Watch and pray, that ye enter not into temptation. *Matt. 26:41*

5. Take heed, beware of the leaven of the Pharisees, and of the leaven of Herod. *Mark 8:15*

6. Take ye heed, watch and pray. *Mark 13:33*

7. Let your loins be girded about, and your lights burning. *Luke 12:35*

8. Watch ye, stand fast in the faith, quit you like men, be strong. *1 Cor. 16:13*

9. Be sober, be vigilant; because your adversary the devil, as a roaring lion, walketh about, seeking whom he may devour. *1 Peter 5:8*

CELEBRATION (See also Dancing; Ritual; Song.)

1. Celebrate your sabbath. *Lev. 23:32*

2. Ye shall hallow the fiftieth year, and proclaim liberty throughout all the land . . . it shall be a jubilee. *Lev. 25:10*

3. Thou hast turned for me my mourning into dancing: thou hast put off my sackcloth, and girded me with gladness. *Ps. 30:11*

4. He that is of a merry heart hath a continual feast. *Prov. 15:15*

5. Thou shalt have joy and gladness; and many shall rejoice at his birth. *Luke 1:14*

6. Take thine ease, eat, drink, and be merry. *Luke 12:19*

7. It was meet that we should make merry, and be glad. *Luke 15:32*

CELEBRITY   See Fame.

CELIBACY   (See also Marriage; Virginity.)

1. All men cannot receive this saying, save they to whom it is given. For there are some eunuchs . . . which have made themselves eunuchs for the kingdom of heaven's sake. He that is able to receive it, let him receive it. *Matt. 19:11,12*

2. They neither marry, nor are given in marriage, but are as the angels of God in heaven. *Matt. 22:30*

3. It is good for a man not to touch a woman. *1 Cor. 7:1*

4. I say therefore to the unmarried and widows, It is good for them if they abide even as I. *1 Cor. 7:8*

5. He that is unmarried careth for the things that belong to the Lord. *1 Cor. 7:32*

6. These are they which were not defiled with women; for they are virgins. *Rev. 14:4*

CENSURE   See Chastisement; Blame.

CEREMONY   See Celebration; Ritual.

CHANCE   See Opportunity.

CHANGE   See Conversion; Reform; Transfiguration.

CHAOS   (See also Disaster.)

1. Therefore is the name of it called Babel; because the Lord did there confound the language of all the earth: and from thence did the Lord scatter them abroad upon the face of all the earth. *Gen. 11:9*

2. [God] makest men as the fishes of the sea, as the creeping things, that have no ruler over them. *Hab. 1:14*

3. God is not the author of confusion, but of peace. *1 Cor. 14:33*

4. Where envying and strife is, there is confusion and every evil work. *James 3:16*

5. He that believeth on him [Jesus] shall not be confounded. *1 Peter 2:6*

CHARACTER

1. Who shall abide in thy tabernacle? Who shall dwell in thy holy

hill? He that walketh uprightly, and worketh righteousness, and speaketh the truth in his heart. *Ps. 15:1,2*
2. Mark the perfect man, and behold the upright: for the end of that man is peace. *Ps. 37:37*
3. A good name is rather to be chosen than great riches. *Prov. 22:1*
4. Ye are the salt of the earth. *Matt. 5:13*
5. Let your light so shine before men, that they may see your good works, and glorify your Father. *Matt. 5:16*
6. Ye shall be hated of all men for my name's sake: but he that endureth to the end shall be saved. *Matt. 10:22*
7. God hath not given us the spirit of fear; but of power, and of love, and of a sound mind. *2 Tim. 1:7*
8. Follow righteousness, faith, charity, peace, with them that call on the Lord out of a pure heart. *2 Tim. 2:22*
9. In all things showing thyself a pattern of good works: in doctrine showing uncorruptness, gravity, sincerity, sound speech, that cannot be condemned. *Titus 2:7,8*
10. Add to your faith virtue; and to virtue knowledge; And to knowledge temperance; and to temperance patience; and to patience godliness; And to godliness brotherly kindness; and to brotherly kindness charity. *2 Peter 1:5-7*

CHARITY   (See also Generosity; Giving; Love; Unselfishness.)
1. He hath dispersed, he hath given to the poor; his righteousness endureth for ever. *Ps. 112:9*
2. Inasmuch as ye have done it unto one of the least of these my brethren, ye have done it unto me. *Matt. 25:40*
3. Give, and it shall be given unto you . . . For with the same measure that ye mete withal it shall be measured to you again. *Luke 6:38*
4. Knowledge puffeth up, but charity edifieth. *1 Cor. 8:1*
5. I have the gift of prophecy, and understand all mysteries, and all knowledge; and though I have all faith, so that I could remove mountains, and have not charity, I am nothing. *1 Cor. 13:2*
6. Charity suffereth long, and is kind; charity envieth not; charity vaunteth not itself. . . . Charity never faileth. *1 Cor. 13:4,8*
7. Faith, hope, charity . . . the greatest of these is charity. *1 Cor. 13:13*

8. Above all things have fervent charity among yourselves: for charity shall cover the multitude of sins. *1 Peter 4:8*

9. Thou doest faithfully whatsoever thou doest to the brethren, and to strangers; which have borne witness of thy charity before the church. *3 John 1:5,6*

CHASTISEMENT   (See also Discipline; Punishment.)

1. Despise not the chastening of the Lord; neither be weary of his correction: for whom the Lord loveth he correcteth. *Prov. 3:11,12*

2. Reprove not a scorner, lest he hate thee: rebuke a wise man, and he will love thee. *Prov. 9:8*

3. From the first day that thou didst set thine heart to understand, and to chasten thyself before thy God, thy words were heard. *Dan. 10:12*

4. Let no man strive, nor reprove another. *Hos. 4:4*

5. If ye endure chastening, God dealeth with you as with sons. *Heb. 12:7*

6. As many as I love, I rebuke and chasten: be zealous therefore, and repent. *Rev. 3:19*

CHASTITY   See Celibacy; Purity; Virginity.

CHEATING (See also Deceit; Falsehood.)

1. Swear unto me here by God that thou wilt not deal falsely with me. *Gen. 21:23*

2. Ye shall not steal, neither deal falsely, neither lie one to another. *Lev. 19:11*

3. Thou shalt not defraud thy neighbor, neither rob him: the wages of him that is hired shall not abide with thee all night until the morning. *Lev. 19:13*

4. The getting of treasures by a lying tongue is a vanity tossed to and fro of them that seek death. *Prov. 21:6*

5. Woe unto him that . . . useth his neighbor's service without wages, and giveth him not for his work. *Jer. 22:13*

6. The hire of the laborers who have reaped down your fields, which is of you kept back by fraud, crieth. *James 5:4*

CHILD ABUSE

1. Do not sin against the child. *Gen. 42:22*

2. Do not prostitute thy daughter, to cause her to be a whore. *Lev. 19:29*

3. They built the high places of Baal . . . to cause their sons and their daughters to pass through the fire unto Molech; which I commanded them not . . . that they should do this abomination. *Jer. 32:35*

4. Take heed that ye despise not one of these little ones. *Matt. 18:10*

CHILDLESSNESS   See Sterility.

CHILDLIKENESS   (See also Innocence; Simplicity.)

1. I have behaved and quieted myself, as a child that is weaned of his mother: my soul is even as a weaned child. *Ps. 131:2*

2. Except ye be converted, and become as little children, ye shall not enter into the kingdom of heaven. *Matt. 18:3*

3. When I was a child, I spake as a child, I understood as a child, I thought as a child: but when I became a man, I put away childish things. *1 Cor. 13:11*

4. Be not children in understanding: howbeit in malice be ye children, but in understanding be men. *1 Cor. 14:20*

5. Be ye therefore followers of God, as dear children. *Eph. 5:1*

6. As newborn babes, desire the sincere milk of the word, that ye may grow thereby. *1 Peter 2:2*

CHILDREN   (See also Family; Father; God, Family of; Mother; Orphan; Parent.)

1. Out of the mouth of babes and sucklings hast thou ordained strength. *Ps. 8:2*

2. A child is known by his doings, whether his work be pure, and whether it be right. *Prov. 20:11*

3. Train up a child in the way he should go: and when he is old, he will not depart from it. *Prov. 22:6*

4. Better is a poor and a wise child than an old and foolish king. *Eccl. 4:13*

5. A little child shall lead them. *Isa. 11:6*

6. Suffer the little children to come unto me . . . for of such is the kingdom of God. *Mark 10:14*

7. In him we live, and move, and have our being; . . . For we are also his offspring. *Acts 17:28*

8. We are the children of God: And if children, then heirs. *Rom. 8:16,17*

9. Ye are all the children of light, and the children of the day. *Thess. 5:5*

CHOICE   (See also Decision; Election; Indecision.)

1. Moses . . . said, Who is on the Lord's side? let him come unto me. *Exod. 32:26*

2. The Lord thy God hath chosen thee to be a special people unto himself. *Deut. 7:6*

3. I have set before you life and death, blessing and cursing: therefore choose life, that both thou and thy seed may live. *Deut. 30:19*

4. Give therefore thy servant an understanding heart to judge thy people, that I may discern between good and bad. *1 Kings 3:9*

5. Many be called, but few chosen. *Matt. 20:16*

6. Hath not God chosen the poor of this world rich in faith, and heirs of the kingdom which he hath promised to them that love him? *James 2:5*

CHRIST (See also God; Lamb; Lord; Savior; Trinity, Holy.)

1. Thou art the Christ, the Son of the living God. *Matt. 16:16*

2. Unto you is born this day in the city of David a Savior, which is Christ the Lord. *Luke 2:11*

3. The Word was made flesh, and dwelt among us, (and we beheld his glory, the glory as of the only begotten of the Father), full of grace and truth. *John 1:14*

4. Jesus said unto them, I am the bread of life. *John 6:35*

5. I am the good shepherd: the good shepherd giveth his life for the sheep. *John 10:11*

6. Jesus said . . . I am the resurrection, and the life. *John 11:25*

7. Jesus saith . . . I am the way, the truth, and the life: no man cometh unto the Father, but by me. *John 14:6*

8. There is one God, and one mediator between God and men, the man Christ Jesus. *1 Tim. 2:5*

9. Jesus Christ . . . is the blessed and only Potentate, the King of kings, and the Lord of lords. *1 Tim. 6:14,15*

10. I am Alpha and Omega, the beginning and the end, the first and the last. *Rev. 22:13*

CHRIST, BELIEF IN (See also Belief; Faith.)

1. Let Christ the King of Israel descend now from the cross, that we may see and believe. *Mark 15:32*

2. He that believeth on the Son hath everlasting life: and he that believeth not the Son shall not see life; but the wrath of God abideth on him. *John 3:36*

3. We believe and are sure that thou art that Christ, the Son of the living God. *John 6:69*

4. Whosoever liveth and believeth in me shall never die. *John 11:26*

5. Ye might believe that Jesus is the Christ, the Son of God; and that believing ye might have life through his name. *John 20:31*

6. I believe that Jesus Christ is the Son of God. *Acts 8:37*

7. Believe on the Lord Jesus Christ, and thou shalt be saved, and thy house. *Acts 16:31*

8. Whom having not seen, ye love; in whom, though now ye see him not, yet believing, ye rejoice with joy unspeakable and full of glory. *1 Peter 1:8*

CHRIST, COMPANIONSHIP OF   (See also Brotherhood; Fellowship; Friendship.)

1. There is a friend that sticketh closer than a brother. *Prov. 18:24*

2. Whosoever therefore shall confess me before men, him will I confess also before my Father. *Matt. 10:32*

3. Whosoever shall do the will of God, the same is my brother, and my sister, and mother. *Mark 3:35*

4. Ye are my friends, if ye do whatsoever I command you. . . . I have called you friends; for all things that I have heard of my Father I have made known unto you. *John 15:14,15*

5. We are . . . willing rather to be absent from the body, and to be present with the Lord. *2 Cor. 5:8*

6. That I may know . . . the fellowship of his sufferings. *Phil. 3:10*

7. Salute thee . . . my fellow prisoner in Christ Jesus. *Philem. 1:23*

8. I . . . am your brother, and companion in tribulation, and in the kingdom and patience of Jesus Christ. *Rev. 1:9*

CHRIST, CRUCIFIXION OF   (See also Atonement.)

1. He is brought as a lamb to the slaughter. *Isa. 53:7*

2. I send unto you prophets, and wise men, and scribes: and some of them ye shall kill and crucify. *Matt. 23:34*

3. Let him be crucified. *Matt. 27:22*

4. When they were come to the place, which is called Calvary, there they crucified him. *Luke 23:33*

5. It is expedient for us, that one man should die for the people, and that the whole nation perish not. *John 11:50*

6. I am crucified with Christ: nevertheless I live. *Gal. 2:20*

7. They that are Christ's have crucified the flesh with the affections and lusts. *Gal. 5:24*

8. It is impossible . . . If they shall fall away, to renew them again unto repentance; seeing they crucify to themselves the Son of God afresh. *Heb. 6:4-6*

CHRIST, DEATH OF See Christ, Crucifixion of; Christ, Purpose of; Christ, Resurrection of.

CHRIST, DIVINITY OF (See also God; Miracle; Trinity, Holy.)

1. A virgin shall be with child, and shall bring forth a son, and they shall call his name Immanuel, which being interpreted is, God with us. *Matt. 1:23*

2. A voice from heaven, saying, This is my beloved Son, in whom I am well pleased. *Matt. 3:17*

3. Thou art the Christ, the Son of the living God. *Matt. 16:16*

4. God so loved the world, that he gave his only begotten Son, that whosoever believeth in him should not perish, but have everlasting life. *John 3:16*

5. When the Comforter is come, whom I will send unto you from the Father, even the Spirit of truth, which proceedeth from the Father, he shall testify of me: And ye also shall bear witness, because ye have been with me from the beginning. *John 15:26,27*

6. God sending his own Son in the likeness of sinful flesh. *Rom. 8:3*

7. Christ Jesus: Who, being in the form of God, thought it not robbery to be equal with God. *Phil. 2:5,6*

8. In him dwelleth all the fullness of the Godhead bodily. *Col. 2:9*

9. God was manifest in the flesh, justified in the Spirit, seen of angels, preached unto the Gentiles, believed on in the world, received up into glory. *1 Tim. 3:16*

CHRIST, LEADERSHIP OF (See also Guidance; Leadership.)

1. Follow me, and I will make you fishers of men. *Matt. 4:19*

2. If any man serve me, let him follow me. *John 12:26*

3. Jesus saith . . . I am the way, the truth, and the life: no man cometh unto the Father, but by me. *John 14:6*

4. The Lord said unto him, Go thy way: for he is a chosen vessel unto me, to bear my name before the Gentiles, and kings, and the children of Israel. *Acts 9:15*

5. The head of every man is Christ. *1 Cor. 11:3*

6. Christ is the head of the church. *Eph. 5:23*

7. Lord Jesus Christ, direct our way unto you. *1 Thess. 3:11*

8. The Lamb which is in the midst of the throne shall feed them, and shall lead them unto living fountains of waters. *Rev. 7:17*

CHRIST, LOVE OF **(See also Love.)**

1. He that loveth father or mother more than me is not worthy of me: and he that loveth son or daughter more than me is not worthy of me. *Matt. 10:37*

2. If ye love me, keep my commandments. *John 14:15*

3. [Jesus said] If a man love me, he will keep my words: and my Father will love him, and we will come unto him, and make our abode with him. *John 14:23*

4. If any man love not the Lord Jesus Christ, let him be Anathema Maranatha. *1 Cor. 16:22*

5. The love of Christ constraineth us. *2 Cor. 5:14*

6. Walk in love, as Christ also hath loved us. *Eph. 5:2*

7. Grace be with all them that love our Lord Jesus Christ in sincerity. *Eph. 6:24*

8. Perceive we the love of God, because he laid down his life for us. *1 John 3:16*

9. Unto him [Christ] that loved us, and washed us from our sins in his own blood. *Rev. 1:5*

10. As many as I love, I rebuke and chasten. *Rev. 3:19*

CHRIST, PURPOSE OF **(See also Atonement; Reason; Redemption; Salvation; Savior.)**

1. The Son of man came not to be ministered unto, but to minister, and to give his life a ransom for many. *Matt. 20:28*

2. The Son of man is not come to destroy men's lives, but to save them. *Luke 9:56*

3. God so loved the world, that he gave his only begotten Son, that whosoever believeth in him should not perish, but have everlasting life . . . that the world through him might be saved. *John 3:16,17*

4. My meat is to do the will of him that sent me, and to finish his work. *John 4:34*

5. I must work the works of him that sent me, while it is day: the night cometh, when no man can work. *John 9:4*

6. To this end was I born, and for this cause came I into the world, that I should bear witness unto the truth. *John 18:37*

7. I have appeared unto thee for this purpose, to make thee a minister and a witness. *Acts 26:16*

8. I am made all things to all men, that I might by all means save some. *1 Cor. 9:22*

9. He died for all, that they which live should not henceforth live unto themselves, but unto him. *2 Cor. 5:15*

CHRIST, RESURRECTION OF (See also **Christ, Second Coming of.**)

1. As Jonas was three days and three nights in the whale's belly; so shall the Son of man be three days and three nights in the heart of the earth. *Matt. 12:40*

2. Thus it is written, and thus it behooved Christ to suffer, and to rise from the dead the third day. *Luke 24:26*

3. Jesus answered and said unto them, Destroy this temple, and in three days I will raise it up. . . . he spake of the temple of his body. *John 2:19,21*

4. I am the resurrection, and the life: he that believeth in me, though he were dead, yet shall he live. *John 11:25*

5. Christ was raised up from the dead by the glory of the Father. *Rom. 6:4*

6. [God] raised him from the dead, and set him at his own right hand in the heavenly places. *Eph. 1:20*

7. I am he that liveth, and was dead; and, behold, I am alive for evermore. *Rev. 1:18*

CHRIST, SECOND COMING OF (See also **Christ, Resurrection of.**)

1. As the lightning cometh out of the east, and shineth even unto the west; so shall also the coming of the Son of man be. *Matt. 24:27*

2. Then shall appear the sign of the Son of man in heaven: and then shall all the tribes of the earth mourn, and they shall see the Son of man coming in the clouds of heaven with power and great glory. *Matt. 24:30*

3. Be ye also ready: for in such an hour as ye think not the Son of man cometh. *Matt. 24:44*

4. I will come again, and receive you unto myself. *John 14:3*

5. Jesus, which is taken up from you into heaven, shall so come in like manner as ye have seen him go into heaven. *Acts 1:11*

6. When Christ, who is our life, shall appear, then shall ye also appear with him in glory. *Col. 3:4*

7. The day of the Lord so cometh as a thief in the night. *1 Thess. 5:2*

8. Christ was once offered to bear the sins of many; and unto them that look for him shall he appear the second time without sin unto salvation. *Heb. 9:28*

9. The Lord cometh with ten thousands of his saints, To execute judgment upon all, and to convince all that are ungodly among them of their ungodly deeds which they have ungodly committed. *Jude 1:14,15*

10. Behold, he cometh with clouds; and every eye shall see him, and they also which pierced him: and all kindreds of the earth shall wail because of him. *Rev. 1:7*

CHRIST, TRANSFIGURATION OF   See Transfiguration.

CHRISTENING   See Baptism.

CHRISTIAN   See Disciple; Follower; God, Family of.

CHRISTIAN ARMY   See Army, Christian.

CHRISTIAN OBLIGATION   (See also Church, Attendance at; Duty; God, Law of; Obedience; Responsibility; Tithe.)

1. What doth the Lord require of thee, but to do justly, and to love mercy, and to walk humbly with thy God? *Mic. 6:8*

2. Thou shalt love the Lord thy God with all thy heart, and with all thy soul, and with all thy mind. This is the first and great commandment . . . the second is . . . Thou shalt love thy neighbor as thyself. *Matt. 22:37–39*

3. The true worshipers shall worship the Father in spirit and in truth: for the Father seeketh such to worship him. *John 4:23*

4. Forasmuch as ye are zealous of spiritual gifts, seek that ye may excel to the edifying of the church. *1 Cor. 14:12*

5. Hold fast the profession of our faith. *Heb. 10:23*

6. Remember them which have . . . spoken unto you the word of God. . . . Obey them . . . and submit yourselves: for they watch for your souls. *Heb. 13:7,17*

CHURCH   (See also Fellowship; God, Family of; Ministry.)

1. How good and how pleasant it is for brethren to dwell together in unity! *Ps. 133:1*

2. Thou art Peter, and upon this rock I will build my church; and the gates of hell shall not prevail against it. *Matt. 16:18*

3. God . . . dwelleth not in temples made with hands. *Acts 17;24*

4. Now are they many members, yet but one body. *1 Cor. 12:20*

5. I am the least of the apostles, that am not meet to be called an apostle, because I persecuted the church of God. *1 Cor. 15:9*

6. [God] hath put all things under his feet, and gave him to be the head over all things to the church, Which is his body. *Eph. 1:22,23*

7. The church is subject unto Christ. *Eph. 5:24*

8. Christ also loved the church, and gave himself for it. *Eph. 5:25*

9. We are members of his body, of his flesh, and of his bones. *Eph. 5:30*

10. He [Christ] is the head of the body, the church. *Col. 1:18*

CHURCH, ATTENDANCE AT   (See also Sabbath.)

1. My sabbaths ye shall keep: for it is a sign between me and you throughout your generations. *Exod. 31:13*

2. He that regardeth the day, regardeth it unto the Lord; and he that regardeth not the day, to the Lord he doth not regard it. *Rom. 14:6*

3. Not forsaking the assembling of ourselves together, as the manner of some is; but exhorting one another: and so much the more, as ye see the day approaching. *Heb. 10:25*

CHURCH, CRITICISM OF   (See also Blasphemy; Heresy.)

1. Thine enemies roar in the midst of thy congregations. *Ps. 74:4*

2. When the Jews saw the multitudes, they were filled with envy, and spake against those things which were spoken by Paul, contradicting and blaspheming. *Acts. 13:45*

3. Mark them which cause divisions and offenses contrary to the doctrine which ye have learned. *Rom. 16:17*

4. Give none offense, neither to the Jews, nor to the Gentiles, nor to the church of God. *1 Cor. 10:32*

CHURCH, LEADERSHIP OF   See Apostle; Bishop; Deacon; Elder; Ministry; Shepherd.

CHURCH, MISSION OF   (See also Christ, Purpose of; Evangelism; Missionary.)

1. He [Jesus] said unto them, Go ye into all the world, and preach the gospel to every creature. *Mark 16:15*

2. The Spirit of the Lord is upon me, because he hath annointed me to preach the gospel of the poor; he hath sent me to heal the broken-hearted, to preach deliverance to the captives, and recovering of sight to the blind, to set at liberty them that are bruised, to preach the acceptable year of the Lord. *Luke 4:18,19*

3. Go thou and preach the kingdom of God. *Luke 9:60*

4. When they . . . had gathered the church together, they rehearsed all that God had done with them, and how he had opened the door of faith unto the Gentiles. *Acts 14:27*

5. God hath set some in the church, first apostles, secondarily prophets, thirdly teachers, after that miracles, then gifts of

healings, helps, governments, diversities of tongues. *1 Cor. 12:28*
6. Let the word of Christ dwell in you richly in all wisdom; teaching and admonishing one another in psalms and hymns and spiritual songs. *Col. 3:16*

CHURCH, OBLIGATION TO   See Church, Attendance at; Tithe.

CHURCH, PURPOSE OF   See Church, Mission of.

CIRCUMCISION
1. Ye shall circumcise the flesh of your foreskin; and it shall be a token of the covenant betwixt me and you. *Gen. 17:11*
2. He that is eight days old shall be circumcised among you. *Gen. 17:12*
3. The uncircumcised man child whose flesh of his foreskin is not circumcised, that soul shall be cut off from his people: he hath broken my covenant. *Gen. 17:14*
4. Circumcise therefore the foreskin of your heart. *Deut. 10:16*
5. When eight days were accomplished for the circumcising of the child, his name was called JESUS. *Luke 2:21*
6. Except ye be circumcised after the manner of Moses, ye cannot be saved. *Acts 15:1*
7. If thou be a breaker of the law, thy circumcision is made uncircumcision. *Rom. 2:25*
8. He is not a Jew, which is one outwardly; neither is that circumcision, which is outward in the flesh. But he is a Jew, which is one inwardly; and circumcision is that of the heart, in the spirit, and not in the letter; whose praise is not of men, but of God. *Rom. 2:28,29*
9. He received the sign of circumcision, a seal of the righteousness of the faith which he had yet being uncircumcised. *Rom. 4:11*
10. We are the circumcision, which worship God in the spirit, and rejoice in Christ Jesus, and have no confidence in the flesh. *Phil. 3:3*

CLERGY   See Bishop; Deacon; Elder; Ministry.

CLOTHING   See Dress.

COMFORT   (See also Relief; Sympathy.)
1. Thou art with me; thy rod and thy staff they comfort me. *Ps. 23:4*
2. Thou, Lord, hast helped me, and comforted me. *Ps. 86:17*
3. Comfort ye, comfort ye my people, saith your God. *Isa. 40:1*

4. The Lord hath anointed me . . . to comfort all that mourn. *Isa. 61:1,2*

5. Blessed are they that mourn: for they shall be comforted. *Matt. 5:4*

6. We through patience and comfort of the scriptures might have hope. *Rom. 15:4*

7. Blessed be God, . . . the Father of mercies, and the God of all comfort; Who comforteth us in all our tribulation, that we may be able to comfort them which are in any trouble, by the comfort wherewith we ourselves are comforted of God. *2 Cor. 1:3,4*

8. God shall wipe away all tears from their eyes; and there shall be no more death, neither sorrow, nor crying, neither shall there be any more pain. *Rev. 21:4*

COMFORTER   See Holy Spirit.

COMMANDMENT   See Doctrine; God, Law of; Golden Rule; Law.

COMMERCE   See Business; Consumerism.

COMMERCIALISM   (See also Worldliness.)

1. Thou hast defiled thy sanctuaries by the multitude of thine iniquities, by the iniquity of thy traffic. *Ezek. 28:18*

2. The heads thereof judge for reward, and the priests thereof teach for hire, and the prophets thereof divine for money; yet will they . . . say, Is not the Lord among us? none evil can come upon us. Therefore shall Zion . . . be plowed as a field, and Jerusalem shall become heaps. *Mic. 3:11,12*

3. Jesus went into the temple of God, and cast out all them that sold and bought in the temple, and overthrew the tables of the money changers . . . And said . . . My house shall be called the house of prayer, but ye have made it a den of thieves. *Matt. 21:12,13*

4. Thy money perish with thee, because thou hast thought that the gift of God may be purchased with money. *Acts 8:20*

COMMON SENSE   See Prudence; Wisdom.

COMMUNION, HOLY   See Eucharist.

COMPANIONS, EVIL   (See also Enemy; Influence; Obstacle; Ruffian; Temptation.)

1. Thou shalt not follow a multitude to do evil. *Exod. 23:2*

2. Depart, I pray you, from the tents of these wicked men, and touch nothing of theirs, lest ye be consumed in all their sins. *Num. 16:26*

3. Blessed is the man that walketh not in the counsel of the ungodly, nor standeth in the way of sinners, nor sitteth in the seat of the scornful. *Ps.1:1*

4. He that walketh with wise men shall be wise: but a companion of fools shall be destroyed. *Prov. 13:20*

5. Be not thou envious against evil men, neither desire to be with them. *Prov. 24:1*

6. He that is a companion of riotous men shameth his father. *Prov. 28:7*

7. He that keepeth company with harlots spendeth his substance. *Prov. 29:3*

8. Brethren, mark them which cause divisions and offenses contrary to the doctrine which ye have learned; and avoid them. For they that are such serve not our Lord Jesus Christ, but their own belly; and by good words and fair speeches deceive the hearts of the simple. *Rom. 16:17,18*

9. Have no fellowship with the unfruitful works of darkness. *Eph. 5:11*

10. Withdraw yourselves from every brother that walketh disorderly, and not after the tradition which he received of us. *2 Thess. 3:6*

COMPANIONSHIP   See Brotherhood; Christ, Companionship of; Companions, Evil; Friendship.

COMPASSION   See Comfort; God, Mercy of; Mercy; Pity; Sympathy.

COMPENSATION   See Reward; Wages.

COMPETITION

1. Let there be no strife . . . between me and thee . . for we be brethren. *Gen. 13:8*

2. There was also a strife among them [the apostles], which of them should be accounted the greatest. *Luke 22:24*

3. If a man also strive for masteries, yet is he not crowned, except he strive lawfully. *2 Tim. 2:5*

COMPLAINT   (See also Discontent; Unrest.)

1. Even today is my complaint bitter. *Job 23:2*

2. I complained, and my spirit was overwhelmed. *Ps. 77:3*

3. I poured out my complaint before him; I showed before him my trouble. *Ps. 142:2*

4. Wherefore doth a living man complain, a man for the punishment of his sins? *Lam. 3:39*

5. Murmur not among yourselves. *John 6:43*

6. Complainers, walking after their own lusts. *Jude 1:16*

   COMPLETION   See Accomplishment; Ending; Fulfillment.

   COMPREHENSION   See Understanding.

   CONCEALMENT   See Hiding; Secrecy.

   CONCEIT   See Boasting; Pride; Self-Centeredness; Vanity.

   CONCERN   See Worry.

   CONCLUSION   See Ending.

   CONDEMNATION   See Guilt; Punishment.

   CONDUCT   See Behavior.

   CONFESSION OF SINS   (See also Atonement; Forgiveness; Remission of Sins; Repentance.)

1. He shall confess that he hath sinned . . . And he shall bring his trespass offering unto the Lord. *Lev. 5:5,6*

2. I acknowledged my sin unto thee, and mine iniquity have I not hid . . . I will confess my transgressions unto the Lord; and thou forgavest the iniquity of my sin. *Ps. 32:5*

3. Through his name whosoever believeth in him shall receive remission of sins. *Acts 10:43*

4. Confess your faults one to another . . . that ye may be healed. *James 5:16*

5. If we confess our sins, he is faithful and just to forgive us our sins, and to cleanse us from all unrighteousness. *1 John 1:9*

   CONFIDENCE   See Faith; Trust.

   CONFINEMENT   See Captivity; Imprisonment.

   CONFUSION   See Chaos; Indecision.

   CONSCIENCE   (See also Guilt; Mind.)

1. My righteousness I hold fast, and will not let it go: my heart shall not reproach me so long as I live. *Job 27:6*

2. Have always a conscience void of offense toward God, and toward men. *Acts 24:16*

3. My conscience also bearing me witness in the Holy Ghost. *Rom. 9:1*

4. When ye sin so against the brethren, and wound their weak conscience, ye sin against Christ. *1 Cor. 8:12*

5. Speaking lies in hypocrisy; having their conscience seared with a hot iron. *1 Tim. 4:2*

   CONSCRIPTION   See Draft, Military.

   CONSENT   See Approval.

   CONSEQUENCE   See Result.

CONSERVATION See Environment; Pollution.

CONSERVATISM (See also Liberalism.)

1. The thing that hath been, it is that which shall be; and that which is done is that which shall be done: and there is no new thing under the sun. *Eccl. 1:9*

2. Ask for the old paths, where is the good way, and walk therein. *Jer. 6:16*

3. Can the Ethiopian change his skin, or the leopard his spots? *Jer. 13:23*

4. The fashion of this world passeth away. *1 Cor. 7:31*

5. Stand fast, and hold the traditions which ye have been taught. *2 Thess. 2:15*

CONSOLATION See Comfort.

CONSPIRACY (See also Deceit; Treachery.)

1. Put not thine hand with the wicked to be an unrighteous witness. Thou shalt not follow a multitude to do evil; neither shall thou speak in a cause to decline after many to wrest judgment. *Exod. 23:1,2*

2. Why do the heathen rage, and the people imagine a vain thing? The kinds of the earth set themselves, and the rulers take counsel together, against the Lord and against his anointed. *Ps. 2:1,2*

3. They intended evil against thee: they imagined a mischievous device. *Ps. 21:11*

4. The wicked plotteth against the just. *Ps. 37:12*

5. All that hate me whisper together against me: against me do they devise my hurt. *Ps. 41:7*

6. Thy tongue deviseth mischiefs; like a sharp razor, working deceitfully. *Ps. 52:2*

7. The Pharisees . . . took counsel with the Herodians against him [Jesus], how they might destroy him. *Mark 3:6*

CONSTANCY (See also Faithfulness; God, Faithfulness of Permanence.)

1. My foot hath held his steps, his way have I kept, and not declined. *Job 23:11*

2. His heart is fixed, trusting in the Lord. *Ps. 112:7*

3. None of these things move me. *Acts 20:24*

4. Be ye stedfast, unmoveable, always abounding in the work of the Lord. *1 Cor. 15:58*

5. The foundation of God standeth sure. *2 Tim. 2:19*

6. Jesus Christ the same yesterday, and today, and for ever. Be not carried about with divers and strange doctrines. For it is a good thing that the heart be established with grace. *Heb. 13:8,9*

CONSUMERISM   **(See also Borrowing and Lending.)**

1. It is naught saith the buyer: but when he is gone his way, then he boasteth. *Prov. 20:14*

2. Let not the buyer rejoice, nor the seller mourn: for wrath is upon all the multitude thereof. *Ezek. 7:12*

3. Which of you, intending to build a tower, sitteth not down first, and counteth the cost, whether he have sufficient to finish it? *Luke 14:28*

CONSUMMATION   **See Fulfillment.**

CONTEMPLATION   **See Meditation; Thought.**

CONTEMPT   **(See also Hatred; Scorn.)**

1. Because he hath despised the word of the Lord, and hath broken his commandment, that soul shall utterly be cut off. *Num. 15:31*

2. Them that honor me I will honor, and they that despise me shall be lightly esteemed. *1 Sam. 2:30*

3. Our soul is exceedingly filled with the scorning of those that are at ease, and with the contempt of the proud. *Ps. 123:4*

4. He that is void of wisdom despiseth his neighbor. *Prov. 11:12*

5. When the wicked cometh, then cometh also contempt, and with ignominy reproach. *Prov. 18:3*

6. He that despiseth you despiseth me; and he that despiseth me despiseth him that sent me. *Luke 10:16*

7. Let not him that eateth despise him that eateth not. *Rom. 14:3*

8. Let no man despise thee. *Titus 2:15*

CONTENTION   **See Argument.**

CONTENTMENT   **(See also Happiness.)**

1. I shall be satisfied, when I awake, with thy likeness. *Ps. 17:15*

2. To be spiritually minded is life and peace. *Rom. 8:6*

3. I have learned, in whatsoever state I am, therewith to be content. *Phil. 4:11*

4. Godliness with contentment is great gain. For we brought nothing into this world, and it is certain we can carry nothing out. And having food and raiment let us be therewith content. *1 Tim. 6:6–8*

5. Be content with such things as ye have. *Heb. 13:5*

   CONTEST   See Competition.

   CONTINENCE   See Celibacy; Moderation; Self-Control; Virginity.

   CONTRACT   See Covenant.

   CONTRITION   See Regret; Repentance.

   CONTROL   See Authority; God, Power of; Power.

   CONTROVERSY   See Argument.

   CONVERSION   (See also Baptism; Born Again; Reformation.)

1. Then will I teach transgressors thy ways; and sinners shall be converted unto thee. *Ps. 51:13*

2. Let the wicked forsake his way, and the unrighteous man his thoughts: and let him return unto the Lord, and he will have mercy upon him. *Isa. 55:7*

3. Turn thou to thy God: keep mercy and judgment, and wait on thy God continually. *Hos. 12:6*

4. When thou art converted, strengthen thy brethren. *Luke 22:32*

5. Repent ye therefore, and be converted, that your sins be blotted out. *Acts 3:19*

6. He which converteth the sinner from the error of his way shall save a soul from death, and shall hide a multitude of sins. *James 5:20*

   COOPERATION   See Brotherhood; Fellowship.

   CORRUPTION   (See also Decadence; Depravity; Evil; Impurity; Perversion; Sin.)

1. I have said to corruption, Thou art my father. *Job 17:14*

2. The creature itself also shall be delivered from the bondage of corruption into the glorious liberty of the children of God. *Rom. 8:21*

3. We shall all be changed . . . For this corruptible must put on incorruption. *1 Cor. 15:51,53.*

4. He that soweth to his flesh shall of the flesh reap corruption. *Gal. 6:8*

5. Natural brute beasts . . . shall utterly perish in their own corruption. *2 Peter 2:12*

6. While they promise them liberty, they themselves are the servants of corruption: for of whom a man is overcome, of the same is he brought in bondage. *2 Peter 2:19*

   COUNSEL   (See also Guidance; Leadership.)

1. Hearken now unto my voice, I will give thee counsel, and God shall be with thee. *Exod. 18:19*

2. We took sweet counsel together, and walked unto the house of God in company. *Ps. 55:14*

3. Where no counsel is, the people fall: but in the multitude of counselors there is safety. *Prov. 11:14*

4. He that hearkeneth unto counsel is wise. *Prov. 12:15*

5. With the well advised is wisdom. *Prov. 13:10*

6. Hear counsel, and receive instruction, that thou mayest be wise in thy latter end. *Prov. 19:20*

7. Every purpose is established by counsel: and with good advice make war. *Prov. 20:18*

8. Come now, and let us reason together, saith the Lord. *Isa. 1:18*

9. Hear the counsel of the Lord. *Jer. 49:20*

COUNTRY See Kingdom; Land; Nation.

COUNTRY, LOVE OF See Patriotism.

COURAGE (See also Strength.)

1. Be strong and of good courage, fear not, nor be afraid of them: for the Lord thy God, he it is that doth go with thee; he will not fail thee, nor forsake thee. *Deut. 31:6*

2. And thou, son of man, be not afraid of them, neither be afraid of their words, . . . nor be dismayed at their looks. *Ezek. 2:6*

3. They were all filled with the Holy Ghost, and they spake the word of God with boldness. *Acts 4:31*

4. Watch ye, stand fast in the faith, quit you like men, be strong. *1 Cor. 16:13*

5. Stand fast in one spirit, with one mind striving together for the faith of the gospel; And in nothing terrified by your adversaries. *Phil. 1:27,28*

6. I can do all things through Christ which strengtheneth me. *Phil. 4:13*

7. God hath not given us the spirit of fear; but of power, and of love, and of a sound mind. *2 Tim. 1:7*

COURT OF LAW See Trial.

COURTESY (See also Behavior; Kindness; Respect.)

1. Three men stood by him: and when he saw them, he ran to meet them from the tent door, and bowed himself toward the ground. *Gen. 18:2*

2. Thou hast spoken friendly unto thine handmaid. *Ruth 2:13*

3. A soft answer turneth away wrath: but grievous words stir up anger. *Prov. 15:1*

4. Pleasant words are as a honeycomb, sweet to the soul, and health to the bones. *Prov. 16:24*

5. Evil communications corrupt good manners. *1 Cor. 15:33*

6. Let your speech be always with grace, seasoned with salt, that ye may know how ye ought to answer every man. *Col. 4:6*

7. Be courteous. *1 Peter 3:8*

COVENANT   (See also Vow.)

1. I do set my bow in the cloud, and it shall be for a token of a covenant between me and the earth. *Gen. 9:13*

2. My covenant shall be in your flesh for an everlasting covenant. *Gen. 17:13*

3. They entered into a covenant to seek the Lord God of their fathers with all their heart and with all their soul. *2 Chron. 15:12*

4. This is my blood of the new testament, which is shed for many for the remission of sins. *Matt. 26:28*

5. Though it be but a man's covenant, yet if it be confirmed, no man disannulleth, or addeth thereto. *Gal. 3:15*

6. This is the covenant that I will make . . . I will put my laws into their mind, and write them in their hearts: and I will be to them a God, and they shall be to me a people. *Heb. 8:10*

COVETOUSNESS   (See also Desire; Greed; Lust; Worldliness.)

1. Thou shalt not covet thy neighbor's house, thou shalt not covet thy neighbor's wife, nor his manservant, nor his maidservant, nor his ox, nor his ass, nor any thing that is thy neighbor's. *Exod. 20:17*

2. Incline my heart unto thy testimonies, and not to covetousness. *Ps. 119:36*

3. The desire of the slothful killeth him; for his hands refuse to labor. He coveteth greedily all the day long. *Prov. 21:25,26.*

4. Beware of covetousness: for a man's life consisteth not in the abundance of the things which he possesseth. *Luke 12:15*

5. Let your conversation be without covetousness; and be content with such things as ye have. *Heb. 13:5*

COWARDICE   (See also Fear; Hiding.)

1. I will send a faintness into their hearts in the lands of their enemies; and the sound of a shaken leaf shall chase them; and they shall flee. *Lev. 26:36*

2. As soon as we had heard these things, our hearts did melt, neither did there remain any more courage in any man. *Josh. 2:11*

3. My flesh trembleth for fear of thee; and I am afraid of thy judgments. *Ps. 119:120*

4. The wicked flee when no man pursueth. *Prov. 28:1*

5. All the disciples forsook him, and fled. *Matt. 26:56*

CRAFTINESS   See Cunning.

CREATION   See Beginning; God, The Creator; Life.

CREDIT   See Borrowing and Lending.

CREMATION   (See also Burial; Death.)

1. All Israel stoned him with stones, and burned them with fire, after they had stoned them with stones. *Josh. 7:25*

2. The valiant men arose . . . and took the body of Saul and the bodies of his sons . . . and burnt them. *1 Sam. 31:12*

3. He slew all the priests of the high places that were there upon the altars, and burned men's bones upon them. *2 Kings 23:20*

4. I[the Lord]will not turn away the punishment thereof; because he burned the bones of the king of Edom into lime. *Amos 2:1*

5. A man's uncle shall take him up, and he that burneth him, to bring out the bones out of the house. *Amos 6:10*

CRIME   (See also Evil; Murder; Sin.)

1. If they say, Come with us, let us lay wait for blood, let us lurk privily for the innocent without cause . . . walk not thou in the way with them; refrain thy foot from their path. *Prov. 1:11,15*

2. Put away the evil of your doings from before mine eyes; cease to do evil. *Isa. 1:16*

3. As the partridge sitteth on eggs, and hatcheth them not; so he that getteth riches, and not by right, shall leave them in the midst of his days, and at his end shall be a fool. *Jer. 17:11*

4. The land is full of bloody crimes, and the city is full of violence. *Ezek. 7:23*

5. The world of the flesh are manifest . . . adultery, fornication, uncleanness, lasciviousness, Idolatry, witchcraft, hatred, variance, emulations, wrath, strife, seditions, heresies, Envyings, murders, drunkenness, revellings, and such like . . . they which do such things shall not inherit the kingdom of God. *Gal. 5:19–21*

CRITICISM   See Church, Criticism of.

CROSS   See Burden; Christ, Crucifixion of.

CROWN   (See also Reward.)

1. The hoary head is a crown of glory. *Prov. 16:31*

2. The Lord of hosts be for a crown of glory, and for a diadem of beauty, unto the residue of his people. *Isa. 28:5*

3. Jesus [came] forth, wearing the crown of thorns, and the purple robe. *John 19:5*

4. Every man that striveth for the mastery is temperate in all things. Now they do it to obtain a corruptible crown; but we an incorruptible. *1 Cor. 9:25*

5. There is laid up for me a crown of righteousness, which the Lord, the righteous judge, shall give me at that day: and not to me only, but unto all them also that love his appearing. *2 Tim. 4:8*

6. We see Jesus . . . crowned with glory and honor; that he by the grace of God should taste death for every man. *Heb. 2:9*

7. Blessed is the man that endureth temptation: for when he is tried, he shall receive the crown of life, which the Lord hath promised to them that love him. *James 1:12*

8. Be thou faithful unto death, and I will give thee a crown of life. *Rev. 2:10*

CRUCIFIXION **See Christ, Crucifixion of.**

CRUELTY **(See also Child Abuse; Terrorism.)**

1. Instruments of cruelty are in their habitations. *Gen. 49:5*

2. My father made your yoke heavy. . . . my father also chastised you with whips, but I will chastise you with scorpions. *1 Kings 12:14*

3. He that is cruel troubleth his own flesh. *Prov. 11:17*

4. The tender mercies of the wicked are cruel. *Prov. 12:10*

5. Ye beat my people to pieces, and grind the faces of the poor. *Isa. 3:15*

6. His father, because he cruelly oppressed, spoiled his brother by violence, and did that which is not good among his people, lo, even he shall die in his iniquity. *Ezek. 18:18*

7. The men that held Jesus mocked him, and smote him. And when they had blindfolded him, they struck him on the face. *Luke 22:63,64*

8. Others had trial of cruel mockings and scourgings, yea, moreover of bonds and imprisonment: They were stoned, they were sawn asunder . . . were slain with the sword . . . being destitute, afflicted, tormented. *Heb. 11:36,37*

CULTS, RELIGIOUS **(See also False Prophet; Heresy; Idolatry; Occult; Paganism.)**

1. The soul that turneth after such as have familiar spirits, and after wizards, to go a whoring after them, I will even set my face against that soul, and will cut him off from among his people. *Lev. 20:6*

2. That prophet, or that dreamer of dreams, shall be put to death; because he hath spoken to turn you away from the Lord your God . . . to thrust thee out of the way which the Lord thy God commanded thee to walk in. *Deut. 13:5*

3. They sacrificed unto devils, not to God; to gods whom they knew not, to new gods that came newly up. *Deut. 32:17*

4. Blessed is the man that walketh not in the counsel of the ungodly. *Ps. 1:1*

5. I am the Lord thy God . . . there is no savior beside me. *Hos. 13:4*

6. There shall arise false Christs, and false prophets, and shall show great signs and wonders; insomuch that, if it were possible, they shall deceive the very elect. *Matt. 24:24*

7. Howbeit then, when ye knew not God, ye did service unto them which by nature are no gods. *Gal. 4:8*

8. Let no man deceive you . . . who opposeth and exalteth himself above all that is called God, or that is worshipped; so that he as God sitteth in the temple of God, showing himself that he is God. *2 Thess. 2:3,4*

9. There are certain men crept in unawares, who were before of old ordained to this condemnation, ungodly men, turning the grace of our God into lasciviousness, and denying the only Lord God, and our Lord Jesus Christ. *Jude 1:4*

10. If any man worship the beast and his image, and receive his mark in his forehead, or in his hand, The same shall drink of the wine of the wrath of God. *Rev. 14:9,10*

CUNNING   (See also Deceit.)

1. Thy brother[Jacob] came with subtilty, and hath taken away thy blessing. *Gen. 27:35*

2. He taketh the wise in their own craftiness. *Job 5:13*

3. [Christians] have renounced the hidden things of dishonesty, not walking in craftiness, nor handling the word of God deceitfully. *2 Cor. 4:2*

4. Henceforth be no more children, tossed to and fro . . . by the sleight of men, and cunning craftiness, whereby they lie in wait to deceive. *Eph. 4:14*

CURIOSITY (See also Question.)

1. Take heed . . . that thou inquire not after their gods. *Deut. 12:30*

2. Hell and destruction are never full; so the eyes of man are never satisfied. *Prov. 27:20*

3. They came not for Jesus' sake only, but that they might see Lazarus also, whom he had raised from the dead. *John 12:9*

4. The Athenians and strangers which were there spent their time in nothing else, but either to tell, or to hear some new thing. *Acts 17:21*

5. Foolish and unlearned questions avoid, knowing that they do gender strifes. *2 Tim. 2:23*

> **CURSING**   See Blasphemy; Profanity.
> **CYNICISM**   See Pessimism.

DAMNATION See Hell; Punishment.

DANCING (See also Song.)

1. The women came out of all the cities of Israel, singing and dancing, to meet king Saul. *1 Sam. 18:6*

2. David danced before the Lord with all his might. *2 Sam. 6:14*

3. Thou hast turned for me my mourning into dancing. *Ps. 30:11*

4. Praise his name in the dance. *Ps. 149:3*

5. A time to mourn, and a time to dance. *Eccl. 3:4*

6. The virgin [shall] rejoice in the dance, both young men and old together: for I will turn their mourning into joy. *Jer. 31:13*

7. We have piped unto you, and ye have not danced. *Matt. 11:17*

DANGER (See also Temptation.)

1. Is not this the blood of the men that went in jeopardy of their lives? *2 Sam. 23:17*

2. Thou shalt not kill; and whosoever shall kill shall be in danger of the judgment: But I say unto you, That whosoever is angry with his brother without a cause shall be in danger of the judgment. *Matt. 5:21,22*

3. He that shall blaspheme against the Holy Ghost hath never forgiveness, but is in danger of eternal damnation. *Mark 3:29*

DARKNESS (See also Evil; Ignorance; Light.)

1. Where there is no vision, the people perish. *Prov. 29:18*

2. The fool walketh in darkness. *Eccl. 2:14*

3. We wait for light, but behold obscurity; for brightness, but we walk in darkness. *Isa. 59:9*

4. If thine eye be evil, thy whole body shall be full of darkness. If therefore the light that is in thee be darkness, how great is that darkness! *Matt. 6:23*

5. If the blind lead the blind, both shall fall into the ditch. *Matt. 15:14*

6. The light shineth in darkness; and the darkness comprehended it not. *John 1:5*

7. Then spake Jesus . . . saying, I am the light of the world: he that followeth me shall not walk in darkness, but shall have the light of life. *John 8:12*

8. He that saith he is in the light, and hateth his brother, is in darkness. *1 John 2:9*

9. [They are] wandering stars, to whom is reserved the blackness of darkness for ever. *Jude 1:13*

DEACON   (See also Bishop; Elder; Ministry.)

1. Brethren, look ye out among you seven men of honest report, full of the Holy Ghost and wisdom, whom we may appoint over this business. *Acts 6:3*

2. I commend unto you Phoebe our sister, which is a servant of the church . . . That ye receive her in the Lord. *Rom. 16:1,2*

3. The deacons [must] be grave, not double-tongued, not given to much wine, not greedy of filthy lucre; Holding the mystery of the faith in a pure conscience. *1 Tim. 3:8,9*

4. Let the deacons be the husbands of one wife, ruling their children and their own houses well. *1 Tim. 3:12*

5. They that have used the office of a deacon well purchase to themselves a good degree, and great boldness in the faith which is in Christ Jesus. *1 Tim. 3:13*

DEAD, RESURRECTION OF   See Resurrection of the Dead.

DEADLY SINS   See Anger; Covetousness; Envy; Gluttony; Lust; Pride; Sloth.

DEATH   (See also Assassination; Burial; Christ, Crucifixion of; Euthanasia; Life; Mortality; Murder; Resurrection of the Dead; Suicide.)

1. Thou return unto the ground; for out of it wast thou taken: for dust thou art, and unto dust shalt thou return. *Gen. 3:19*

2. Naked came I out of my mother's womb, and naked shall I return thither: the Lord gave, and the Lord hath taken away. *Job 1:21*

3. Precious in the sight of the Lord is the death of his saints. *Ps. 116:15*

4. To every thing there is a season . . . A time to be born, and a time to die. *Eccl. 3:1,2*

5. A good name is better than precious ointment; and the day of death than the day of one's birth. *Eccl. 7:1*

6. There is no man that hath power over the spirit to retain the spirit; neither hath he power in the day of death. *Eccl. 8:8*

7. Jesus . . . said, Father, into thy hands I commend my spirit: and having said thus, he gave up the ghost. *Luke 23:46*

8. The last enemy that shall be destroyed is death. *1 Cor. 15:26*

9. Death is swallowed up in victory. O death, where is thy sting? O grave, where is thy victory? The sting of death is sin; and the strength of sin is the law. *1 Cor. 15:54–56*

10. We brought nothing into this world, and it is certain we can carry nothing out. *1 Tim. 6:7*

11. Behold a pale horse: and his name that sat on him was Death. *Rev. 6:8*

12. Blessed are the dead which die in the Lord from henceforth: Yea, saith the Spirit, that they may rest from their labors. *Rev. 14:13*

DEATH SENTENCE   See Capital Punishment.

DEBT   See Borrowing and Lending.

DECADENCE   (See also Corruption; Depravity; Evil; Sin.)

1. [He] wasted his substance with riotous living. *Luke 15:13*

2. Let us walk honestly, as in the day; not in rioting and drunkenness, not in chambering and wantonness, not in strife and envying. *Rom. 13:13*

3. Every one of you should know how to possess his vessel in sanctification and honor; Not in the lust of concupiscence. *1 Thess. 4:4,5*

4. The time past of our life . . . we walked in lasciviousness, lusts, excess of wine, revellings, banquetings, and abominable idolatries. *1 Peter 4:3*

5. As Sodom and Gomorrah, and the cities about them in like manner, giving themselves over to fornication, and going after strange flesh, are set forth for an example, suffering the vengeance of eternal fire. Likewise also these filthy dreamers defile the flesh. *Jude 1:7,8*

DECEIT   (See also Conspiracy; Cunning; Flattery; Treachery.)

1. Thou shalt destroy them that speak leasing: the Lord will abhor the bloody and deceitful man. *Ps. 5:6*

c

2. He that worketh deceit shall not dwell within my house: he that telleth lies shall not tarry in my sight. *Ps. 101:7*

3. Bread of deceit is sweet to a man; but afterwards his mouth shall be filled with gravel. *Prov. 20:17*

4. The kisses of an enemy are deceitful. *Prov. 27:6*

5. The heart is deceitful above all things. *Jer. 17:9*

6. Take heed that no man deceive you. For many shall come in my name, saying, I am Christ; and shall deceive many. *Matt. 24:4,5*

7. Their throat is an open sepulcher; with their tongues they have used deceit; the poison of asps is under their lips. *Rom. 3:13*

8. If a man think himself to be something, when he is nothing, he deceiveth himself. *Gal. 6:3*

DECEPTION   See Deceit; False Prophet.

DECISION   (See also Choice; Indecision; Judgment.)

1. But Daniel purposed in his heart that he would not defile himself. *Dan. 1:8*

2. The day of the Lord is near in the valley of decision. *Joel 3:14*

3. This one thing I do . . . I press toward the mark for the prize of the high calling of God in Christ Jesus. *Phil 3:13,14*

DEEDS   See Performance; Service; Work.

DEFEAT   (See also Failure; Surrender; Victory.)

1. How are the mighty fallen, and the weapons of war perished! *2 Sam. 1:27*

2. Know ye not that there is a prince and a great man fallen this day in Israel? *2 Sam. 3:38*

3. The Lord upholdeth all that fall, and raiseth up all those that be bowed down. *Ps. 145:14*

4. I beheld Satan as lightning fall from heaven. *Luke 10:18*

DEFECT   See Imperfection.

DEFIANCE   (See also Disobedience; Rebellion; Rejection.)

1. The Lord said unto Moses . . . this people . . . is a stiffnecked people. *Exod. 32:9*

2. How shall I defy, whom the Lord hath not defied? *Num. 23:8*

3. He hath defied the armies of the living God. *1 Sam. 17:36*

4. They are like the deaf adder that stoppeth her ear; which will not hearken to the voice of charmers. *Ps. 58:4,5*

5. They kept not the covenant of God, and refused to walk in his law. *Ps. 78:10*

6. Woe to them that . . . look not unto the Holy One of Israel, neither seek the Lord! *Isa. 31:1*

7. Ye stiffnecked and uncircumcised in heart and ears, ye do always resist the Holy Ghost: as your fathers did, so do ye. *Acts 7:51*

8. It is hard for thee to kick against the pricks. *Acts 26:14*

DEFILEMENT   See Blasphemy; Corruption; Pollution.

DEITY   See Christ; Cults, Religious; God; Idolatry; Trinity, Holy.

DELAY   See Procrastination; Tardiness.

DELIVERANCE   (See also Liberty; Redemption; Release; Salvation.)

1. I am come down to deliver them . . . unto a land flowing with milk and honey. *Exod. 3:8*

2. The Lord that delivered me out of the paw of the lion . . . will deliver me out of the hand of this Philistine. *1 Sam. 17:37*

3. I sought the Lord, and he heard me, and delivered me from all my fears. *Ps. 34:4*

4. Thou hast delivered my soul from death: wilt not thou deliver my feet from falling, that I may walk before God in the light of the living? *Ps. 56:13*

5. [God] shall deliver thee from the snare of the fowler, and from the noisome pestilence. *Ps. 91:3*

6. Thou hast in love to my soul delivered it from the pit of corruption: for thou hast cast all my sins behind thy back. *Isa. 38:17*

7. Our God whom we serve is able to deliver us from the burning fiery furnace. *Dan. 3:17*

8. Whosoever shall call on the name of the Lord shall be delivered. *Joel 2:32*

9. Deliver us from evil. *Matt. 6:13*

10. The Lord knoweth how to deliver the godly out of temptations, and to reserve the unjust unto the day of judgment to be punished. *2 Peter 2:9*

DEMONS   (See also Angel; Exorcism; Hell; Occult.)

1. The Lord said unto Satan, Behold, all that he [Job] hath is in thy power; only upon himself put not forth thine hand. So Satan went forth from the presence of the Lord. *Job 1:12*

2. How art thou fallen from heaven, O Lucifer, son of the morning! how art thou cut down to the ground! *Isa. 14:12*

3. Get thee behind me, Satan. *Matt. 16:23*

4. My name is Legion: for we are many. *Mark 5:9*

5. Lord, even the devils are subject unto us through thy name. And he said unto them, I beheld Satan as lightning fall from heaven. *Luke 10:17,18*

6. Ye are of your father the devil, and the lusts of your father ye will do. He was a murderer from the beginning, and abode not in the truth, because there is no truth in him . . . he is a liar, and the father of it. *John 8:44*

7. Satan himself is transformed into an angel of light. *2 Cor. 11:14*

8. Resist the devil, and he will flee from you. *James 4:7*

9. Be sober, be vigilant; because your adversary the devil, as a roaring lion, walketh about, seeking whom he may devour. *1 Peter 5:8*

10. The angels which kept not their first estate, but left their own habitation, he [God] hath reserved in everlasting chains under darkness unto the judgment of the great day. *Jude 1:6*

11. That old serpent, called the Devil, and Satan, which deceiveth the whole world: he was cast out into the earth, and his angels were cast out with him. *Rev. 12:9*

DENIAL   See Defiance; Rejection.

DEPARTURE   (See also Journey.)

1. Entreat me not to leave thee, or to return from following after thee: for whither thou goest, I will go . . . thy people shall be my people, and thy God my God. *Ruth 1:16*

2. Lord, now lettest thou thy servant depart in peace, according to thy word. *Luke 2:29*

3. The hour cometh, yea, is now come, that ye shall be scattered, every man to his own, and shall leave me alone: and yet I am not alone, because the Father is with me. *John 16:32*

4. He [Christ] hath said, I will never leave thee, nor forsake thee. *Heb. 13:5*

DEPENDENCE   (See also Faith; Trust.)

1. The Lord God of Israel, under whose wings thou art come to trust. *Ruth 2:12*

2. Thou hast relied on the king of Syria, and not relied on the Lord thy God, therefore is the host of the king of Syria escaped out of thine hand. *2 Chron. 16:7*

3. The Lord thinketh upon me: thou art my help and my deliverer. *Ps. 40:17*

4. The Son can do nothing of himself, but what he seeth the Father do: for what things soever he doeth, these also doeth the Son likewise. *John 5:19*

DEPRAVITY   (See also Corruption; Decadence; Evil; Perversion.)

1. The imagination of man's heart is evil from his youth. *Gen. 8:21*

2. Thy way is perverse before me. *Num. 22:32*

3. The way of man is froward and strange. *Prov. 21:8*

4. A corrupt tree bringeth forth evil fruit. *Matt. 7:17*

5. From within, out of the heart of men, proceed evil thoughts, adulteries, fornications, murders, Thefts, covetousness, wickedness, deceit, lasciviousness, an evi) eye, blasphemy, pride, foolishness: All these evil things come from within, and defile the man. *Mark 7:21–23*

6. Evil men and seducers shall wax worse and worse, deceiving, and being deceived. *2 Tim. 3:13*

DEPRESSION   (See also Despair; Hopelessness; Sadness.)

1. Why art thou cast down, O my soul? and why art thou desquieted within me? Hope in God: for I shall yet praise him, who is the health of my countenance. *Ps. 43:5*

2. By the rivers of Babylon, there we sat down, yea, we wept, when we remembered Zion. *Ps. 137:1*

3. As he that taketh away a garment in cold weather . . . so is he that singeth songs to a heavy heart. *Prov. 25:20*

DERISION   See Scorn.

DESERTION   (See also Departure; Rejection.)

1. Leave me not, neither forsake me, O God of my salvation. *Ps. 27:9*

2. My lovers and my friends stand aloof from my sore; and my kinsmen stand afar off. *Ps. 38:11*

3. This is thy lot, the portion of thy measures from me, saith the Lord; because thou hast forgotten me, and trusted in falsehood. *Jer. 13:25*

DESIRE   (See also Covetousness; Expectation; Greed; Hope; Lust; Need.)

1. Behold, my desire is, that the Almighty would answer me, and that mine adversary had written a book. *Job 31:35*

2. Thou hast given him his heart's desire. *Ps. 21:2*

3. One thing have I desired of the Lord, that will I seek after; that I may dwell in the house of the Lord all the days of my life. *Ps. 27:4*

4. Delight thyself also in the Lord; and he shall give thee the desires of thine heart. *Ps. 37:4*

5. As the hart panteth after the water brooks, so panteth my soul after thee, O God. My soul thirsteth for God. *Ps. 42:1,2*

6. Thou openest thine hand, and satisfiest the desire of every living thing. *Ps. 145:16*

7. Better is the sight of the eyes than the wandering of the desire. *Eccl. 6:9*

8. Desire spiritual gifts. *1 Cor. 14:1*

DESPAIR   (See also Depression; Hopelessness; Pessimism.)

1. Out of the depths have I cried unto thee, O Lord. *Ps. 130:1*

2. Therefore is my spirit overwhelmed within me; my heart within me is desolate. *Ps. 143:4*

3. The harvest is past, the summer is ended, and we are not saved. *Jer. 8:20*

4. We despaired even of life. *2 Cor. 1:8*

5. We are troubled on every side, yet not distressed; we are perplexed, but not in despair. *2 Cor. 4:8*

6. The sorrow of the world worketh death. *2 Cor. 7:10*

DESTINY   See Predestination.

DESTITUTION   See Beggar; Poverty.

DESTRUCTION   See Disaster; Nuclear Holocaust.

DETERMINATION   (See also Decision; Predestination; Zeal.)

1. I will speak of thy testimonies also before kings, and will not be ashamed. And I will delight myself in thy commandments. *Ps. 119:46,47*

2. He that shall endure unto the end, the same shall be saved. *Mark 13:13*

3. Lord, I will follow thee whithersoever thou goest. *Luke 9:57*

4. The Son of man goeth, as it was determined. *Luke 22:22*

5. If ye continue in my word, then are ye my disciples indeed. *John 8:31*

6. [God] hath determined the times before appointed. *Acts 17:26*

DEVELOPMENT   See Growth; Improvement; Maturity; Self-Improvement.

DEVIL   See Demons; Exorcism; Hell.

DEVOTION   See Constancy, Faithfulness; Loyalty; Worship; Zeal.

DIFFICULTY See Trouble.

DIPLOMACY (See also Discretion; Mediation; Peacemaking.)

1. A soft answer turneth away wrath: but grievous words stir up anger. *Prov. 15:1*

2. By long forbearing is a prince persuaded, and a soft tongue breaketh the bone. *Prov. 25:15*

3. I made myself servant unto all, that I might gain the more. And unto the Jews I became as a Jew, that I might gain the Jews; to them that are under the law, as under the law, that I might gain them . . . To them that are without law, as without law, (being not without law to God, but under the law of Christ,) that I might gain them . . . To the weak became I as weak, that I might gain the weak: I am made all things to all men, that I might by all means save some. *1 Cor. 9:19–22*

DIRECTION See Guidance; Leadership.

DISABILITY See Handicap.

DISAGREEMENT See Argument.

DISAPPOINTMENT (See also Failure; Frustration.)

1. He disappointeth the devices of the crafty, so that their hands cannot perform their enterprise. *Job 5:12*

2. O Lord, disappoint him, cast him down: deliver my soul from the wicked. *Ps. 17:13*

3. The Lord . . . frustrateth the tokens of the liars. *Isa. 44:24,25*

4. Behold, these three years I come seeking fruit on this fig tree, and find none. *Luke 13:7*

5. The days will come, when ye shall desire to see one of the days of the Son of man, and ye shall not see it. *Luke 17:22*

6. I lay in Sion a chief corner stone, elect, precious: and he that believeth on him shall not be confounded. *1 Peter 2:6*

DISASTER

1. [I will] bring a flood of waters upon the earth, to destroy all flesh, wherein is the breath of life, from under heaven; and every thing that is in the earth shall die. *Gen. 6:17*

2. The Lord rained upon Sodom and upon Gomorrah brimstone and fire. *Gen. 19:24*

3. The day of their calamity is at hand. *Deut. 32:35*

4. The Lord passed by, and a great and strong wind rent the mountains, and brake in pieces the rocks before the Lord; but the Lord was not in the wind: and after the wind an earthquake: but the Lord was not in the earthquake: And after the earthquake a fire; but the Lord was not in the fire: and after the fire a still small voice. *1 Kings 19:11,12*

5. I will wipe Jerusalem as a man wipeth a dish, wiping it, and turning it upside down. *2 Kings 21:13*

6. The earth shall reel to and fro like a drunkard . . . and it shall fall, and not rise again. *Isa. 24:20*

7. Thou shalt be visited of the Lord of hosts with thunder, and with earthquake, and great noise, with storm and tempest, and the flame of devouring fire. *Isa. 29:6*

8. Nation shall rise against nation, and kingdom against kingdom: and there shall be famines, and pestilences, and earthquakes, in divers places. *Matt. 24:7*

9. Jesus . . . yielded up the ghost. And, behold . . . the veil of the temple was rent in twain from the top to the bottom; and the earth did quake, and the rocks rent. *Matt. 27:50,51*

10. Therefore shall her plagues come in one day, death, and mourning, and famine; and she shall be utterly burned with fire: for strong is the Lord God who judgeth. *Rev. 18:8*

DISCIPLE   (See also Apostle; Army, Christian; Follower.)

1. The disciple is not above his master, nor the servant above his lord. *Matt. 10:24*

2. Whosoever will come after me, let him deny himself, and take up his cross, and follow me. *Mark 8:34*

3. The Lord appointed other seventy also, and sent them two and two before his face into every city and place. *Luke 10:1*

4. Whosoever he be of you that forsaketh not all that he hath, he cannot be my disciple. *Luke 14:33*

5. If ye continue in my word, then are ye my disciples indeed. *John 8:31*

6. If any man serve me, let him follow me; and where I am, there shall also my servant be: if any man serve me, him will my Father honor. *John 12:26*

7. By this shall all men know that ye are my disciples, if ye have love one to another. *John 13:35*

8. The disciples were called Christians. *Acts 11:26*

DISCIPLINE   (See also Chastisement; Punishment.)

1. He openeth also their ear to discipline, and commandeth that they return from iniquity. *Job 36:10*

2. He that spareth his rod hateth his son: but he that loveth him chasteneth him betimes. *Prov. 13:24*

3. Chasten thy son while there is hope, and let not thy soul spare for his crying. *Prov. 19:18*

4. The rod and reproof give wisdom: but a child left to himself bringeth his mother to shame. . . . Correct thy son, and he shall give thee rest. *Prov. 29:15,17*

5. Despise not thou the chastening of the Lord, nor faint when thou art rebuked of him: For whom the Lord loveth he chasteneth, and scourgeth every son whom he receiveth. If ye endure chastening, God dealeth with you as with sons . . . But if ye be without chastisement . . . then are ye bastards, and not sons. *Heb. 12:5–8*

DISCONTENT   (See also Complaint; Unrest.)

1. The Lord heareth your murmurings which ye murmur against him. *Exod. 16:8*

2. I am feeble and sore broken: I have roared by reason of the disquietness of my heart. *Ps. 38:8*

3. The eye is not satisfied with seeing, nor the ear filled with hearing. *Eccl. 1:8*

4. He that loveth silver shall not be satisfied with silver; nor he that loveth abundance with increase. *Eccl. 5:10*

5. Jesus . . . said unto them, Murmur not among yourselves. *John 6:43*

6. Do all things without murmurings and disputings. *Phil. 2:14*

DISCOURAGEMENT   (See also Depression; Despair; Hopelessness; Weariness.)

1. My punishment is greater than I can bear. *Gen. 4:13*

2. The soul of the people was much discouraged. *Num. 21:4*

3. Hope deferred maketh the heart sick. *Prov. 13:12*

4. He shall not fail nor be discouraged, till he have set judgment in the earth. *Isa. 42:4*

5. Fathers, provoke not your children to anger, lest they be discouraged. *Col. 3:21*

DISCOVERY   (See also Revelation.)

1. Ahab said to Elijah, Hast thou found me, O mine enemy? And he answered, I have found thee: because thou hast sold thyself to work evil in the sight of the Lord. *1 Kings 21:20*

2. Canst thou by searching find out God? *Job 11:7*

3. He [God] discovereth deep things out of darkness, and bringeth out to light the shadow of death. *Job 12:22*

4. Ye shall seek me, and find me, when ye shall search for me with all your heart. *Jer. 29:13*

DISCRETION (See also Diplomacy.)

1. Give subtilty to the simple, to the young man knowledge and discretion. *Prov. 1:4*

2. Discretion shall preserve thee. *Prov. 2:11*

3. As a jewel of gold in a swine's snout, so is a fair woman which is without discretion. *Prov. 11:22*

4. The discretion of a man deferreth his anger; and it is his glory to pass over a transgression. *Prov. 19:11*

5. Teach the young women . . . to be discreet. *Titus 2:4,5*

DISCRIMINATION See Favoritism; Segregation.

DISEASE See Illness; Venereal Disease.

DISGRACE See Dishonor.

DISHONESTY See Bribery; Cheating; Deceit; Falsehood.

DISHONOR (See also Shame.)

1. Let them be ashamed and brought to confusion together that rejoice at mine hurt: let them be clothed with shame and dishonor that magnify themselves against me. *Ps. 35:26*

2. He that saith unto the wicked, Thou art righteous; him shall the people curse, nations shall abhor him. *Prov. 24:24*

3. Do not disgrace the throne of thy glory. *Jer. 14:21*

4. Ye are taken up in the lips of talkers, and are an infamy of the people. *Ezek. 36:3*

5. Many of them that sleep in the dust of the earth shall awake, some to everlasting life, and some to shame and everlasting contempt. *Dan. 12:2*

DISOBEDIENCE (See also Defiance; Obedience; Rebellion; Sin.)

1. Whosoever will not hearken unto my words which he shall speak in my name, I will require it of him. *Deut. 18:19*

2. Thou hast done foolishly: thou hast not kept the commandment of the Lord thy God. *1 Sam. 13:13*

3. Cursed be the man that obeyeth not the words of this covenant. *Jer. 11:3*

4. The wrath of God [cometh] upon the children of disobedience. *Eph. 5:6*

5. Vengeance on them that know not God, and that obey not the gospel of our Lord Jesus Christ. *2 Thess. 1:8*

6. The law is not made for a righteous man, but for the lawless and disobedient. *1 Tim. 1:9*

7. Every transgression and disobedience received a just recompense. *Heb. 2:2*

DISPUTE   See Argument.

DISSATISFACTION   See Complaint; Discontent.

DISTRESS   (See also Sorrow; Suffering; Trouble.)

1. In my distress I called upon the Lord, and cried to my God: and he did hear my voice out of his temple, and my cry did enter into his ears. *2 Sam. 22:7*

2. This poor man cried, and the Lord heard him, and saved him out of all his troubles. *Ps. 34:6*

3. The Lord . . . delivered them out of their distresses. *Ps. 107:6*

4. Tribulation and anguish, upon every soul of man that doeth evil. *Rom. 2:9*

5. I take pleasure . . . in distresses for Christ's sake. *2 Cor. 12:10*

DIVINITY   See Christ, Divinity of; God.

DIVISION   (See also Heresy; Segregation; Unity.)

1. Every kingdom divided against itself is brought to desolation; and every . . . house divided against itself shall not stand. *Matt. 12:25*

2. Before him shall be gathered all nations: and he shall separate them one from another, as a shepherd divideth his sheep from the goats. *Matt. 25:32*

3. Blessed are ye, when men . . . shall separate you from their company . . . for the Son of man's sake. *Luke 6:22*

4. I beseech you . . . that ye all speak the same thing, and that there be no divisions among you; but that ye be perfectly joined together in the same mind and in the same judgment. *1 Cor. 1:10*

DIVORCE   (See also Marriage.)

1. When a man hath taken a wife, and married her, and . . . she find no favor in his eyes . . . let him write her a bill of divorcement, and . . . send her out of his house. And when she is departed . . . she may go and be another man's wife. *Deut. 24:1,2*

2. The queen Vashti refused to come at the king's commandment by his chamberlains. . . . let the king give her royal estate unto another that is better than she. *Esth. 1:12,19*

3. Whosoever shall put away his wife, saving for the cause of fornication, causeth her to commit adultery: and whosoever shall marry her that is divorced committeth adultery. *Matt. 5:32*

4. What therefore God hath joined together, let not man put asunder. *Matt. 19:6*

5. Let not the wife depart from her husband: But and if she depart, let her remain unmarried, or be reconciled to her husband: and let not the husband put away his wife. *1 Cor. 7:10,11*

DOCTOR   See Physician.

DOCTRINE   (See also Gospel; Scripture; Word.)

1. My doctrine shall drop as the rain. *Deut. 32:2*

2. When Jesus had ended these sayings, the people were astonished at his doctrine: For he taught them as one having authority, and not as the scribes. *Matt. 7:28,29*

3. My doctrine is not mine, but his that sent me. If any man will do his will, he shall know of the doctrine, whether it be of God, or whether I speak of myself. *John 7:16,17*

4. May we know what this new doctrine, whereof thou speakest, is? For thou bringest certain strange things to our ears: we would know therefore what these things mean. *Acts 17:19,20*

5. If any man . . . consent not to wholesome words, even the words of our Lord Jesus Christ, and to the doctrine which is according to godliness; He is proud, knowing nothing. *1 Tim. 6:3,4*

6. All scripture is given by inspiration of God, and is profitable for doctrine. *2 Tim. 3:16*

7. Whosoever transgresseth, and abideth not in the doctrine of Christ, hath not God. He that abideth in the doctrine of Christ, he hath both the Father and the Son. *2 John 1:9*

DONATION   See Giving; Tithe.

DOUBT   (See also Faith; Question.)

1. Thy life shall hang in doubt before thee. *Deut. 28:66*

2. No man is sure of life. *Job 24:22*

3. O thou of little faith, wherefore didst thou doubt? *Matt. 14:31*

4. If ye have faith, and doubt not . . . ye shall say unto this mountain, Be thou removed, and be thou cast into the sea; it shall be done. *Matt. 21:21*

5. Except I [Thomas] shall see in his hands the print of nails, and put my finger into the print of the nails, and thrust my hand into his side, I will not believe . . . Jesus saith unto him, Thomas, because thou hast seen me, thou hast believed: blessed are they that have not seen, and yet have believed. *John 20:25–29*

DRAFT, MILITARY

1. [Take every male] from twenty years old and upward, all that are able to go forth to war. *Num. 1:3*

2. What man is there that hath built a new house, and hath not dedicated it? let him go and return to his house, lest he die in the battle, and another man dedicate it. And what man is he that hath planted a vineyard, and hath not yet eaten of it? let him also go and return unto his house, lest he die in the battle, and another man eat of it. And what man is there that hath betrothed a wife, and hath not taken her? let him go and return unto his house, lest he die in the battle, and another man take her . . . What man is there that is fearful and fainthearted? let him go and return unto his house, lest his brethren's heart faint as well as his heart. *Deut. 20:5–8*

3. Take ten men of an hundred throughout all the tribes of Israel, and a hundred of a thousand, and a thousand out of ten thousand. *Judg. 20:10*

4. There was sore war . . . and when Saul saw any strong man, or any valiant man, he took him unto him. *1 Sam. 14:52*

DREAM   (See also Interpretation.)

1. He [Jacob] dreamed, and behold a ladder set up on the earth, and the top of it reached to heaven: and behold the angels of God ascending and descending on it. *Gen. 28:12*

2. If there be a prophet among you, I the Lord will make myself known unto him in a vision, and will speak unto him in a dream. *Num. 12:6*

3. That [false] prophet, or that dreamer of dreams, shall be put to death. *Deut. 13:5*

4. In a dream, in a vision of the night, when deep sleep falleth upon men, in slumberings upon the bed; then he openeth the ears of men, and sealeth their instruction. *Job 33:15,16*

5. Your old men shall dream dreams, your young men shall see visions. *Joel 2:28*

6. The angel of the Lord appeared unto him [Joseph] in a dream. *Matt. 1:20*

7. These filthy dreamers defile the flesh, despise dominion, and speak evil of dignities. *Jude 1:8*

DRESS   (See also Modesty; Nakedness.)

1. The eyes of them both [Adam and Eve] were opened, and they knew that they were naked; and they sewed fig leaves together, and made themselves aprons. *Gen. 3:7*

2. The woman shall not wear that which pertaineth unto a man, neither shall a man put on a woman's garment: for all that do so are abomination unto the Lord. *Deut. 22:5*

3. They part my garments among them, and cast lots upon my vesture. *Ps. 22:18*

4. Strength and honor are her clothing. *Prov. 31:25*

5. The Lord . . . hath clothed me with the garments of salvation, he hath covered me with the robe of righteousness. *Isa. 61:10*

6. If any man . . . take away thy coat, let him have thy cloak also. *Matt. 5:40*

7. Take no thought . . . for your body, what ye shall put on. Is not the life more than meat, and the body than raiment? *Matt. 6:25*

8. [I was] Naked, and ye clothed me. *Matt. 25:36*

9. Women [should] adorn themselves in modest apparel, with shamefacedness and sobriety; not with braided hair, or gold, or pearls, or costly array. *1 Tim. 2:9*

DRUG ABUSE   (See also Drunkenness.)

1. If any man defile the temple of God, him shall God destroy; for the temple of God is holy, which temple ye are. *1 Cor. 3:17*

2. Let us cleanse ourselves from all filthiness of the flesh and spirit. *2 Cor. 7:1*

DRUNKENNESS   (See also Sobriety; Wine.)

1. Be not among winebibbers . . . For the drunkard and the glutton shall come to poverty. *Prov. 23:20,21*

2. Who hath woe? Who hath sorrow? Who hath contentions? Who hath babbling? Who hath wounds without cause? Who hath redness of eyes? They that tarry long at the wine; they that go to seek mixed wine. *Prov. 23:29,30*

3. Give strong drink unto him that is ready to perish, and wine unto those that be of heavy hearts. Let him drink, and forget his poverty, and remember his misery no more. *Prov. 31:6,7*

4. Woe unto them that rise up early in the morning, that they may follow strong drink; that continue until night, till wine inflame them! *Isa. 5:11*

5. Strong drink shall be bitter to them that drink it. *Isa. 24:9*

6. Awake, ye drunkards, and weep; and howl, all ye drinkers of wine, because of the new wine; for it is cut off from your mouth. *Joel 1:5*

7. They have . . . sold a girl for wine, that they might drink. *Joel 3:3*

8. Drunkards . . . shall [not] inherit the kingdom of God. *1 Cor. 6:10*

9. Be not drunk with wine, wherein is excess; but be filled with the Spirit. *Eph. 5:18*

DULLNESS   See Boredom.

DUTY   (See also Christian Obligation; Responsibility; Taxation.)

1. Thou shalt love thy neighbor as thyself. *Lev. 19:18*

2. Thou shalt love the Lord thy God with all thine heart, and with all thy soul, and with all thy might. *Deut. 6:5*

3. Thou shalt do that which is right and good in the sight of the Lord. *Deut. 6:18*

4. Give unto the Lord the glory due unto his name . . . worship the Lord in the beauty of holiness. *1 Chron. 16:29*

5. Fear God, and keep his commandments: for this is the whole duty of man. *Eccl. 12:13*

6. All things whatsoever ye would that men should do to you, do ye even so to them: for this is the law and the prophets. *Matt. 7:12*

7. Wist ye not that I must be about my Father's business. *Luke 2:49*

8. I [Jesus] came down from heaven, not to do mine own will, but the will of him that sent me. *John 6:38*

9. Render therefore to all their dues: tribute to whom tribute is due; custom to whom custom; fear to whom fear; honor to whom honor. *Rom. 13:7*

10. Honor all men. Love the brotherhood. Fear God. Honor the King. *1 Peter 2:17*

EAGERNESS　See Zeal.

EARTH　(See also Creation; Heaven; Land; Pollution.)

1. In the beginning God created the heaven and the earth. And the earth was without form, and void. *Gen. 1:1,2*

2. While the earth remaineth, seed-time and harvest, and cold and heat, and summer and winter, and day and night shall not cease. *Gen. 8:22*

3. The earth is the Lord's, and the fullness thereof; the world, and they that dwell therein. *Ps. 24:1*

4. One generation passeth away, and another generation cometh: but the earth abideth for ever. *Eccl. 1:4*

5. The earth shall be full of the knowledge of the Lord, as the waters cover the sea. *Isa. 11:9*

6. The heavens shall vanish away like smoke, and the earth shall wax old like a garment, and they that dwell therein shall die in like manner. *Isa. 51:6*

7. Thy will be done in earth, as it is in heaven. *Matt. 6:10*

8. The earth is the Lord's, and the fullness thereof. *1 Cor. 10:26*

9. We [Christians] . . . look for new heavens and a new earth, wherein dwelleth righteousness. *2 Peter 3:13*

10. I saw a great white throne, and him that sat on it, from whose face the earth and the heaven fled away; and there was found no place for them. *Rev. 20:11*

EATING　See Food; Gluttony; Vegetarianism.

ECOLOGY　See Conservation; Environment; Pollution.

EDEN, GARDEN OF　See Paradise.

EDUCATION　(See also Teaching.)

1. Thou shalt teach them diligently unto thy children. *Deut. 6:7*

2. I will teach you the good and the right way. *1 Sam. 12:23*

3. Whoso loveth instruction loveth knowledge. *Prov. 12:1*

4. Hear counsel, and receive instruction, that thou mayest be wise in thy latter end. *Prov. 19:20*

5. Learn of me . . . and ye shall find rest unto your souls. *Matt. 11:29*

6. Jesus increased in wisdom and stature, and in favor with God and man. *Luke 2:52*

7. The law was our schoolmaster to bring us unto Christ. *Gal. 3:24*

8. The heir, as long as he is a child . . . is under tutors and governors until the time appointed of the father. *Gal. 4:1,2*

EGOTISM   See Boasting; Pride; Self-Centeredness; Selfishness; Vanity.

EGYPT   (See also Israel, Middle East Conflict.)

1. Pharaoh said unto Joseph . . . take your father and your households, and come unto me: and I will give you the good of the land of Egypt, and ye shall eat the fat of the land. *Gen. 45:17,18*

2. The Egyptians shall know that I am the Lord, when I stretch forth mine hand upon Egypt, and bring out the children of Israel from among them. *Exod. 7:5*

3. Blessed be Egypt my people. *Isa. 19:25*

4. They also that uphold Egypt shall fall; and the pride of her power shall come down. *Ezek. 30:6*

ELDER   (See also Bishop; Deacon; Ministry.)

1. Why do thy disciples transgress the tradition of the elders? *Matt. 15:2*

2. Neglect not the gift that is in thee, which was given thee by prophecy, with the laying on of the hands of the presbytery. *1 Tim. 4:14*

3. Rebuke not an elder, but entreat him as a father. *1 Tim. 5:1*

4. Let the elders that rule well be counted worthy of double honor, especially they who labor in the word and doctrine. *1 Tim. 5:17*

5. Ordain elders in every city. *Titus 1:5*

6. Is any sick among you? let him call for the elders of the church; and let them pray over him, anointing him with oil in the name of the Lord. *James 5:14*

7. The elders which are among you I exhort . . . Feed the flock of God . . . taking the oversight thereof. *1 Peter 5:1,2*

ELDERLY   See Aged.

ELECTION   (See also Choice.)

1. The people also cast lots, to bring one of ten to dwell in Jerusalem the holy city, and nine parts to dwell in other cities. *Neh. 11:1*

2. The last shall be first, and the first last: for many be called, but few chosen. *Matt. 20:16*

3. Ye have not chosen me, but I have chosen you. *John 15:16*

4. The purpose of God according to election might stand, not of works, but of him that calleth. *Rom. 9:11*

5. Elect according to the foreknowledge of God the Father, through sanctification of the Spirit, unto obedience and sprinkling of the blood of Jesus Christ. *1 Peter 1:2*

EMBARRASSMENT   See Shame.

EMPATHY   See Sympathy.

EMPLOYMENT   See Business; Unemployment; Work.

ENDING   (See also Beginning; Death.)

1. There is a way which seemeth right unto a man; but the end thereof are the ways of death. *Prov. 14:12*

2. Better is the end of a thing than the beginning thereof. *Eccl. 7:8*

3. The last state of that [wicked] man is worse than the first. *Matt. 12:45*

4. The harvest is the end of the world. *Matt. 13:39*

5. He that shall endure unto the end, the same shall be saved. *Matt. 24:13*

6. Of his kingdom there shall be no end. *Luke 1:33*

7. Jesus . . . said, It is finished: and he bowed his head, and gave up the ghost. *John 19:30*

8. In the last days perilous times shall come. *2 Tim. 3:1*

9. I am Alpha and Omega, the beginning and the end, the first and the last. *Rev. 22:13*

ENDURANCE   See Constancy; Patience; Tolerance.

ENEMY   (See also Companions, Evil; Demons; Hostility.)

1. I will be an enemy unto thine enemies, and an adversary unto thine adversaries. *Exod. 23:22*

2. Let them be confounded and consumed that are adversaries to my soul; let them be covered with reproach and dishonor that seek my hurt. *Ps. 71:13*

3. His [Solomon's] enemies shall lick the dust. *Ps. 72:9*

4. I hate them with perfect hatred: I count them mine enemies. *Ps. 139:22*

5. Rejoice not when thine enemy falleth, and let not thine heart be glad when he stumbleth. *Prov. 24:17*

6. If thine enemy be hungry, give him bread to eat; and if he be thirsty, give him water to drink: for thou shalt heap coals of fire upon his head, and the Lord shall reward thee. *Prov. 25:21,22*

7. The kisses of an enemy are deceitful. *Prov. 27:6*

8. Thine hand shall be lifted up upon thine adversaries, and all thine enemies shall be cut off. *Mic. 5:9*

9. A man's enemies are the men of his own house. *Mic. 7:6*

10. Love your enemies, bless them that curse you, do good to them that hate you, and pray for them which despitefully use you, and persecute you. *Matt. 5:44*

11. The last enemy that shall be destroyed is death. *1 Cor. 15:26*

12. Your adversary the devil, as a roaring lion, walketh about, seeking whom he may devour. *1 Peter 5:8*

ENGAGEMENT   See Betrothal.

ENJOYMENT   See Amusement; Pleasure.

ENLIGHTENMENT   See Realization; Revelation; Teaching.

ENMITY   See Hatred; Hostility; Malice.

ENTERTAINMENT   See Amusement; Pleasure.

ENTHUSIASM   See Zeal.

ENTICEMENT   See Seduction; Temptation.

ENVIRONMENT   (See also Earth; Pollution.)

1. Blessed of the Lord be his land, for the precious things of heaven, for the dew . . . for the precious fruits brought forth by the sun . . . and for the precious things of the earth and fulness thereof. *Deut. 33:13–16*

2. Be in the league with the stones of the field: and the beasts of the field shall be at peace with thee. *Job 5:23*

3. Speak to the earth, and it shall teach thee. *Job 12:8*

4. The earth is full of thy riches. *Ps. 104:24*

5. As the mountains are round about Jerusalem, so the Lord is round about his people from henceforth even for ever. *Ps. 125:2*

ENVY   (See also Covetousness; Jealousy.)

1. Wrath killeth the foolish man, and envy slayeth the silly one. *Job 5:2*

2. Envy thou not the oppressor, and choose none of his ways. *Prov. 3:31*

3. A sound heart is the life of the flesh: but envy the rottenness of the bones. *Prov. 14:30*

4. Fret not thyself because of evil men, neither be thou envious at the wicked. *Prov. 24:19*

5. Let us walk honestly, as in the day . . . not in strife and envying. *Rom. 13:13*

6. Charity envieth not. *1 Cor. 13:4*

7. If ye have bitter envying and strife in your hearts, glory not. *James 3:14*

8. The spirit that dwelleth in us lusteth to envy. *James 4:5*

EPISTLE   See Book; Gospel; Scripture; Writing.

EQUALITY   (See also Impartiality; Inequality; Prejudice.)

1. Eve . . . the mother of all living. *Gen. 3:20*

2. The rich and the poor meet together: the Lord is the maker of them all. *Prov. 22:2*

3. The profit of the earth is for all. *Eccl. 5:9*

4. Have we not all one father? hath not one God created us? *Mal. 2:10*

5. Be not ye called Rabbi: for one is your Master, even Christ; and all ye are brethren. *Matt. 23:8*

6. [God] hath made of one blood all nations of men for to dwell on all the face of the earth. *Acts 17:26*

7. I mean not that other men be eased, and ye burdened: But by an equality, that now at this time your abundance may be a supply for their want, that their abundance also may be a supply for your want: that there may be equality. *2 Cor. 8:13,14*

8. There is neither Jew nor Greek, there is neither bond nor free, there is neither male nor female: for ye are all one in Christ Jesus. *Gal. 3:28*

9. Observe these things without preferring one before another, doing nothing by partiality. *1 Tim. 5:21*

EROTICISM   See Promiscuity.

ERROR   See Mistake; Sin.

ESCAPE   (See also Deliverance; Passover; Release.)

1. The eyes of the wicked shall fail, and they shall not escape. *Job 11:20*

2. I am escaped with the skin of my teeth. *Job 19:20*

3. O that I had wings like a dove! For then would I fly away. *Ps. 55:6*

4. He that speaketh lies shall not escape. *Prov. 19:5*

5. The angel of the Lord appeareth to Joseph in a dream, saying, Arise, and take the young child and his mother, and flee into Egypt. *Matt. 2:13*

6. Ye serpents, ye generation of vipers, how can ye escape the damnation of hell? *Matt. 23:33*

7. Pray always, that ye may be accounted worthy to escape all these things that shall come to pass, and to stand before the Son of man. *Luke 21:36*

8. Thinkest thou this, O man, that judgest them which do such things, and doest the same, that thou shalt escape the judgment of God. *Rom. 2:3*

9. The kings of the earth, and the great men, and the rich men, and the chief captains, and the mighty men, and every bondman, and every free man, hid themselves in the dens and in the rocks of the mountains; And said to the mountains and rocks, Fall on us, and hide us from the face of him that sitteth on the throne, and from the wrath of the Lamb: For the great day of his wrath is come. *Rev. 6:15–17*

ESPIONAGE   (See also Exploration.)

1. Moses sent them to spy out the land of Canaan . . . And see the land, what it is; and the people that dwelleth therein, whether they be strong or weak, few or many. *Num. 13:17,18*

2. We will send men before us, and they shall search us out the land, and bring us word again by what way we must go up, and into what cities we shall come. *Deut. 1:22*

3. Go, I pray you, prepare yet, and know and see his place where his haunt is, and who hath seen him there: for it is told me that he dealeth very subtly. *1 Sam. 23:22*

4. Hath not David rather sent his servants unto thee, to search the city, and to spy it out, and to overthrow it? *2 Sam. 10:3*

5. False brethren . . . who came privily to spy out our liberty which we have in Christ Jesus, that they might bring us into bondage. *Gal. 2:4*

ESTEEM   See Respect.

ETERNITY   (See also Immortality; Permanence.)

1. The Lord shall reign for ever and ever. *Exod. 15:18*

2. His name shall endure for ever: his name shall be continued as long as the sun. *Ps. 72:17*

3. Lord, thou hast been our dwelling place in all generations. Before the mountains were brought forth, or ever thou hadst formed the earth and the world, even from everlasting to everlasting, thou art God. *Ps. 90:1,2*

4. The Lord is good; his mercy is everlasting; and his truth endureth to all generations. *Ps. 100:5*

5. Thine is the kingdom, and the power, and the glory, for ever. *Matt. 6:13*

6. I am with you alway, even unto the end of the world. *Matt. 28:20*

7. This is life eternal, that they might know thee the only true God, and Jesus Christ, whom thou hast sent. *John 17:3*

8. The things which are not seen are eternal. *2 Cor. 4:18*

9. Lay hold on eternal life. *1 Tim. 6:12*

EUCHARIST   (See also Blood; Body; Ritual; Wine.)

1. He [Jesus] took bread, and gave thanks, and brake it, and gave unto them, saying, This is my body which is given for you: this do in remembrance of me. Likewise also the cup after supper, saying, This cup is the new testament in my blood, which is shed for you. *Luke 22:19,20*

2. Except ye eat the flesh of the Son of man, and drink his blood, ye have no life in you. Whoso eateth my flesh, and drinketh my blood, hath eternal life. *John 6:53,54*

3. He that eateth my flesh, and drinketh my blood, dwelleth in me, and I in him. *John 6:56*

4. The cup of blessing which we bless, is it not the communion of the blood of Christ? The bread which we break, is it not the communion of the body of Christ? *1 Cor. 10:16*

5. As often as ye eat this bread, and drink this cup, ye do show the Lord's death till he come. . . . Whosoever shall eat this bread, and drink this cup of the Lord, unworthily, shall be guilty of the body and blood of the Lord . . . For he . . . eateth and drinketh damnation to himself, not discerning the Lord's body. *1 Cor. 11:26–29*

6. Blessed are they which are called unto the marriage supper of the Lamb. *Rev. 19:9*

EUTHANASIA   (See also Murder; Suicide.)

1. Thou shalt not kill. *Exod. 20:13*

2. I am not able to bear all this . . . because it is too heavy for me. And if thou deal thus with me, kill me, I pray thee, out of hand, if I have found favor in thy sight; and let me not see my wretchedness. *Num. 11:14,15*

3. He requested for himself that he might die; and said, It is enough; now, O Lord, take away my life. *1 Kings 19:4*

4. My soul is weary of life . . . Are not my days few? cease then, and let me alone. *Job 10:1,20*

5. Their torment was as the torment of a scorpion, when he striketh a man. And in those days shall men seek death, and shall not find it; and shall desire to die. *Rev. 9:5,6*

EVANGELISM   (See also Church, Mission of; Gospel; Ministry; Missionary; Teaching.)

1. He that winneth souls is wise. *Prov. 11:30*

2. Follow me, and I will make you fishers of men. *Matt. 4:19*

3. Go ye therefore, and teach all nations, baptizing them in the name of the Father, and of the Son, and of the Holy Ghost: Teaching them to observe all things whatsoever I have commanded you. *Matt. 28:19,20*

4. Go ye into all the world, and preach the gospel to every creature. *Mark 16:15*

5. How shall they believe in him of whom they have not heard? and how shall they hear without a preacher? And how shall they preach, except they be sent? as it is written, How beautiful are the feet of them that preach the gospel of peace, and bring glad tidings of good things! *Rom. 10:14,15*

6. Preach the word . . . reprove, rebuke, exhort with all long-suffering and doctrine. *2 Tim. 4:2*

7. Do the work of an evangelist, make full proof of thy ministry. *2 Tim. 4:5*

EVIDENCE   See God, Existence of; Miracle; Sign.

EVIL   (See also Companions, Evil; Corruption; Crime; Demons; Depravity; Perversion; Sin.)

1. Wickedness proceedeth from the wicked. *1 Sam. 24:13*

2. Though I walk through the valley of the shadow of death, I will fear no evil: for thou art with me. *Ps. 23:4*

3. Ye that love the Lord, hate evil. *Ps. 97:10*

4. Blessings are upon the head of the just: but violence covereth the mouth of the wicked . . . the name of the wicked shall rot. *Prov. 10:6,7*

5. A wise man feareth, and departeth from evil. *Prov. 14:16*

6. There is no peace, saith the Lord, unto the wicked. *Isa. 48:22*

7. Let the wicked forsake his way, and the unrighteous man his thoughts. *Isa. 55:7*

8. Lead us not into temptation, but deliver us from evil. *Matt. 6:13*

9. If thine eye be evil, thy whole body shall be full of darkness. *Matt. 6:23*

10. The good that I would I do not: but the evil which I would not, that I do. *Rom. 7:19*

11. Abhor . . . evil. *Rom. 12:9*

12. Be not overcome of evil, but overcome evil with good. *Rom. 12:21*

EVIL COMPANIONS   See Companions, Evil.

EVIL SPIRIT   See Demons; Exorcism.

EVOLUTION   See Creation.

EXAMPLE   (See also Guidance; Light.)

1. Ye shall not walk in the manners of the nation, which I cast out before you: for they committed all these things, and therefore I abhorred them. *Lev. 20:23*

2. When thou art come into the land which the Lord thy God giveth thee, thou shalt not learn to do after the abominations of those nations. *Deut. 18:9*

3. Be not ye like your fathers,and like your brethren, which trespassed against the Lord God. *2 Chron. 30:7*

4. Let your light so shine before men, that they may see your good works, and glorify your Father which is in heaven. *Matt. 5:16*

5. Be ye therefore merciful, as your Father also is merciful. *Luke 6:36*

6. That ye may be blameless and harmless, the sons of God, without rebuke, in the midst of a crooked and perverse nation, among whom ye shine as lights in the world. *Phil. 2:15*

7. Those things, which ye have both learned, and received, and heard, and seen in me, do: and the God of peace shall be with you. *Phil. 4:9*

8. Be thou an example of the believers, in word, in conversation, in charity, in spirit, in faith, in purity. *1 Tim. 4:12*

EXCOMMUNICATION   (See also Exile; Result.)
1. Whosoever hath sinned against me, him will I blot out of my book. *Exod. 32:33*
2. I did cast them out as dirt in the streets. *Ps. 18:42*
3. Let them be blotted out of the book of the living, and not be written with the righteous. *Ps. 69:28*
4. Depart from me, ye cursed, into everlasting fire. *Matt. 25:41*
5. If any man love not the Lord Jesus Christ, let him be Anathema Maranatha. *1 Cor. 16:2*
6. Some having put away concerning faith have made shipwreck . . . whom I have delivered unto Satan, that they may learn not to blaspheme. *1 Tim. 1:19,20*

EXCUSE   See Justification.

EXILE   (See also Excommunication; Loneliness; Stranger.)
1. A fugitive and a vagabond shalt thou be in the earth. *Gen. 4:12*
2. I have been a stranger in a strange land. *Exod. 2:22*
3. The wicked is driven away in his wickedness. *Prov. 14:32*
4. For the wickedness of their doings I will drive them out of mine house, I will love them no more. *Hos. 9:15*
5. Blessed are ye, when men shall hate you, and when they shall separate you from their company, and shall reproach you, and cast out your name as evil, for the Son of man's sake. *Luke 6:22*
6. He that leadeth into captivity shall all go into captivity. *Rev. 13:10*

EXISTENCE   See God, Existence of; Life.

EXORCISM   (See also Demons.)
1. I will cause . . . the unclean spirit to pass out of the land. *Zech. 13:2*
2. [Jesus] met . . . two possessed with devils . . . And he said unto them, Go. And when they were come out, they went into the herd of swine: and, behold, the whole herd of swine ran violently down a steep place into the sea, and perished. *Matt. 8:28–32*
3. He [Jesus] gave them power against unclean spirits, to cast them out. *Matt. 10:1*
4. If I cast out devils by the Spirit of God, then the kingdom of God is come unto you. *Matt. 12:28*
5. Certain of the vagabond Jews, exorcists, took upon them to call

over them which had evil spirits the name of the Lord Jesus. *Acts 19:13*

6. Resist the devil, and he will flee from you. *James 4:7*

EXPECTATION   (See also Desire; Hope.)

1. My soul, wait thou only upon God; for my expectation is from him. *Ps. 62:5*

2. The eyes of all wait upon thee [the Lord]. *Ps. 145:15*

3. It is good that a man should both hope and quietly wait for the salvation of the Lord. *Lam. 3:26*

4. He gave heed unto them, expecting to receive something of them. *Acts 3:5*

5. My earnest expectation and my hope, that . . . Christ shall be magnified in my body, whether it be by life, or by death. *Phil. 1:20*

6. Looking for and hasting unto the coming of the day of God. *2 Peter 3:12*

EXPLANATION   See Interpretation.

EXPLORATION   (See also Espionage; Land.)

1. Send thou men, that they may search the land of Canaan. *Num. 13:2*

2. They went up, and searched the land. *Num. 13:21*

3. The land, which we passed through to search it, is an exceeding good land. *Num. 14:7*

4. We will send men before us, and they shall search us out the land. *Deut. 1:22*

5. Go and walk through the land, and describe it. *Josh. 18:8*

EXPULSION   See Excommunication; Exile; Exorcism.

FAILURE (See also Defeat; Disappointment; Frustration; Loss.)

1. Unstable as water, thou shalt not excel. *Gen. 49:4*

2. Because ye believed me not . . . therefore ye shall not bring this congregation into the land which I have given them. *Num. 20:12*

3. My flesh and my heart faileth. *Ps. 73:26*

4. I was afraid, and went and hid thy talent in the earth. *Matt. 25:25*

5. He cometh, and findeth them sleeping, and saith unto Peter, Simon, sleepest thou? couldest not thou watch one hour? *Mark 14:37*

6. We have toiled all the night, and have taken nothing. *Luke 5:5*

FAIRNESS See Equality; Impartiality; Justice.

FAITH (See also Belief; Christ, Belief in; Constancy; Faithfulness; Trust.)

1. Thou wilt keep him in perfect peace, whose mind is stayed on thee. *Isa. 26:3*

2. If ye have faith as a grain of mustard seed . . . nothing shall be impossible unto you. *Matt. 17:20*

3. Blessed are they that have not seen, and yet have believed. *John 20:29*

4. Hast thou faith? have it to thyself before God. *Rom. 14:22*

5. We walk by faith, not by sight. *2 Cor. 5:7*

6. Fight the good fight of faith. *1 Tim. 6:12*

7. Hold fast the profession of our faith without wavering. *Heb. 10:23*

8. Faith is the substance of things hoped for, the evidence of things not seen. *Heb. 11:1*

FAITHFULNESS (See also Constancy; Faith; God, Faithfulness of; Loyalty; Trust.)

1. He clave to the Lord, and departed not from following him, but kept his commandments. *2 Kings 18:6*

2. Well done, thou good and faithful servant: thou hast been faithful over a few things, I will make thee ruler over many things: enter thou into the joy of thy lord. *Matt. 25:21*

3. He that is faithful in that which is least is faithful also in much. *Luke 16:10*

4. It is required in stewards, that a man be found faithful. *1 Cor. 4:2*

5. Be thou faithful unto death, and I will give thee a crown of life. *Rev. 2:10*

FAITHLESSNESS (See also Agnosticism; Atheism; Rejection.)

1. They are a very froward generation, children in whom is no faith. *Deut. 32:20*

2. O ye of little faith. *Matt. 6:30*

3. Whosoever shall deny me before men, him will I also deny before my Father. *Matt. 10:33*

4. O faithless and perverse generation. *Matt. 17:17*

5. Ye also have seen me, and believe not. *John 6:36*

6. Be not faithless, but believing. *John 20:27*

7. For what if some did not believe? shall their unbelief make the faith of God without effect? *Rom. 3:3*

8. Whosoever denieth the Son, the same hath not the Father. *1 John 2:23*

FALL   See Defeat.

FALSEHOOD   (See also Deceit; Perjury; Truth.)

1. Thou shalt not bear false witness against thy neighbor. *Exod. 20:16*

2. God is not a man, that he should lie. *Num. 23:19*

3. They delight in lies. *Ps. 62:4*

4. He that telleth lies shall not tarry in my sight. *Ps. 101:7*

5. The lip of truth shall be established for ever: but a lying tongue is but for a moment. *Prov. 12:19*

6. Lying lips are abomination to the Lord: but they that deal truly are his delight. *Prov. 12:22*

7. A righteous man hateth lying. *Prov. 13:5*

8. Thou hast not lied unto men, but unto God. *Acts 5:4*

9. Thou hast tried them which say they are apostles, and are not, and hast found them liars. *Rev. 2:2*

FALSE PROPHET (See also Cults, Religious; Heresy; Idolatry; Prophet.)

1. If there arise among you a prophet . . . saying, Let us go after other gods . . . thou shalt stone him with stones, that he die; because he hath sought to thrust thee away from the Lord. *Deut. 13:1,2,10*

2. I am against them that prophesy false dreams. *Jer. 23:32*

3. They prophesy falsely unto you in my name: I have not sent them, saith the Lord. *Jer. 29:9*

4. Beware of false prophets, which come to you in sheep's clothing, but inwardly they are ravening wolves. *Matt. 7:15*

5. There shall arise false Christs, and false prophets, and shall show great signs and wonders . . . they shall deceive the very elect. *Matt. 24:24*

6. I have a few things against thee, because thou sufferest that woman Jezebel, which calleth herself a prophetess, to teach and to seduce my servants to commit fornication. *Rev. 2:20*

7. I beheld another beast coming up out of the earth; and he had two horns like a lamb, and he spake as a dragon . . . And deceiveth them that dwell on the earth by the means of those miracles which he had power to do. *Rev. 13:11,14*

8. The devil that deceived them was cast into the lake of fire and brimstone, where the beast and false prophet are, and shall be tormented day and night for ever and ever. *Rev. 20:10*

FALSE WITNESS   See Falsehood; Perjury.

FAME   (See also Reputation.)

1. I will bless thee, and make thy name great. *Gen. 12:2*

2. Thou shalt become an astonishment, a proverb, and a byword, among all nations. *Deut. 28:37*

3. His fame was noised throughout all the country. *Josh. 6:27*

4. His name may be famous in Israel. *Ruth 4:14*

5. Thy wisdom and prosperity exceedeth the fame which I heard. *1 Kings 10:7*

6. They . . . spread abroad his fame in all that country. *Matt. 9:31*

7. Herod . . . heard of the fame of Jesus. *Matt. 14:1*

8. Your faith is spoken of throughout the whole world. *Rom. 1:8*

FAMILY   (See also Children; Church; Father; Genealogy; God, Family of; Mother; Parent; Unity.)
1. In thee shall all families of the earth be blessed. *Gen. 12:3*
2. He that smiteth his father, or his mother, shall be surely put to death. *Exod. 21:15*
3. God setteth the solitary in families. *Ps. 68:6*
4. A wise son maketh a glad father: but a foolish son is the heaviness of his mother. *Prov. 10:1*
5. He shall turn the heart of the fathers to the children, and the heart of the children to their fathers. *Mal. 4:6*

FAMILY OF GOD   See God, Family of.

FAMINE   See Hunger.

FARMING   (See also Abundance.)
1. He that tilleth his land shall be satisfied with bread. *Prov. 12:11*
2. The sluggard will not plow by reason of the cold; therefore shall he beg in harvest, and have nothing. *Prov. 20:4*
3. A time to plant, and a time to pluck up that which is planted. *Eccl. 3:2*
4. Doth the plowman plow all day to sow? doth he open and break the clods of his ground? *Isa. 28:24*
5. Plant gardens, and eat the fruit of them. *Jer. 29:5*
6. They shall plant vineyards, and drink the wine thereof; they shall also make gardens, and eat the fruit of them. *Amos 9:14*
7. The earth bringeth forth fruit of herself; first the blade, then the ear, after that the full corn in the ear. *Mark 4:28*
8. He which soweth sparingly shall reap also sparingly; and he which soweth bountifully shall reap also bountifully. *2 Cor. 9:6*

FASTING   (See also Sacrifice.)
1. He [Moses] was there with the Lord forty days and forty nights; he did neither eat bread, nor drink water. *Exod. 34:28*
2. Now he is dead, wherefore should I fast? *2 Sam. 12:23*
3. He [Elijah] arose, and did eat and drink, and went in the strength of that meat forty days and forty nights. *1 Kings 19:8*
4. I humbled my soul with fasting. *Ps. 35:13*
5. My knees are weak through fasting; and my flesh faileth of fatness. *Ps. 109:24*
6. I [Daniel] ate no pleasant bread, neither came flesh nor wine in my mouth, neither did I anoint myself at all, till three whole weeks were fulfilled. *Dan. 10:3*

7. When he [Jesus] had fasted forty days and forty nights, he was afterward ahungered. *Matt. 4:2*

8. When thou fastest, anoint thine head, and wash thy face; That thou appear not unto men to fast. *Matt 6:17,18*

9. Ye may give yourselves to fasting and prayer. *1 Cor. 7:5*

FATE   See Predestination.

FATHER   (See also Children; Family; God, Fatherhood of; Mother; Parent.)

1. Thou shalt be a father of many nations. *Gen. 17:4*

2. Honor thy father and thy mother. *Exod. 20:12*

3. A wise son maketh a glad father. *Prov. 10:1*

4. The glory of children are their fathers. *Prov. 17:6*

5. Whoso curseth his father or his mother, his lamp shall be put out in obscure darkness. *Prov. 20:20*

6. The father of the righteous shall greatly rejoice: and he that begetteth a wise child shall have joy of him. *Prov. 23:24*

7. Fathers, provoke not your children to wrath: but bring them up in the nurture and admonition of the Lord. *Eph. 6:4*

8. We have had fathers of our flesh which corrected us, and we gave them reverence. *Heb. 12:9*

FATHERHOOD   See Father; God, Fatherhood of.

FATIGUE   See Weariness.

FAULT   See Blame; Guilt; Imperfection; Mistake; Sin.

FAVORITISM   (See also Impartiality; Inequality; Prejudice.)

1. Issac loved Esau . . . but Rebekah loved Jacob. *Gen. 25:28*

2. He went in also unto Rachel, and he loved also Rachel more than Leah. *Gen. 29:30*

3. Israel loved Joseph more than all his children, because he was the son of his old age. *Gen. 37:3*

4. Benjamin's mess was five times so much as any of theirs. *Gen. 43:34*

5. The Lord thy God hath chosen thee to be a special people unto himself, above all people that are upon the face of the earth. *Deut. 7:6*

6. As the apple tree among the trees of the wood, so is my beloved among the sons. *Song of Sol. 2:3*

7. Hail, thou that art highly favored, the Lord is with thee: blessed art thou among women. *Luke 1:28*

8. [I charge thee] that thou observe these things without preferring one before another, doing nothing by partiality. *1 Tim. 5:21*

FEAR **(See also Cowardice.)**

1. Fear came upon me, and trembling . . . the hair of my flesh stood up. *Job 4:14,15*

2. I am afraid, and trembling taketh hold on my flesh. *Job 21:6*

3. Fearfulness and trembling are come upon me, and horror hath overwhelmed me. *Ps. 55:5*

4. Be not afraid of sudden fear. *Prov. 3:25*

5. Why are ye fearful, O ye of little faith? *Matt. 8:26*

6. I was with you in weakness, and in fear, and in much trembling. *1 Cor. 2:3*

7. Deliver them who through fear of death were all their lifetime subject to bondage. *Heb. 2:15*

8. There is no fear in love; but perfect love casteth out fear: because fear hath torment. He that feareth is not made perfect in love. *1 John 4:18,19*

FEAR OF THE LORD **(See also Respect.)**

1. I heard thy voice in the garden, and I was afraid, because I was naked; and I hid myself. *Gen. 3:10*

2. Thou shalt fear the Lord thy God. *Deut. 6:13*

3. The fear of the Lord, that is wisdom; and to depart from evil is understanding. *Job 28:28*

4. Let all the earth fear the Lord: let all the inhabitants of the world stand in awe of him. *Ps. 33:8*

5. The fear of the Lord is the beginning of knowledge. *Prov. 1:7*

6. The fear of the Lord is a fountain of life. *Prov. 14:27*

7. Better is little with the fear of the Lord, than great treasure and trouble therewith. *Prov. 15:16*

8. The fear of the Lord tendeth to life: and he that hath it shall abide satisfied. *Prov. 19:23*

9. Be thou in the fear of the Lord all the day long. *Prov. 23:17*

10. A woman that feareth the Lord, she shall be praised. *Prov. 31:30*

11. Fear God, and keep his commandments: for this is the whole duty of man. *Eccl. 12:13*

12. Knowing therefore the terror of the Lord, we persuade men. *2 Cor. 5:11*

FEARLESSNESS **See Courage.**

FEAST **See Celebration; Passover.**

FEEBLENESS   See Weakness.

FELLOWSHIP   (See also Brotherhood; Church; Friendship; Unity.)

1. We took sweet counsel together, and walked unto the house of God in company. *Ps. 55:14*

2. Two are better than one . . . For if they fall, the one will lift up his fellow. *Eccl. 4:9,10*

3. Can two walk together, except they be agreed? *Amos 3:3*

4. Where two or three are gathered together in my name, there am I in the midst of them. *Matt. 18:20*

5. Be ye not unequally yoked together with unbelievers: for what fellowship hath righteousness with unrighteousness? and what communion hath light with darkness? *2 Cor. 6:14*

6. They gave to me and Barnabas the right hands of fellowship. *Gal. 2:9*

7. [I thank my God] For your fellowship in the gospel from the first day until now. *Phil. 1:5*

8. Truly our fellowship is with the Father, and with his Son Jesus Christ . . . If we say that we have fellowship with him, and walk in darkness, we lie, and do not the truth: But if we walk in the light . . . we have fellowship one with another. *1 John 1:3,6,7*

9. I stand at the door, and knock: if any man hear my voice, and open the door, I will come in to him, and will sup with him, and he with me. *Rev. 3:20*

FEMALE   See Feminism; Sex; Woman.

FEMINISM   (See also Woman.)

1. [The daughters of Zelophehad] stood before Moses . . . saying . . . Why should the name of our father be done away from among his family, because he hath no son? Give unto us therefore a possession among the brethren of our father. And Moses brought their cause before the Lord. And the Lord spake unto Moses, saying, The daughters of Zelophehad speak right. *Num. 27:1–7*

2. Hilkiah the priest [and four other men] . . . went unto Huldah the prophetess . . . and they communed with her. *2 Kings 22:14*

3. As for my people . . . women rule over them. *Isa. 3:12*

4. A woman shall compass a man. *Jer. 31:22*

5. As the woman is of the man, even so is the man also by the woman; but all things of God. *1 Cor. 11:12*

D

6. There is neither male nor female: for ye are all one in Christ Jesus. *Gal. 3:28*

7. There appeared a great wonder in heaven; a woman clothed with the sun, and the moon under her feet, and upon her head a crown of twelve stars. *Rev. 12:1*

FERTILITY   (See also Abundance; Sterility.)

1. Be fruitful, and multiply, and replenish the earth. *Gen. 1:28*

2. I will multiply thy seed as the stars of the heaven, and as the sand which is upon the sea shore. *Gen. 22:17*

3. God hath caused me to be fruitful in the land of my affliction. *Gen. 41:52*

4. The Almighty, who shall bless thee with blessings of heaven above, blessings of the deep that lieth under, blessings of the breasts, and of the womb. *Gen. 49:25*

5. Those that be planted in the house of the Lord shall flourish in the courts of our God. *Ps. 92:13*

6. Thy wife shall be as fruitful vine by the sides of thine house. *Ps. 128:3*

7. Blessed art thou among women, and blessed is the fruit of thy womb. *Luke 1:42*

FERVOR   See Zeal.

FICKLENESS   See Instability.

FIDELITY   See Constancy; Faithfulness; God, Faithfulness of; Loyalty.

FIGHTING   (See also Army, Christian; War.)

1. One man of you shall chase a thousand: for the Lord your God, he it is that fighteth for you, as he hath promised you. *Josh. 23:10*

2. The Lord saveth not with sword and spear: for the battle is the Lord's, and he will give you into our hands. *1 Sam. 17:47*

3. Be not afraid nor dismayed by reason of this great multitude; for the battle is not yours, but God's. *2 Chron. 20:15*

4. Be not ye afraid of them: remember the Lord, which is great and terrible, and fight for your brethren, your sons, and your daughters, your wives, and your houses. *Neh. 4:14*

5. They shall fight every one against his brother, and every one against his neighbor; city against city, and kingdom against kingdom. *Isa. 19:2*

6. Every man's sword shall be against his brother. *Ezek. 38:21*

7. If it be of God, ye cannot overthrow it; lest haply ye be found even to fight against God. *Acts 5:39*

8. Fight the good fight of faith. *1 Tim. 6:12*

FIND   See Discovery.

FIRE   (See also Arson; Cremation.)

1. The angel of the Lord appeared unto him in a flame of fire out of the midst of a bush . . . and the bush was not consumed. *Exod. 3:2*

2. [The Lord went before them] by night in a pillar of fire, to give them light. *Exod. 13:21*

3. Mount Sinai was altogether on a smoke, because the Lord descended upon it in fire. *Exod. 19:18*

4. There appeared a chariot of fire, and horses of fire, and parted them both asunder; and Elijah went up by a whirlwind into heaven. *2 Kings 2:11*

5. A fire goeth before him [the Lord], and burneth up his enemies round about. *Ps. 97:3*

6. Can a man take fire in his bosom, and his clothes not be burned? Can one go upon hot coals, and his feet not be burned? *Prov. 6:27,28*

7. When thou walkest through the fire, thou shalt not be burned. *Isa. 43:2*

8. There appeared unto them cloven tongues like as of fire, and it sat upon each of them. *Acts 2:3*

9. Behold, how great a matter a little fire kindleth! And the tongue is a fire, a world of iniquity: . . . it defileth the whole body, and setteth on fire the course of nature; and it is set on fire of hell. *James 3:5,6*

FLATTERY   (See also Deceit.)

1. He that speaketh flattery to his friends, even the eyes of his children shall fail. *Job 17:5*

2. I know not to give flattering titles; in so doing my Maker would soon take me away. *Job 32:22*

3. The Lord shall cut off all flattering lips, and the tongue that speaketh proud things. *Ps. 12:3*

4. The words of his mouth were smoother than butter, but war was in his heart: his words were softer than oil, yet were they drawn swords. *Ps. 55:21*

5. Meddle not with him that flattereth with his lips. *Prov. 20:19*

6. A flattering mouth worketh ruin. *Prov. 26:28*

7. A man that flattereth his neighbor spreadeth a net for his feet. *Prov. 29:5*

8. Such as do wickedly against the covenant shall he corrupt by flatteries. *Dan. 11:32*

FLAW   See Imperfection.

FLESH   See Body; Lust; Worldliness.

FLOOD   See Disaster; Weather.

FOE   See Enemy.

FOLLOWER   (See also Apostle; Army, Christian; Disciple; Leadership.)

1. That which is altogether just shalt thou follow, that thou mayest live, and inherit the land which the Lord thy God giveth thee. *Deut. 16:20*

2. If the Lord be God, follow him. *1 Kings 18:21*

3. Follow me, and I will make you fishers of men. *Matt. 4:19*

4. Jesus said unto him, Follow me; and let the dead bury their dead. *Matt. 8:22*

5. They forsook all, and followed him. *Luke 5:11*

6. If any man will come after me, let him deny himself, and take up his cross daily, and follow me. *Luke 9:23*

7. I am the light of the world: he that followeth me shall not walk in darkness, but shall have the light of life. *John 8:12*

8. Let us therefore follow after the things which make for peace, and things wherewith one may edify another. *Rom. 14:19*

9. Be ye followers of me, even as I also am of Christ. *1 Cor. 11:1*

10. But thou, O man of God, flee these things; and follow after righteousness, godliness, faith, love, patience, meekness. *1 Tim. 6:11*

FOLLY   See Foolishness.

FOOD   (See also Gluttony; Hunger; Vegetarianism.)

1. The woman said unto the serpent, We may eat of the fruit of the trees of the garden: But of the fruit of the tree which is in the midst of the garden, God hath said, Ye shall not eat of it, neither shall ye touch it, lest ye die. *Gen. 3:2,3*

2. When the children of Israel saw it, they said one to another, It is manna: for they wist not what it was. And Moses said unto them, This is the bread which the Lord hath given you to eat. *Exod. 16:15*

3. Whatsoever parteth the hoof, and is clovenfooted, and cheweth the cud, among the beasts, that shall ye eat. *Lev. 11:3*

4. Man doth not live by bread only, but by every word that proceedeth out of the mouth of the Lord. *Deut. 8:3*

5. The ravens brought him bread and flesh in the morning, and bread and flesh in the evening; and he drank of the brook. *1 Kings 17:6*

6. Better is a dinner of herbs where love is, than a stalled ox and hatred therewith. *Prov. 15:17*

7. Cast thy bread upon the waters: for thou shalt find it after many days. *Eccl. 11:1*

8. [Jesus] took the five loaves, and the two fishes, and looking up to heaven, he blessed, and brake, and gave the loaves to his disciples, and the disciples to the multitude. *Matt. 14:19*

9. Give us day by day our daily bread. *Luke 11:3*

10. I am that bread of life. . . . I am the living bread which came down from heaven: if any man eat of this bread, he shall live for ever: and the bread that I will give is my flesh, which I will give for the life of the world. *John 6:48,51*

FOOLISHNESS (See also Ignorance; Imprudence.)

1. The way of a fool is right in his own eyes. *Prov. 12:15*

2. Fools make a mock at sin. *Prov. 14:9*

3. The foolishness of fools is folly. *Prov. 14:24*

4. A fool's mouth is his destruction, and his lips are the snare of his soul. *Prov. 18:7*

5. Answer not a fool according to his folly, lest thou also be like unto him. *Prov. 26:4*

6. As a dog returneth to his vomit, so a fool returneth to his folly. *Prov. 26:11*

7. Though thou shouldest bray a fool in a mortar among wheat with a pestle, yet will not his foolishness depart from him. *Prov. 27:22*

8. He that trusteth in his own heart is a fool. *Prov. 28:26*

9. A fool uttereth all his mind. *Prov. 29:11*

10. As the crackling of thorns under a pot, so is the laughter of the fool. *Eccl. 7:6*

11. They that were foolish took their lamps, and took no oil with them. *Matt. 25:3*

FORBEARANCE See Patience; Self-Control; Tolerance.

FOREIGNER See Stranger.

FORERUNNER (See also Angel; Prophet.)

1. He shall send his angel before thee. *Gen. 24:7*

2. The voice of him that crieth in the wilderness, Prepare ye the way of the Lord, make straight in the desert a highway for our God. *Isa. 40:3*

3. Behold, I will send my messenger, and he shall prepare the way before me. *Mal. 3:1*

4. Behold, I will send you Elijah the prophet before the coming of the great and dreadful day of the Lord. *Mal. 4:5*

5. There cometh one mightier than I after me, the latchet of whose shoes I am not worthy to stoop down and unloose. *Mark 1:7*

6. Thou, child, shalt be called the prophet of the Highest: for thou shalt go before the face of the Lord to prepare his ways. *Luke 1:76*

7. He that cometh after me is preferred before me: for he was before me. *John 1:15*

8. I am the voice of one crying in the wilderness, Make straight the way of the Lord, as said the prophet Isaiah. *John 1:23*

FORESIGHT See Prudence.

FORGETFULNESS (See also Ingratitude: Memory; Neglect.)

1. Yet did not the chief butler remember Joseph, but forgat him. *Gen. 40:23*

2. For God, said he, hath made me forget all my toil, and all my father's house. *Gen. 41:51*

3. Of the Rock that begat thee thou art unmindful, and hast forgotten God that formed thee. *Deut. 32:18*

4. The children of Israel did evil in the sight of the Lord, and forgat the Lord their God. *Judg. 3:7*

5. Thou shalt forget thy misery, and remember it as waters that pass away. *Job 11:16*

6. The womb shall forget him; the worm shall feed sweetly on him; he shall be no more remembered. *Job 24:20*

7. How long wilt thou forget me, O Lord? *Ps. 13:1*

8. I am forgotten as a dead man out of mind: I am like a broken vessel. *Ps. 31:12*

9. If I forget thee, O Jerusalem, let my right hand forget her cunning. If I do not remember thee, let my tongue cleave to the roof of my mouth. *Ps. 137:5,6*

10. For the living know that they shall die: but the dead know not any thing, neither have they any more a reward; for the memory of them is forgotten. *Eccl. 9:5*

11. Seeing thou hast forgotten the law of thy God, I will also forget thy children. *Hos. 4:6*

12. Because they delivered up the whole captivity to Edom, and remembered not the brotherly covenant. *Amos 1:9*

FORGIVENESS   (See also Atonement; Mercy; Remission.)

1. Forgive, I pray thee now, the trespass of thy brethren, and their sin; for they did unto thee evil. *Gen. 50:17*

2. Who can understand his errors? Cleanse thou me from secret faults. *Ps. 19:12*

3. Purge me with hyssop, and I shall be clean: wash me, and I shall be whiter than snow. *Ps. 51:7*

4. Though your sins be as scarlet, they shall be as white as snow; though they be red like crimson, they shall be as wool. *Isa. 1:18*

5. I will forgive their iniquity, and I will remember their sin no more. *Jer. 31:34*

6. Whosoever shall smite thee on thy right cheek, turn to him the other also. *Matt. 5:39*

7. Forgive us our debts, as we forgive our debtors. *Matt. 6:12*

8. If ye forgive men their trespasses, your heavenly Father will also forgive you: But if ye forgive not men their trespasses, neither will your Father forgive your trespasses. *Matt. 6:14,15*

9. [Peter] said, Lord, how oft shall my brother sin against me, and I forgive him? till seven times? Jesus saith unto him, I say not unto thee, Until seven times: but, Until seventy times seven. *Matt. 18:21,22*

10. Her sins, which are many, are forgiven; for she loved much: but to whom little is forgiven, the same loveth little. *Luke 7:47*

11. Father, forgive them; for they know not what they do. *Luke 23:34*

12. Be ye kind one to another, tenderhearted, forgiving one another, even as God for Christ's sake hath forgiven you. *Eph. 4:32*

FORNICATION   See Adultery; Promiscuity; Prostitution; Sex.

FORTITUDE   See Courage; Strength.

FORTUNETELLING   (See also Astrology; Occult.)

1. Regard not them that have familiar spirits, neither seek after wizards, to be defiled by them. *Lev. 19:31*

2. The soul that turneth after such as have familiar spirits, and after wizards, to go a whoring after them, I will even set my face against that soul, and will cut him off from among his people. *Lev. 20:6*

3. Seek unto them that have familiar spirits, and unto wizards that peep, and that mutter: should not a people seek unto their God? *Isa. 8:19*

4. Let not your prophets and your diviners . . . deceive you . . . For they prophesy falsely. *Jer. 29:8,9*

5. There shall be no more any vain vision nor flattering divination within the house of Israel. *Ezek. 12:24*

6. The prophets thereof divine for money. *Mic. 3:11*

7. A certain damsel possessed with a spirit of divination met us, which brought her masters much gain by soothsaying. *Acts 16:16*

    FOUNDATION   See Rock.

    FRATERNITY   See Brotherhood; Christ, Companionship of; Fellowship; Friendship.

    FREEDOM   See Liberty.

    FRIEND   See Friendship; Neighbor.

    FRIENDLINESS   See Hospitality; Kindness.

    FRIENDSHIP   (See also Brotherhood; Christ, Companionship of; Fellowship; Love; Loyalty; Neighbor.)

1. The soul of Jonathan was knit with the soul of David, and Jonathan loved him as his own soul. *1 Sam. 18:1*

2. When Job's three friends heard of all this evil that was come upon him, they came every one from his own place . . . to mourn with him and to comfort him. *Job 2:11*

3. The rich hath many friends. *Prov. 14:20*

4. A friend loveth at all times. *Prov. 17:17*

5. A man that hath friends must show himself friendly: and there is a friend that sticketh closer than a brother. *Prov. 18:24*

6. A man sharpeneth the countenance of his friend. *Prov. 27:17*

7. Two are better than one. *Eccl. 4:9*

8. Woe to him that is alone when he falleth; for he hath not another to help him up. *Eccl. 4:10*

9. This is my friend. *Song of Sol. 5:16*

10. The friend of the bridegroom, which standeth and heareth him, rejoiceth greatly. *John 3:29*

11. Greater love hath no man than this, that a man lay down his life for his friends. *John 15:13*

FRUITFULNESS See Fertility.

FRUSTRATION (See also Defeat; Disappointment; Distress; Failure.)

1. How long will ye vex my soul, and break me in pieces with words? *Job 19:2*

2. I go forward, but he is not there; and backward, but I cannot perceive him: on the left hand, where he doth work, but I cannot behold him: he hideth himself on the right hand, that I cannot see him: but he knoweth the way that I take. *Job 23:8–10*

3. The children are come to the birth, and there is not strength to bring forth. *Isa. 37:3*

4. [I am the Lord] That frustrateth the tokens of the liars. *Isa. 44:25*

5. She shall follow after her lovers, but she shall not overtake them; and she shall seek them, but shall not find them. *Hos. 2:7*

6. The spirit indeed is willing, but the flesh is weak. *Matt. 26:41*

7. We have toiled all the night, and have taken nothing. *Luke 5:5*

8. I do not frustrate the grace of God. *Gal. 2:21*

FULFILLMENT (See also Accomplishment; Answer; Christ, Resurrection of.)

1. The Lord fulfill all thy petitions. *Ps. 20:5*

2. The word that I [the Lord] speak shall come to pass . . . I [will] say the word, and will perform it. *Ezek. 12:25*

3. I am not come to destroy, but to fulfill. For verily I say unto you, Till heaven and earth pass, one jot or one tittle shall in no wise pass from the law, till all be fulfilled. *Matt. 5:17,18*

4. The time is fulfilled, and the kingdom of God is at hand. *Mark 1:15*

5. Tell us, when shall these things be? and what shall be the sign when all these things shall be fulfilled? *Mark 13:4*

6. These are the words which I spake unto you, while I was yet with you, that all things must be fulfilled, which were written in the law of Moses, and in the prophets, and in the psalms, concerning me. *Luke 24:44*

7. For these things were done, that the scripture should be fulfilled. *John 19:36*

8. That the righteousness of the law might be fulfilled in us, who walk not after the flesh, but after the Spirit. *Rom. 8:4*

9. All the law is fulfilled in one word, even in this; Thou shalt love thy neighbor as thyself. *Gal.* 5:14

10. Bear ye one another's burdens, and so fulfill the law of Christ. *Gal.* 6:2

    FUNERAL   **See Burial; Cremation.**

    FUTILITY   **See Despair; Frustration; Hopelessness.**

GAMBLING

1. The lot is cast into the lap. *Prov. 16:33*

2. They have cast lots for my people. *Joel 3:3*

3. [Foreigners] cast lots upon Jerusalem. *Obad. 1:11*

4. They cast lots for her honorable men. *Nah. 3:10*

5. They crucified him, and parted his garments, casting lots: that it might be fulfilled which was spoken by the prophet, They parted my garments among them, and upon my vesture did they cast lots. *Matt. 27:35*

GENEALOGY   (See also Family; Inheritance.)

1. She [Eve] was the mother of all living. *Gen. 3:20*

2. All Israel were reckoned by genealogies. *1 Chron. 9:1*

3. All the generations from Abraham to David are fourteen generations; and from David until the carrying away into Babylon are fourteen generations; and from the carrying away into Babylon unto Christ are fourteen generations. *Matt. 1:17*

4. Jesus . . . the son of Joseph . . . was the son of Adam, which was the son of God. *Luke 3:23,38*

5. Avoid . . . genealogies. *Titus 3:9*

6. Without father, without mother, without descent, having neither beginning of days, nor end of life; but made like unto the Son of God. *Heb. 7:3*

GENEROSITY   (See also Benevolence; Charity; Giving; Kindness; Unselfishness.)

1. Every man shall give as he is able, according to the blessing of the Lord thy God which he hath given thee. *Deut. 16:17*

2. All things come of thee, and of thine own have we given thee. *1 Chron. 29:14*

3. He that giveth unto the poor shall not lack. *Prov. 28:27*

4. Is it not to deal thy bread to the hungry, and that thou bring the poor that are cast out to thy house? when thou seest the naked, that thou cover him; and that thou hide not thyself from thine own flesh? *Isa. 58:7*

5. If thou wilt be perfect, go and sell that thou hast, and give to the poor. *Matt. 19:21*

6. A certain poor widow casting in thither two mites . . . hath cast in more than they all: For all these have of their abundance cast in unto the offerings of God: but she of her penury hath cast in all the living that she had. *Luke 21:2-4*

7. Silver and gold have I none; but such as I have give I thee. *Acts 3:6*

8. It is more blessed to give than to receive. *Acts 20:35*

9. He that spared not his own Son, but delivered him up for us all, how shall he not with him also freely give us all things? *Rom. 8:32*

10. Every man according as he purposeth in his heart, so let him give; not grudgingly, or of necessity: for God loveth a cheerful giver. *2 Cor. 9:7*

GENTILE   See Paganism.

GIFT   (See Also Abundance; Blessing; Giving; Grace; Holy Spirit; Talent; Tithe; Tongues, Gift of.)

1. They that seek the Lord shall not want any good thing. *Ps. 34:10*

2. The kings of Tarshish and of the isles shall bring presents: the kings of Sheba and Seba shall offer gifts. *Ps. 72:10*

3. They [the wise men] presented unto him gifts; gold, and frankincense, and myrrh. *Matt. 2:11*

4. This is my body which is given for you. *Luke 22:19*

5. God so loved the world, that he gave his only begotten Son. *John 3:16*

6. The gift of God is eternal life through Jesus Christ our Lord. *Rom. 6:23*

7. Every man hath his proper gift of God, one after this manner, and another after that. *1 Cor. 7:7*

8. There are diversities of gifts, but the same Spirit. *1 Cor. 12:4*

9. When he ascended up on high, he led captivity captive, and gave gifts unto men. *Eph. 4:8*

10. Every good gift and every perfect gift is from above. *James 1:17*

GIRL   See Children; Woman; Youth.

GIVING   (See also Abundance; Charity; Generosity; Gift.)
1. They shall not appear before the Lord empty: Every man shall give as he is able. *Deut. 16:16,17*
2. Go not empty unto thy mother-in-law. *Ruth. 3:17*
3. If ye then, being evil, know how to give good gifts unto your children, how much more shall your Father which is in heaven give good things to them that ask him? *Matt. 7:11*
4. Freely ye have received, freely give. *Matt. 10:8*
5. Give to every man that asketh of thee. *Luke 6:30*
6. Whatsoever ye shall ask the Father in my name, he will give it you . . . ask, and ye shall receive, that your joy may be full. *John 16:23,24*
7. It is more blessed to give than to receive. *Acts 20:35*
8. He that giveth, let him do it with simplicity. *Rom. 12:8*
9. Every man according as he purposeth in his heart, so let him give; not grudgingly, or of necessity: for God loveth a cheerful giver. *2 Cor. 9:7*

GLORY   (See also Grandeur; Praise.)
1. Holy, holy, holy, is the Lord of hosts: the whole earth is full of his glory. *Isa. 6:3*
2. The glory of the Lord is risen upon thee. *Isa. 60:1*
3. Even Solomon in all his glory was not arrayed like one of these. *Matt. 6:29*
4. The glory of the Lord shone round about them [the shepherds]. *Luke 2:9*
5. Glory to God in the highest. *Luke 2:14*
6. Now is the Son of man glorified, and God is glorified in him. *John 13:31*
7. Glorify thy Son, that thy Son also may glorify thee. *John 17:1*
8. The glory of the celestial is one, and the glory of the terrestrial is another. There is one glory of the sun, and another glory of the moon, and another glory of the stars: for one star differeth from another star in glory. *1 Cor. 15:40,41*
9. We all, with open face beholding as in a glass the glory of the Lord, are changed into the same image from glory to glory. *2 Cor. 3:18*

10. This man [Christ] was counted worthy of more glory than Moses, inasmuch as he who hath builded the house hath more honor than the house. *Heb. 3:3;*

11. Our Lord Jesus Christ, the Lord of glory. *James 2:1*

12. All the glory of man [is] as the flower of grass. *1 Peter 1:24*

GLUTTONY (See also Food.)

1. He is a glutton, and a drunkard. And all the men of his city shall stone him with stones, that he die. *Deut. 21:20,21*

2. Put a knife to thy throat, if thou be a man given to appetite. Be not desirous of his dainties: for they are deceitful meat. *Prov. 23:2,3*

3. Be not among winebibbers; among riotous eaters of flesh: for the drunkard and the glutton shall come to poverty: and drowsiness shall clothe a man with rags. *Prov. 23:20,21*

4. Let us eat and drink; for tomorrow we shall die. *Isa. 22:13*

5. The Son of man came eating and drinking, and they say, Behold a man gluttonous, and a winebibber. *Matt. 11:19*

6. Woe unto you that are full! for ye shall hunger. *Luke 6:25*

7. They are the enemies of the cross of Christ . . . whose God is their belly. *Phil. 3:18,19*

GOD (See also Christ; Holy Spirit; Infallibility; Lord; Trinity, Holy; Universality.)

1. God said unto Moses, I AM THAT I AM. *Exod. 3:14*

2. To whom then will ye liken God? or what likeness will ye compare unto him? *Isa. 40:18*

3. I am the Lord, your Holy One, the creator of Israel, your King. *Isa. 43:15*

4. I am the Lord, and there is none else, there is no God beside me. *Isa. 45:5*

5. The Lord is the true God, he is the living God, and an everlasting king. *Jer. 10:10*

6. Wisdom and might are his: and he changeth the times and the seasons: he removeth kings, and setteth up kings: he giveth wisdom unto the wise, and knowledge to them that know understanding: he revealeth the deep and secret things: he knoweth what is in the darkness, and the light dwelleth with him. *Dan. 2:20,22*

7. In the beginning was the Word, and the Word was with God, and the Word was God. *John 1:1*

8. All things were made by him; and without him was not any thing made that was made. In him was life, and the life was the light of men. *John 1:3,4*

9. There is but one God, the Father, of whom are all things, and we in him. *1 Cor. 8:6*

10. One God and Father of all, who is above all, and through all, and in you all. *Eph. 4:6*

11. The King eternal, immortal, invisible, the only wise God. *1 Tim. 1:17*

12. God was manifest in the flesh, justified in the Spirit, seen of angels, preached unto the Gentiles, believed on in the world, received up into glory. *1 Tim. 3:16*

13. God is light. *1 John 1:5*

14. God is love. *1 John 4:8*

GOD, THE ALMIGHTY (See also God, Power of; Strength.)

1. I am the Almighty God; walk before me, and be thou perfect. *Gen. 17:1*

2. God Almighty bless thee, and make thee fruitful, and multiply thee. *Gen. 28:3*

3. God hath power to help, and to cast down. *2 Chron. 25:8*

4. Thou canst do every thing, and that no thought can be withholden from thee. *Job 42:2*

5. The Lord strong and mighty, the Lord mighty in battle. *Ps. 24:8*

6. Power belongeth unto God. *Ps. 62:11*

7. With God all things are possible. *Matt. 19:26*

8. They were all amazed at the mighty power of God. *Luke 9:43*

9. If it be of God, ye cannot overthrow it. *Acts 5:39*

10. Holy, holy, holy, Lord God Almighty, which was, and is, and is to come. *Rev. 4:8*

GOD, THE CREATOR (See also Beginning; Life.)

1. In the beginning God created the heaven and the earth. *Gen. 1:1*

2. Thine hands have made me and fashioned me together round about. *Job 10:8*

3. Know ye that the Lord he is God: it is he that hath made us, and not we ourselves; we are his people, and the sheep of his pasture. *Ps. 100:3*

4. This is the day which the Lord hath made; we will rejoice and be glad in it. *Ps. 118:24*

5. O Lord, thou art our father; we are the clay, and thou our potter; and we all are the work of thy hand. *Isa. 64:8*

6. By him [God] were all things created, that are in heaven, and that are in earth, visible and invisible, whether they be thrones, or dominions, or principalities, or powers: all things were created by him, and for him. *Col. 1:16*

7. Thou art worthy, O Lord, to receive glory and honor and power: for thou hast created all things, and for thy pleasure they are and were created. *Rev. 4:11*

GOD, EXISTENCE OF (See also Miracle; Natural Religion.)

1. They heard the voice of the Lord God walking in the garden. *Gen. 3:8*

2. God called unto him out of the midst of the bush, and said Moses, Moses. . . . I am the God of thy father, the God of Abraham, the God of Isaac, and the God of Jacob. *Exod. 3:4,6*

3. God said unto Moses, I AM THAT I AM. *Exod. 3:14*

4. This sign shalt thou have of the Lord, that the Lord will do the thing that he hath spoken. *2 Kings 20:9*

5. The earth shall be full of the knowledge of the Lord, as the waters cover the sea. *Isa. 11:9*

6. Thou [shalt] call, and the Lord shall answer; thou shalt cry, and he shall say, Here I am. *Isa. 58:9*

7. The Lord liveth. *Jer. 23:8*

8. God also bearing them witness, both with signs and wonders, and with divers miracles, and gifts of the Holy Ghost. *Heb. 2:4*

9. No man hath seen God at any time. If we love one another, God dwelleth in us, and his love is perfected in us. Hereby know we that we dwell in him, and he in us, because he hath given us of his Spirit. *1 John 4:12,13*

GOD, FAITHFULNESS OF (See also Constancy; Faithfulness; Loyalty.)

1. The Lord thy God . . . will not forsake thee, neither destroy thee, nor forget the covenant of thy fathers which he sware unto them. *Deut. 4:31*

2. There hath not failed one word of all his good promise. *1 Kings 8:56*

3. This God is our God for ever and ever. *Ps. 48:14*

4. The mercy of the Lord is from everlasting to everlasting upon them that fear him, and his righteousness unto children's children. *Ps. 103:17*

5. He hath remembered his covenant for ever, the word which he commanded to a thousand generations. *Ps. 105:8*

6. Thy faithfulness is unto all generations. *Ps. 119:90*

7. If we believe not, yet he abideth faithful. *2 Tim. 2:13*

8. I will never leave thee, nor forsake thee. *Heb. 13:5*

GOD, FAMILY OF   (See also Church; Family; God, Fatherhood of; Orphan; Unity.)

1. Ye are the children of the Lord your God. *Deut. 14:1*

2. Have we not all one father? hath not one God created us? *Mal. 2:10*

3. Whosoever shall do the will of my Father which is in heaven, the same is my brother, and sister, and mother. *Matt. 12:50*

4. My mother and my brethren are these which hear the word of God, and do it. *Luke 8:21*

5. [God] hath made of one blood all nations of men for to dwell on all the face of the earth. *Acts 17:26*

6. [I] will be a Father unto you, and ye shall be my sons and daughters. *2 Cor. 6:18*

7. Ye are no more strangers and foreigners, but fellow citizens with the saints, and of the household of God. *Eph. 2:19*

8. The Father of our Lord Jesus Christ, of whom the whole family in heaven and earth is named. *Eph. 3:14,15*

GOD, FATHERHOOD OF   (See also God, Family of; Orphan.)

1. I [God] have chosen him to be my son, and I will be his father. *1 Chron. 28:6*

2. A father of the fatherless . . . is God. *Ps. 68:5*

3. Thou shalt call me, My father; and shalt not turn away from me. *Jer. 3:19*

4. Ye may be the children of your Father which is in heaven. *Matt. 5:45*

5. Our Father which art in heaven. *Matt. 6:9*

6. Call no man your father upon the earth: for one is your Father, which is in heaven. *Matt. 23:9*

7. [I] will be a Father unto you, and ye shall be my sons and daughters, saith the Lord Almighty. *2 Cor. 6:18*

8. One God and Father of all. *Eph. 4:6*

GOD, GOODNESS OF   (See also Benevolence; Goodness; Grace; Kindness; God, Help of; God, Mercy of.)

1. I will make all my goodness pass before thee. *Exod. 33:19*

2. Thou art a God ready to pardon, gracious and merciful, slow to anger and of great kindness. *Neh. 9:17*

3. Far be it from God, that he should do wickedness; and from the Almighty, that he should commit iniquity. *Job 34:10*

4. The Lord is my shepherd; I shall not want. He maketh me to lie down in green pastures: he leadeth me beside the still waters. *Ps. 23:1,2*

5. The earth is full of the goodness of the Lord. *Ps. 33:5*

6. The goodness of God endureth continually. *Ps. 52:1*

7. The mountains shall depart, and the hills be removed; but my kindness shall not depart from thee, neither shall the covenant of my peace be removed, saith the Lord. *Isa. 54:10*

8. Why callest thou me good? there is none good but one, that is, God. *Matt. 19:17*

GOD, HELP OF   (See also God, Goodness of; God, Mercy of; Help; Protection.)

1. Hitherto hath the Lord helped us. *1 Sam. 7:12*

2. The hand of our God is upon all them for good that seek him. *Ezra 8:22*

3. Thou art the helper of the fatherless. *Ps. 10:14*

4. The Lord hear thee in the day of trouble; the name of the God of Jacob defend thee; send thee help from the sanctuary, and strengthen thee out of Zion. *Ps. 20:1,2*

5. The Lord is my shepherd; I shall not want. *Ps. 23:1*

6. My help cometh from the Lord, which made heaven and earth. *Ps. 121:2*

7. Fear not; I will help thee. *Isa. 41:13*

8. Thou hast destroyed thyself; but in me is thine help. *Hos. 13:9*

9. Consider the lilies of the field, how they grow; they toil not, neither do they spin. . . . shall he [God] not much more clothe you, O ye of little faith? *Matt. 6:28,30*

GOD, INFALLIBILITY OF   See Infallibility.

GOD, LAW OF   (See also Infallibility; Law; Obedience.)

1. The law of the Lord is perfect. *Ps. 19:7*

2. Blessed are . . . [those] who walk in the law of the Lord. *Ps. 119:1*

3. The commandment is a lamp; and the law is light. *Prov. 6:23*

4. I will put my law in their inward parts, and write it in their hearts. *Jer. 31:33*

5. Think not that I am come to destroy the law . . . I am not come to destroy, but to fulfil. For verily I say unto you, Till heaven and earth pass, one jot or one tittle shall in no wise pass from the law, till all be fulfilled. *Matt. 5:17,18*

6. All things whatsoever ye would that men should do to you, do ye even so to them: for this is the law. *Matt. 7:12*

7. Thou shalt love the Lord thy God with all thy heart, and with all thy soul, and with all thy mind. This is the first and great commandment. And the second is like unto it, Thou shalt love thy neighbor as thyself. On these two commandments hang all the law. *Matt. 22:37–40*

8. Love your enemies, do good to them which hate you, Bless them that curse you, and pray for them which despitefully use you. *Luke 6:27,28*

9. All things must be fulfilled, which were written in the law of Moses, and in the prophets, and in the psalms, concerning me. *Luke 24:44*

10. Love is the fulfilling of the law. *Rom. 13:10*

11. The law is good, if a man use it lawfully; Knowing this, that the law is not made for a righteous man, but for the lawless and disobedient. *1 Tim. 1:8,9*

GOD, MERCY OF   (See also Benevolence; God, Goodness of; God, Help of; Mercy; Pity.)

1. Showing mercy unto thousands of them that love me, and keep my commandments. *Exod. 20:6*

2. The Lord was gracious unto them, and had compassion on them . . . and would not destroy them, neither cast he them from his presence. *2 Kings 13:23*

3. The Lord your God is gracious and merciful, and will not turn away his face from you. *2 Chron. 30:9*

4. Thou, Lord, art good, and ready to forgive; and plenteous in mercy unto all them that call upon thee. *Ps. 86:5*

5. The mercy of the Lord is from everlasting to everlasting upon them that fear him. *Ps. 103:17*

6. The earth, O Lord, is full of thy mercy. *Ps. 119:64*

7. It is of the Lord's mercies that we are not consumed, because his compassions fail not. *Lam. 3:22*

8. Father of mercies, and the God of all comfort. *2 Cor. 1:3*

GOD, OMNIPRESENCE OF   (See also God, Omniscience of.)

1. I am with thee, and will keep thee in all places whither thou goest . . . I will not leave thee. *Gen. 28:15*

2. Whither shall I go from they Spirit? Or whither shall I flee from thy presence? If I ascend up into heaven, thou art there: if I make my bed in hell, behold, thou art there. *Ps. 139:7,8*

3. The eyes of the Lord are in every place, beholding the evil and the good. *Prov. 15:3*

4. Can any hide himself in secret places that I shall not see him? saith the Lord. Do not I fill heaven and earth? *Jer. 23:24*

5. He [God] be not far from every one of us: For in him we live, and move, and have our being. *Acts 17:27,28*

GOD, OMNISCIENCE OF   (See also God, Omnipresence of; Wisdom.)

1. The Lord searcheth all hearts, and understandeth all the imaginations of the thoughts. *1 Chron. 28:9*

2. [God] looketh to the ends of the earth, and seeth under the whole heaven. *Job 28:24*

3. I know . . . that no thought can be withholden from thee. *Job 42:2*

4. O Lord thou hast searched me, and known me. Thou knowest my downsitting and mine uprising, thou understandest my thought afar off . . . there is not a word in my tongue, but, lo, O Lord, thou knowest it altogether. *Ps. 139:1–4*

5. The eyes of the Lord are in every place, beholding the evil and the good. *Prov. 15:3*

6. Your Father knoweth what things ye have need of, before ye ask him. *Matt. 6:8*

7. All things are naked and opened unto the eyes of him with whom we have to do. *Heb. 4:13*

GOD, POWER OF   (See also God, The Almighty; Miracle; Power.)

1. Thy right hand, O Lord, is become glorious in power: thy right hand, O Lord, hath dashed in pieces the enemy. *Exod. 15:6*

2. The Lord killeth, and maketh alive: he bringeth down to the grave, and bringeth up. The Lord maketh poor, and maketh rich: he bringeth low, and lifteth up. *1 Sam. 2:6,7*

3. He ruleth by his power for ever. *Ps. 66:7*

4. The Lord is a great God, and a great King above all gods. *Ps. 95:3*

5. They shall speak of the glory of thy kingdom, and talk of thy power. *Ps. 145:11*

6. Our God whom we serve is able to deliver us. *Dan. 3:17*

7. With God nothing shall be impossible. *Luke 1:37*

8. Strengthened with all might, according to his glorious power. *Col. 1:11*

9. The voice of mighty thunderings, saying, Alleluia: for the Lord God omnipotent reigneth. *Rev. 19:6*

GOD, WRATH OF   (See also Anger.)

1. Great is the wrath of the Lord that is kindled against us. *2 Kings 22:13*

2. God is angry with the wicked every day. *Ps. 7:11*

3. The Lord is merciful and gracious, slow to anger, and plenteous in mercy. *Ps. 103:8*

4. The anger of the Lord [is] kindled against his people, and he hath stretched forth his hand against them, and hath smitten them. *Isa. 5:25*

5. I will punish the world for their evil, and the wicked for their iniquity; and I will cause the arrogancy of the proud to cease, and will lay low the haughtiness of the terrible. *Isa. 13:11*

6. At his wrath the earth shall tremble, and the nations shall not be able to abide his indignation. *Jer. 10:10*

7. Their silver and their gold shall not be able to deliver them in the day of the wrath of the Lord. *Ezek. 7:19*

8. I will execute vengeance in anger and fury upon the heathen, such as they have not heard. *Mic. 5:15*

9. He that believeth on the Son hath everlasting life: and he that believeth not the Son shall not see life; but the wrath of God abideth on him. *John 3:36*

10. For the wrath of God is revealed from heaven against all ungodliness and unrighteousness of men, who hold the truth in unrighteousness. *Rom. 1:18*

GODS, FALSE   See Cults, Religious; False Prophet; Idolatry.

GOLDEN RULE   (See also Christian Obligation.)

1. All things whatsoever ye would that men should do to you, do ye even so to them: for this is the law and the prophets. *Matt. 7:12*

GOODNESS   (See also God, Goodness of; Grace; Kindness; Mercy; Righteousness; Virtue.)

1. Surely goodness and mercy shall follow me all the days of my life. *Ps. 23:6*

2. She will do him good and not evil all the days of her life. *Prov. 31:12*

3. Learn to do well. *Isa. 1:17*

4. Ye are the salt of the earth: but if the salt have lost his savor . . . it is thenceforth good for nothing. *Matt. 5:13*

5. Be ye therefore perfect, even as your Father which is in heaven is perfect. *Matt. 5:48*

6. A good tree cannot bring forth evil fruit, neither can a corrupt tree bring forth good fruit. *Matt. 7:18*

7. Be not overcome of evil, but overcome evil with good. *Rom. 12:21*

8. As we have therefore opportunity, let us do good unto all men. *Gal. 6:10*

GOSPEL   (See also Doctrine; Evangelism; Parable; Scripture; Word.)

1. How beautiful upon the mountains are the feet of him that bringeth good tidings, that publisheth peace; that bringeth good tidings of good, that publisheth salvation; that saith unto Zion, Thy God reigneth! *Isa. 52:7*

2. Jesus went about all Galilee . . . preaching the gospel of the kingdom. *Matt. 4:23*

3. This gospel of the kingdom shall be preached in all the world for a witness unto all nations. *Matt. 24:14*

4. Repent ye, and believe the gospel. *Mark 1:15*

5. I am not ashamed of the gospel of Christ: for it is the power of God unto salvation to every one that believeth. *Rom. 1:16*

6. Though I preach the gospel, I have nothing to glory of: for necessity is laid upon me; yea, woe is unto me, if I preach not the gospel! . . . What is my reward then? Verily that, when I preach the gospel, I may make the gospel of Christ without charge, that I abuse not my power in the gospel. *1 Cor. 9:16,18*

7. There be some that . . . would pervert the gospel of Christ. *Gal. 1:17*

8. Ye heard the word of truth, the gospel of your salvation. *Eph. 1:13*

9. I may open my mouth boldly, to make known the mystery of the gospel. *Eph. 6:19*

10. Be not moved away from the hope of the gospel . . . which was preached to every creature which is under heaven. *Col. 1:23*

11. For this cause was the gospel preached also to them that are dead, that they might be judged according to men in the flesh, but live according to God in the spirit. *1 Peter 4:6*

GOSSIP (See also Meddling; Slander.)

1. Thou shalt not go up and down as a talebearer among thy people. *Lev. 19:16*

2. A talebearer revealeth secrets: but he that is of a faithful spirit concealeth the matter. *Prov. 11:13*

3. He that keepeth his mouth keepeth his life: but he that openeth wide his lips shall have destruction. *Prov. 18:3*

4. He that repeateth a matter separateth very friends. *Prov. 17:9*

5. The words of a talebearer are as wounds, and they go down into the innermost parts of the belly. *Prov. 18:8*

6. Where there is no talebearer, the strife ceaseth. *Prov. 26:20*

7. Curse not the king, no not in thy thought; and curse not the rich in thy bedchamber: for a bird of the air shall carry the voice, and that which hath wings shall tell the matter. *Eccl. 10:20*

8. Every idle word that men shall speak, they shall give account thereof in the day of judgment. *Matt. 12:36*

9. Refuse profane and old wives' fables. *1 Tim. 4:7*

10. [They learn to be] not only idle, but tattlers also and busybodies, speaking things which they ought not. *1 Tim. 5:13*

11. Keep that which is committed to thy trust, avoiding profane and vain babblings. *1 Tim. 6:20*

GOVERNMENT See Politics.

GRACE (See also Blessing; Gift; God, Goodness of.)

1. Where sin abounded, grace did much more abound. *Rom. 5:20*

2. By the grace of God I am what I am: and his grace which was bestowed upon me was not in vain; but I labored more abundantly than they all: yet not I, but the grace of God which was with me. *1 Cor. 15:10*

3. God is able to make all grace abound toward you. *2 Cor. 9:8*

4. My grace is sufficient for thee. *2 Cor. 12:9*

5. (Blessed be the God) In whom we have redemption through his blood, the forgiveness of sins, according to the riches of his grace. *Eph. 1:7*

6. Grace be with all them that love our Lord Jesus Christ. *Eph. 6:24*

7. Ye all are partakers of my grace. *Phil. 1:7*

8. The grace of God that bringeth salvation hath appeared to all men. *Titus 2:11*

9. Let us therefore come boldly unto the throne of grace, that we may obtain mercy, and find grace to help in time of need. *Heb. 4:16*

10. Grow in grace, and in the knowledge of our Lord and Savior Jesus Christ. *2 Peter 3:18*

11. The grace of our Lord Jesus Christ be with you all. Amen. *Rev. 22:21*

GRAFT   See Bribery.

GRANDEUR   (See also Glory; Luxury.)

1. Thine, O Lord, is the greatness, and the power, and the glory, and the victory, and the majesty. *1 Chron. 29:11*

2. And the house which I build is great: for great is our God above all gods. *2 Chron. 2:5*

3. I saw also the Lord sitting upon a throne, high and lifted up, and his train filled the temple. *Isa. 6:1*

4. The city had no need of the sun, neither of the moon, to shine in it: for the glory of God did lighten it. *Rev. 21:23*

GRAPE   See Wine.

GRATITUDE   See Appreciation; Thanksgiving.

GRAVE   See Burial.

GREATNESS   See God, The Almighty; God, Power of; Grandeur.

GREED   (See also Covetousness; Money; Stinginess; Wealth; Worldliness.)

1. Thou shalt not covet . . . any thing that is thy neighbor's. *Exod. 20:17*

2. He hath swallowed down riches, and he shall vomit them up again: God shall cast them out of his belly. *Job 20:15*

3. The Lord abhorreth [the covetous]. *Ps. 10:3*

4. He that is greedy of gain troubleth his own house. *Prov. 15:27*

5. The horseleech hath two daughters, crying, Give, give. *Prov. 30:15*

6. He that loveth silver shall not be satisfied with silver; nor he that loveth abundance with increase. *Eccl. 5:10*

7. They are greedy dogs which can never have enough. *Isa. 56:11*

8. Lay not up for yourselves treasures upon earth . . . For where your treasure is, there will your heart be also. *Matt. 6:19,21*

9. What is a man profited, if he shall gain the whole world, and lose his own soul? *Matt. 16:26*

10. [Be] not greedy of filthy lucre. *1 Tim. 3:3*

11. The love of money is the root of all evil. *1 Tim. 6:10*

GRIEF See Sadness; Sorrow.

GROWTH (See also Education; Improvement; Maturity; Self-Improvement; Teaching.)

1. I will give you rain in due season, and the land shall yield her increase, and the trees of the field shall yield their fruit. *Lev. 26:4*

2. He shall grow up before him as a tender plant, and as a root out of a dry ground. *Isa. 53:2*

3. If a man should cast seed into the ground . . . the seed should spring and grow up . . . For the earth bringeth forth fruit of herself. *Mark 4:26–28*

4. [The kingdom of God] is like a grain of mustard seed, which, when it is sown . . . groweth up, and becometh greater than all herbs, and shooteth out great branches. *Mark 4:31,32*

5. Jesus increased in wisdom and stature, and in favor with God and man. *Luke 2:52*

6. I have planted, Apollos watered; but God gave the increase. *1 Cor. 3:6*

7. As newborn babes, desire the sincere milk of the word, that ye may grow thereby. *1 Peter 2:2*

8. Grow in grace, and in the knowledge of our Lord and Savior Jesus Christ. *2 Peter 3:18*

GUEST (See also Hospitality; Stranger.)

1. [Two angels] turned in unto him [Lot], and entered into his house; and he made them a feast. *Gen. 19:3*

2. Is there room in thy father's house for us to lodge in? *Gen. 24:33*

3. Lodge here this night. *Num. 22:8*

4. Those servants went out into the highways, and gathered together all as many as they found, both bad and good: and the wedding was furnished with guests. *Matt. 22:10*

5. I was ahungered, and ye gave me meat: I was thirsty, and ye gave me drink: I was a stranger, and ye took me in. *Matt. 25:35*

6. Go out into the highways and hedges, and compel them to come in, that my house may be filled. For I say unto you, That none of those men which were bidden shall taste of my supper. *Luke 14:23,24*

7. He [Jesus] was gone to be guest with a man that is a sinner. *Luke 19:7*

8. When ye are entered into the city, there shall a man meet you, bearing a pitcher of water; follow him into the house where he entereth in. And ye shall say unto the goodman of the house, The Master saith unto thee, Where is the guest chambeŕ, where I shall eat the passover with my disciples? *Luke 22:10,11*

9. Be not forgetful to entertain strangers: for thereby some have entertained angels unawares. *Heb. 13:2*

GUIDANCE   (See also Christ, Leadership of; Leadership.)

1. [Moses said unto the Lord] show me now thy way . . . And he said, My presence shall go with thee. *Exod. 33:13,14*

2. He leadeth me in the paths of righteousness for his name's sake. *Ps. 23:3*

3. Send out thy light and thy truth: let them lead me. *Ps. 43:3*

4. He [God] will be our guide even unto death. *Ps. 48:14*

5. Trust in the Lord with all thine heart . . . and he shall direct thy paths. *Prov. 3:5,6*

6. Thine ears shall hear a word behind thee, saying, This is the way, walk ye in it, when ye turn to the right hand, and when ye turn to the left. *Isa. 30:21*

7. I will bring the blind by a way that they knew not; I will lead them in paths that they have not known: I will make darkness light before them, and crooked things straight. *Isa. 42:16*

8. The star, which they saw in the east, went before them, till it came and stood over where the young child was. *Matt. 2:9*

9. I am the light of the world: he that followeth me shall not walk in darkness, but shall have the light of life. *John 8:12*

10. I am the way, the truth, and the life: no man cometh unto the Father, but by me. *John 14:6*

11. God himself and our Father, and our Lord Jesus Christ, direct our way unto you. *1 Thess. 3:11*

GUILT   (See also Blame; Conscience; Innocence; Shame.)

1. The Lord will not hold him guiltless that taketh his name in vain. *Exod. 20:7*

2. If a soul sin . . . he [is] guilty, and shall bear his iniquity. *Lev. 5:17*

3. He [Pilate] took water, and washed his hands before the multitude, saying, I am innocent of the blood of this just person: see ye to it. Then answered all the people, and said, His blood be on us, and on our children. *Matt. 27:24,25*

4. They which heard it, being convicted by their own conscience, went out one by one. *John 8:9*

5. All the world may become guilty before God. *Rom. 3:19*
6. Whosoever shall eat this bread, and drink this cup of the Lord, unworthily, shall be guilty of the body and blood of the Lord. *1 Cor. 11:27*
7. Whosoever shall keep the whole law, and yet offend in one point, he is guilty of all. *James 2:10*

HADES   See Hell.

HANDICAP   (See also Healing.)

1. Thou shalt not curse the deaf, nor put a stumblingblock before the blind. *Lev. 19:14*

2. It is better for thee to enter into life halt or maimed, rather than having two hands or two feet to be cast into everlasting fire. *Matt. 18:8*

3. When thou makest a feast, call the poor, the maimed, the lame, the blind: And thou shalt be blessed. *Luke 14:13,14*

4. I take pleasure in infirmities . . . for Christ's sake: for when I am weak, then am I strong. *2 Cor. 12:10*

HAPPINESS   (See also Celebration.)

1. Happy art thou, O Israel: who is like unto thee, O people saved by the Lord. *Deut. 33:29*

2. Make a joyful noise unto the Lord, all ye lands. Serve the Lord with gladness: come before his presence with singing. *Ps. 100:1,2*

3. They that sow in tears shall reap in joy. *Ps. 126:5*

4. Happy is that people, whose God is the Lord. *Ps. 144:15*

5. A merry heart maketh a cheerful countenance. *Prov. 15:13*

6. Whoso trusteth in the Lord, happy is he. *Prov. 16:20*

7. A merry heart doeth good like a medicine. *Prov. 17:22*

8. Rejoice, and be exceeding glad: for great is your reward in heaven. *Matt. 5:12*

9. These things have I spoken unto you, that my joy might remain in you, and that your joy might be full. *John 15:11*

10. Be of good cheer; I have overcome the world. *John 16:33*

11. The disciples were filled with joy, and with the Holy Ghost. *Acts 13:52*

12. Rejoice in the Lord always: and again I say, Rejoice. *Phil. 4:4*

13. Rejoice, inasmuch as ye are partakers of Christ's sufferings; that, when his glory shall be revealed, ye may be glad also with exceeding joy. *1 Peter 4:13*

HARBINGER See Forerunner.

HARDSHIP See Distress; Trouble.

HARMONY See Peace; Unity.

HARVEST See Abundance; Farming; Maturity.

HASTE See Imprudence.

HATRED (See also Contempt; Hostility; Malice; Scorn.)

1. Thou shalt not hate thy brother in thine heart. *Lev. 19:17*

2. Do not I hate them, O Lord, that hate thee? . . . I hate them with perfect hatred. *Ps. 139:21,22*

3. Hatred stirreth up strifes: but love covereth all sins. *Prov. 10:12*

4. He that hateth dissembleth with his lips, and layeth up deceit within him. *Prov. 26:24*

5. A time to love, and a time to hate. *Eccl. 3:8*

6. Love your enemies, bless them that curse you, do good to them that hate you, and pray for them which despitefully use you, and persecute you. *Matt. 5:44*

7. Blessed are ye, when men shall hate you, and when they shall separate you from their company, and shall reproach you, and cast out your name as evil, for the Son of man's sake. *Luke 6:22*

8. If the world hate you, ye know that it hated me before it hated you. *John 15:18*

9. He that hateth me hateth my Father also. *John 15:23*

10. Whosoever hateth his brother is a murderer. *1 John 3:15*

11. If a man say, I love God, and hateth his brother, he is a liar: for he that loveth not his brother whom he hath seen, how can he love God whom he hath not seen? *1 John 4:20*

HAUGHTINESS See Contempt; Pride.

HEALING (See also Handicap; Health; Physician.)

1. The Lord will take away from thee all sickness. *Deut. 7:15*

2. He healeth the broken in heart, and bindeth up their wounds. *Ps. 147:3*

3. A time to kill, and a time to heal. *Eccl. 3:3*

4. The eyes of the blind shall be opened, and the ears of the deaf shall be unstopped. Then shall the lame man leap as a hart, and the tongue of the dumb sing. *Isa. 35:5,6*

5. He was wounded for our transgressions, he was bruised for our iniquities . . . and with his stripes we are healed. *Isa. 53:5*

6. Unto you that fear my name shall the Sun of righteousness arise with healing in his wings. *Mal. 4:2*

7. They shall lay hands on the sick, and they shall recover. *Mark 16:18*

8. He called his twelve disciples together, and gave them power and authority over all devils, and to cure diseases. And he sent them to preach the kingdom of God, and to heal the sick. *Luke 9:1,2*

9. Rise, take up thy bed, and walk. *John 5:8*

10. The prayer of faith shall save the sick. *James 5:15*

HEALTH   (See also Healing; Illness; Physician.)

1. I will put none of these diseases upon thee, which I have brought upon the Egyptians: for I am the Lord that healeth thee. *Exod. 15:26*

2. I shall yet praise him, who is the health of my countenance, and my God. *Ps. 42:11*

3. God be merciful unto us, and bless us . . . That thy way may be known upon earth, thy saving health among all nations. *Ps. 67:1,2*

4. [My words] are life unto those that find them, and health to all their flesh. *Prov. 4:22*

5. The whole head is sick, and the whole heart faint. From the sole of the foot even unto the head there is no soundness in it. *Isa. 1:5,6*

6. I will restore health unto thee, and I will heal thee of thy wounds, saith the Lord. *Jer. 30:17*

7. Beloved, I wish above all things that thou mayest prosper and be in health, even as thy soul prospereth. *3 John 1:2*

HEARING   See Listening.

HEART   (See also Conscience; Mind; Soul; Spirit, Human.)

1. Thou shalt love the Lord thy God with all thine heart. *Deut. 6:5*

2. The Lord hath sought him a man after his own heart. *1 Sam. 13:14*

3. Man looketh on the outward appearance, but the Lord looketh on the heart. *1 Sam. 16:7*

4. Keep thy heart with all diligence; for out of it are the issues of life. *Prov. 4:23*

5. As he thinketh in his heart, so is he. *Prov. 23:7*

6. He that hardeneth his heart shall fall into mischief. *Prov. 28:14*

7. The heart is deceitful above all things, and desperately wicked. *Jer. 17:9*

8. For with the heart man believeth unto righteousness; and with the mouth confession is made unto salvation. *Rom. 10:10*

HEART, HARDNESS OF See Apathy; Indifference; Ingratitude.

HEARTBREAK (See also Sorrow.)

1. The Lord is nigh unto them that are of a broken heart. *Ps. 34:18*

2. A broken and a contrite heart, O God, thou wilt not despise. *Ps. 51:17*

3. Hope deferred maketh the heart sick. *Prov. 13:12*

4. The spirit of a man will sustain his infirmity; but a wounded spirit who can bear? *Prov. 18:14*

5. Stay me with flagons, comfort me with apples: for I am sick of love. *Song of Sol. 2:5*

6. He [the Lord] hath sent me to bind up the brokenhearted. *Isa. 61:1*

7. Blessed are they that mourn: for they shall be comforted. *Matt. 5:4*

HEATHEN   See Paganism.

HEAVEN (See also Earth; Kingdom; Paradise.)

1. God said, Let there be a firmament in the midst of the waters . . . And God called the firmament Heaven. *Gen. 1:6,8*

2. How dreadful is this place! this is none other but the house of God, and this is the gate of heaven. *Gen. 28:17*

3. The heaven is my throne, and the earth is my footstool. *Isa. 66:1*

4. I will give unto thee [Peter] the keys of the kingdom of heaven: and whatsoever thou shalt bind on earth shall be bound in heaven: and whatsoever thou shalt loose on earth shall be loosed in heaven. *Matt. 16:19*

5. Verily, verily, I say unto you, Hereafter ye shall see heaven open, and the angels of God ascending and descending upon the Son of man. *John 1:51*

6. There was war in heaven . . . And the great dragon was cast out, that old serpent, called the Devil, and Satan . . . he was cast out into the earth, and his angels were cast out with him. *Rev. 12:7,9*

7. I [John] saw a new heaven and a new earth: for the first heaven and the first earth were passed away. *Rev. 21:1*

HELL (See also Demons; Evil; Punishment.)

1. The wicked shall be turned into hell. *Ps. 9:17*

2. Hell hath enlarged herself, and opened her mouth without measure: and their glory, and their multitude, and their pomp, and he that rejoiceth, shall descend into it. *Isa. 5:14*

3. The Son of man shall send forth his angels, and they shall gather out of his kingdom all things that offend, and them which do iniquity; And shall cast them into a furnace of fire: there shall be wailing and gnashing of teeth. *Matt. 13:41,42*

4. God spared not the angels that sinned, but cast them down to hell, and delivered them into chains of darkness. *2 Peter 2:4*

5. I looked, and behold a pale horse: and his name that sat on him was Death, and Hell followed with him. *Rev. 6:8*

6. He opened the bottomless pit; and there arose a smoke out of the pit, as the smoke of a great furnace; and the sun and the air were darkened by reason of the smoke of the pit. *Rev. 9:2*

7. The devil that deceived them was cast into the lake of fire and brimstone, where the beast and the false prophet are, and shall be tormented day and night for ever and ever. *Rev. 20:10*

8. Death and hell were cast into the lake of fire. This is the second death. And whosoever was not found written in the book of life was cast into the lake of fire. *Rev. 20:14,15*

HELP (See also God, Help of; Refuge; Relief.)

1. I delivered the poor that cried, and the fatherless, and him that had none to help him. . . . I was eyes to the blind, and feet was I to the lame. *Job 29:12,15*

2. I will lift up mine eyes unto the hills, from whence cometh my help. My help cometh from the Lord, which made heaven and earth. *Ps. 121:1,2*

3. Thou hast been a strength to the poor, a strength to the needy in his distress, a refuge from the storm, a shadow from the heat. *Isa. 25:4*

4. We then that are strong ought to bear the infirmities of the weak. *Rom. 15:1*

5. Assist her in whatsoever business she hath need of you: for she hath been a succorer of many. *Rom. 16:2*

6. In that he himself hath suffered being tempted, he is able to succor them that are tempted. *Heb. 2:18*

7. The Lord is my helper, and I will not fear what man shall do unto me. *Heb. 13:6*

HERESY (See also Blasphemy; Church, Criticism of; Cults, Religious; False Prophet.)

1. If thy brother . . . entice thee secretly, saying, Let us go and serve other gods . . . Thou shalt not consent unto him, nor hearken unto him . . . But thou shalt surely kill him. *Deut. 13:6-9*

2. This I confess unto thee, that after the way which they call heresy, so worship I the God of my fathers, believing all things which are written in the law and in the prophets. *Acts 24:14*

3. Mark them which cause divisions and offenses contrary to the doctrine which ye have learned; and avoid them. *Rom. 16:17*

4. There be some that . . . would pervert the gospel of Christ. But though we, or an angel from heaven, preach any other gospel unto you than that which we have preached unto you, let him be accursed. *Gal. 1:7,8*

5. A man that is a heretic after the first and second admonition reject; Knowing that he that is such is subverted, and sinneth, being condemned of himself. *Titus 3:10,11*

6. If there come any unto you, and bring not this doctrine, receive him not into your house. *2 John 1:10*

7. There are certain men crept in unawares, who were before of old ordained to this condemnation, ungodly men, turning the grace of our God into lasciviousness, and denying the only Lord God, and our Lord Jesus Christ. *Jude 1:4*

8. Thou hast tried them which say they are apostles, and are not. *Rev. 2:2*

HERITAGE See Genealogy; Inheritance.

HESITATION See Doubt; Indecision; Procrastination; Tardiness.

HIDING (See also Cowardice; Secrecy; Shame; Solitude.)

1. Adam and his wife hid themselves from the presence of the Lord. *Gen. 3:8*

2. The people did hide themselves in caves, and in thickets, and in rocks, and in high places, and in pits. *1 Sam. 13:6*

3. How long wilt thou hide thy face from me? *Ps. 13:1*

4. Hide thyself as it were for a little moment, until the indignation be overpast. *Isa. 26:20*

5. Under falsehood have we hid ourselves. *Isa. 28:15*

6. A man shall be as a hiding place from the wind. *Isa. 32:2*

HINDRANCE See Obstacle.

HOLINESS   (See also Purity; Righteousness.)

1. They made the plate of the holy crown of pure gold, and wrote upon it a writing . . . HOLINESS TO THE LORD. *Exod. 39:30*

2. Put difference between holy and unholy, and between unclean and clean. *Lev. 10:10*

3. Ye shall be holy: for I the Lord your God am holy. *Lev. 19:2*

4. Worship the Lord in the beauty of holiness. *Ps. 29:2*

5. Holiness becometh thine house, O Lord, for ever. *Ps. 93:5*

6. Holy, holy, holy, is the Lord of hosts. *Isa. 6:3*

7. A highway shall be there, and a way, and it shall be called The way of holiness; the unclean shall not pass over it . . . but the redeemed shall walk there. *Isa. 35:8,9*

8. Our Father which art in heaven, Hallowed be thy name. *Matt. 6:9*

9. Give not that which is holy unto the dogs. *Matt. 7:6*

10. The temple of God is holy, which temple ye are. *1 Cor. 3:17*

11. Let us cleanse ourselves from all filthiness of the flesh and spirit, perfecting holiness in the fear of God. *2 Cor. 7:1*

12. According as he hath chosen us in him before the foundation of the world, that we should be holy and without blame before him in love. *Eph. 1:4*

13. As he which hath called you is holy, so be ye holy in all manner of conversation; Because it is written, Be ye holy; for I am holy. *1 Peter 1:15,16*

HOLY COMMUNION   See Eucharist.

HOLY GHOST   See Holy Spirit.

HOLY LAND   See Israel.

HOLY SPIRIT   (See also God; Inspiration; Tongues, Gift of; Trinity, Holy.)

1. The Spirit of God came upon him, and he prophesied among them. *1 Sam. 10:10*

2. The spirit of the Lord shall rest upon him, the spirit of wisdom and understanding, the spirit of counsel and might, the spirit of knowledge and of the fear of the Lord. *Isa. 11:2*

3. The heavens were opened unto him [Jesus], and he saw the Spirit of God descending like a dove, and lighting upon him. *Matt. 3:16*

4. I will pray the Father, and he shall give you another Comforter, that he may abide with you for ever . . . the Comforter, which is the Holy Ghost . . . shall teach you all things. *John 14:16,26*

5. It is expedient for you that I go away: for if I go not away, the Comforter will not come unto you; but if I depart, I will send him unto you. And when he is come he will reprove the world of sin, and of righteousness, and of judgment. *John 16:7*

6. Suddenly there came a sound from heaven as a rushing mighty wind . . . And there appeared unto them cloven tongues like as of fire . . . And they were all filled with the Holy Ghost, and began to speak with other tongues, as the Spirit gave them utterance. *Acts 2:2–4*

7. Your body is the temple of the Holy Ghost which is in you. *1 Cor. 6:19*

8. The fruit of the Spirit is love, joy, peace, long-suffering, gentleness, goodness, faith, Meekness, temperance. . . . If we live in the Spirit, let us also walk in the Spirit. *Gal. 5:22–25*

9. It is the Spirit that beareth witness, because the Spirit is truth. For there are three that bear record in heaven, the Father, the Word, and the Holy Ghost: and these three are one. *1 John 5:6,7*

HOLY TRINITY   See Trinity, Holy.

HOME   See House.

HOMICIDE   See Murder.

HOMOSEXUALITY   (See also Sexual Perversion.)

1. Where are the men which came in to thee this night? bring them out unto us, that we may know them. *Gen. 19:5*

2. Thou shalt not lie with mankind. *Lev. 18:22*

3. If a man also lie with mankind, as he lieth with a woman, both of them have committed an abomination: they shall surely be put to death. *Lev. 20:13*

4. The woman shall not wear that which pertaineth unto a man, neither shall a man put on a woman's garment. *Deut. 22:5*

5. There shall be no . . . sodomite of the sons of Israel. Thou shalt not bring . . . the price of a dog [male homosexual], into the house of the Lord thy God. *Deut. 23:17,18*

6. Even their women did change the natural use into that which is against nature: and likewise also the men, leaving the natural use of the woman, burned in their lust one toward another; men with men working that which is unseemly. *Rom. 1:26,27*

7. Be not . . . effeminate, nor abusers of themselves with mankind. *1 Cor. 6:9*

HONESTY (See also Deceit; Righteousness; Truth.)

1. Tell me nothing but that which is true in the name of the Lord. *1 Kings 22:16*

2. The lip of truth shall be established for ever: but a lying tongue is but for a moment. *Prov. 12:19*

3. Lying lips are abomination to the Lord: but they that deal truly are his delight. *Prov. 12:22*

4. Let us walk honestly. *Rom. 13:13*

5. Providing for honest things, not only in the sight of the Lord, but also in the sight of men. *2 Cor. 8:21*

6. Speak every man truth with his neighbor. *Eph. 4:25*

7. Whatsoever things are honest . . . think on these things. *Phil. 4:8*

8. Lead a quiet and peaceable life in all godliness and honesty. *1 Tim. 2:2*

HONOR (See also Respect.)

1. Honor thy father and thy mother: that thy days may be long upon the land which the Lord thy God giveth thee. *Exod. 20:12*

2. The Lord saith, . . . them that honor me I will honor, and they that despise me shall be lightly esteemed. *1 Sam. 2:30*

3. Thou hast made [man] a little lower than the angels, and hast crowned him with glory and honor. *Ps. 8:5*

4. Honor the Lord with thy substance, and with the firstfruits of all thine increase. *Prov. 3:9*

5. This people . . . with their lips do honor me, but have removed their hearts far from me. *Isa. 29:13*

6. All men should honor the Son, even as they honor the Father. *John 5:23*

7. Honor all men. Love the brotherhood. Fear God. Honor the king. *1 Peter 2:17*

8. Thou art worthy, O Lord, to receive glory and honor and power: for thou hast created all things, and for thy pleasure they are and were created. *Rev. 4:11*

HOPE (See also Desire; Expectation.)

1. Hope deferred maketh the heart sick, but when the desire cometh, it is a tree of life. *Prov. 13:12*

2. Blessed is the man that trusteth in the Lord, and whose hope the Lord is. *Jer. 17:7*

3. Thou art my hope in the day of evil. *Jer. 17:17*

4. Prisoners of hope. *Zech. 9:12*

5. [Abraham] Who against hope believed in hope. *Rom. 4:18*

6. Knowing that tribulation worketh patience; And patience, experience; and experience, hope: And hope maketh not ashamed. *Rom. 5:3–5*

7. We are saved by hope: but hope that is seen is not hope: for what a man seeth, why doth he yet hope for? But if we hope for that we see not, then do we with patience wait for it. *Rom. 8:24,25*

8. He that ploweth should plow in hope; and he that thresheth in hope should be partaker of his hope. *1 Cor. 9:10*

9. Now abideth faith, hope, charity. *1 Cor. 13:13*

10. Hope we have as an anchor of the soul, both sure and stedfast. *Heb. 6:19*

11. Hope to the end for the grace that is to be brought unto you. *1 Peter 1:13*

HOPELESSNESS (See also Depression; Despair; Discouragement.)

1. My days . . . are spent without hope. *Job 7:6*

2. They [the wicked] shall not escape, and their hope shall be as the giving up of the ghost. *Job 11:20*

3. What is the hope of the hypocrite, though he hath gained, when God taketh away his soul? *Job 27:8*

4. Hope deferred maketh the heart sick. *Prov. 13:12*

5. If in this life only we have hope in Christ, we are of all men most miserable. *1 Cor. 15:19*

6. At that time ye were without Christ . . . having no hope, and without God in the world. *Eph. 2:12*

HOSPITALITY (See also Guest; Kindness; Stranger.)

1. [The Lord your God] loveth the stranger, in giving him food and raiment. Love ye therefore the stranger: for ye were strangers in the land of Egypt. *Deut. 10:18,19*

2. I was ahungered, and ye gave me meat: I was thirsty, and ye gave me drink: I was a stranger, and ye took me in . . . Inasmuch as ye have done it unto one of the least of these my brethren, ye have done it unto me. *Matt. 25:35,40*

3. When thou makest a dinner or a supper, call not thy friends, nor thy brethren, neither thy kinsmen, nor thy rich neighbors; lest they also bid thee again, and a recompense be made thee. But when thou makest a feast call the poor, the maimed, the lame, the blind: And thou shalt be blessed; for they cannot recompense thee. *Luke 14:12–14*

4. Paul dwelt two whole years in his own hired house, and received all that came in unto him. *Acts 28:30*

5. [Be] given to hospitality. *Rom. 12:13*

6. A bishop must be . . . a lover of hospitality. *Titus 1:7,8*

7. Be not forgetful to entertain strangers: for thereby some have entertained angels unawares. *Heb. 13:2*

8. Use hospitality one to another without grudging. *1 Peter 4:9*

HOSTILITY   (See also Enemy; Hatred; Malice; War.)

1. I will beat down his foes before his face, and plague them that hate him. *Ps. 89:23*

2. My soul hath long dwelt with him that hateth peace. I am for peace: but when I speak, they are for war. *Ps. 120:6,7*

3. The words of the wicked are to lie in wait for blood. *Prov. 12:6*

4. I will meet them as a bear that is bereaved of her whelps. *Hos. 13:8*

5. I am come to set a man at variance against his father, and the daughter against her mother, and the daughter-in-law against her mother-in-law. And a man's foes shall be they of his own household. *Matt. 10:35,36*

HOUSE

1. Set thine house in order; for thou shalt die, and not live. *2 Kings 20:1*

2. Lord, thou has been our dwelling place in all generations. *Ps. 90:1*

3. Let us go into the house of the Lord. *Ps. 122:1*

4. Better is a dry morsel, and quietness therewith, than an house full of sacrifices with strife. *Prov. 17:1*

5. If a house be divided against itself, that house cannot stand. *Mark 3:25*

6. In my Father's house are many mansions. *John 14:2*

7. If our earthly house of this tabernacle were dissolved, we have a building of God, an house not made with hands, eternal in the heavens. *2 Cor. 5:1*

8. If a man know not how to rule his own house, how shall he take care of the church of God? *1 Tim. 3:5*

HUMAN BEING   See Man; Woman.

HUMAN SPIRIT   See Spirit, Human.

HUMBLENESS   See Humility.

HUMILITY   (See also Unworthiness.)

1. Before honor is humility. *Prov. 15:33*

2. Better it is to be of a humble spirit with the lowly, than to divide the spoil with the proud. *Prov. 16:19*

3. I dwell in the high and holy place, with him also that is of a contrite and humble spirit, to revive the spirit of the humble, and to revive the heart of the contrite ones. *Isa. 57:15*

4. Blessed are the poor in spirit: for theirs is the kingdom of heaven. . . . Blessed are the meek: for they shall inherit the earth. *Matt. 5:3,5*

5. Lord, I am not worthy that thou shouldest come under my roof. *Matt. 8:8*

6. Whosoever therefore shall humble himself as this little child, the same is greatest in the kingdom of heaven. *Matt. 18:4*

7. Whosoever shall exalt himself shall be abased; and he that shall humble himself shall be exalted. *Matt. 23:12*

8. I say . . . to every man that is among you, not to think of himself more highly than he ought to think. *Rom. 12:3*

9. Mind not high things, but condescend to men of low estate. Be not wise in your own conceits. *Rom. 12:16*

10. God resisteth the proud, but giveth grace unto the humble. *James 4:6*

HUNGER   (See also Desire; Food; Need.)

1. The full soul loatheth a honeycomb; but to the hungry soul every bitter thing is sweet. *Prov. 27:7*

2. They shall feed in the ways, and their pastures shall be in all high places. They shall not hunger nor thirst. *Isa. 49:9,10*

3. Every one that thirsteth, come ye to the waters, and he that hath no money; come ye, buy, and eat; yea, come, buy wine and milk without money and without price. *Isa. 55:1*

4. I was ahungered, and ye gave me meat: I was thirsty, and ye gave me drink. *Matt. 25:35*

5. They shall hunger no more, neither thirst any more. . . . For the Lamb . . . shall feed them, and shall lead them unto living fountains of waters. *Rev. 7:16,17*

HUSBAND   See Father; Marriage.

HYPOCRISY   (See also Appearance; Deceit; Prejudice.)

1. They bless with their mouth, but they curse inwardly. *Ps. 62:4*

2. Every one is a hypocrite. *Isa. 9:17*

3. I am holier than thou. *Isa. 65:5*

4. Thou hypocrite, first cast out the beam out of thine own eye;

and then shalt thou see clearly to cast out the mote out of thy brother's eye. *Matt. 7:5*

5. Woe unto you, scribes and Pharisees, hypocrites! for ye make clean the outside of the cup and of the platter, but within they are full of extortion and excess. . . . cleanse first that which is within the cup and platter, that the outside of them may be clean also. Woe unto you, scribes and Pharisees, hypocrites! for ye are like unto whited sepulchres, which indeed appear beautiful outward, but are within full of dead men's bones, and of all uncleanness. *Matt. 23:25–27*

6. He that is without sin among you, let him first cast a stone at her. *John 8:7*

7. In the latter times some shall depart from the faith . . . Speaking lies in hypocrisy. *1 Tim. 4:1,2*

8. Be ye doers of the word, and not hearers only, deceiving your own selves. *James 1:22*

I

IDLENESS   See Sloth; Unemployment.

IDOLATRY   (See also Cults, Religious; False Prophet; Occult; Paganism.)

1. Thou shalt have no other gods before me. Thou shalt not make unto thee any graven image, or any likeness of any thing . . . thou shalt not bow down thyself to them, nor serve them: for I the Lord thy God am a jealous God. *Exod. 20:3–5*

2. They have made them a molten calf, and have worshiped it, and have sacrificed thereunto, and said, These be thy gods, O Israel. *Exod. 32:8*

3. They forsook the Lord God of their fathers . . . and followed other gods, of the gods of the people that were round about them, and bowed themselves unto them, and provoked the Lord to anger. And they forsook the Lord, and served Baal and Ashtaroth. *Judg. 2:12,13*

4. He had broken down the altars and the groves, and had beaten the graven images into powder, and cut down all the idols throughout all the land. *2 Chron. 34:7*

5. Confounded be all they that serve graven images, that boast themselves of idols. *Ps. 97:7*

6. The Lord alone shall be exalted in that day. And the idols he shall utterly abolish . . . In that day a man shall cast his idols of silver, and his idols of gold, which they made each one for himself to worship, to the moles and to the bats. *Isa. 2:17–20*

7. Flee from idolatry. . . . I would not that ye should have fellowship with devils. *1 Cor. 10:14,20*

8. Idolaters . . . shall have their part in the lake which burneth with fire and brimstone: which is the second death. *Rev. 21:8*

IGNORANCE (See also Darkness; Foolishness; Knowledge.)

1. There arose another generation after them, which knew not the Lord, nor yet the works which he had done for Israel. *Judg. 2:10*

2. He knoweth not that which shall be: for who can tell him when it shall be? *Eccl. 8:7*

3. Father, forgive them; for they know not what they do. *Luke 23:34*

4. They have not known the Father, nor me. *John 16:3*

5. The times of this ignorance God winked at; but now commandeth all men every where to repent. *Acts 17:30*

6. If any man be ignorant, let him be ignorant. *1 Cor. 14:38*

7. Henceforth walk not as other Gentiles walk . . . Having the understanding darkened, being alienated from the life of God through the ignorance that is in them, because of the blindness of their heart. *Eph. 4:17,18*

ILL WILL   See Hatred; Malice.

ILLNESS (See also Handicap; Healing; Health; Physician; Venereal Disease.)

1. He [the Lord] will bring upon thee all the diseases of Egypt. . . . Also every sickness, and every plague . . . until thou be destroyed. *Deut. 28:60,61*

2. Jesus went about all Galilee . . . healing all manner of sickness and all manner of disease among the people. *Matt. 4:23*

3. Himself took our infirmities, and bare our sicknesses. *Matt. 8:17*

4. There was given to me a thorn in the flesh. *2 Cor. 12:7*

5. Through infirmity of the flesh I preached the gospel unto you. *Gal. 4:13*

6. The prayer of faith shall save the sick. *James 5:15*

IMMATURITY (See also Childlikeness; Youth.)

1. The wheat and the rie were not smitten: for they were not grown up. *Exod. 9:32*

2. Thou [David] art not able to go against this Philistine to fight with him: for thou art but a youth, and he a man of war from his youth. *1 Sam. 17:33*

3. I am but a little child: I know not how to go out or come in. *1 Kings 3:7*

4. I was ashamed, yea, even confounded, because I did bear the reproach of my youth. *Jer. 31:19*

5. Ephraim is a cake not turned. *Hos. 7:8*

6. When I was a child, I spake as a child, I understood as a child, I thought as a child: but when I became a man, I put away childish things. *1 Cor. 13:11*

7. Be not children in understanding . . . but in understanding be men. *1 Cor. 14:20*

IMMORALITY   See Adultery; Evil; Lust; Promiscuity; Prostitution.

IMMORTALITY   (See also Christ, Resurrection of; Eternity; Permanence; Resurrection of the Dead; Soul.)

1. God will redeem my soul from the power of the grave. *Ps. 49:15*

2. The dust [shall] return to the earth as it was: and the spirit shall return unto God who gave it. *Eccl. 12:7*

3. Neither can they die anymore . . . being the children of the resurrection. *Luke 20:36*

4. He that believeth on the Son hath everlasting life. *John 3:36*

5. Whoso eateth my flesh, and drinketh my blood, hath eternal life. *John 6:54*

6. He that believeth in me, though he were dead, yet shall he live: And whosoever liveth and believeth in me shall never die. *John 11:25,26*

7. Our Savior Jesus Christ, who hath abolished death, and hath brought life and immortality. *2 Tim. 1:10*

IMPARTIALITY   (See also Equality; Favoritism; Inequality; Judgment; Justness.)

1. Ye shall do no unrighteousness in judgment: thou shalt not respect the person of the poor, nor honor the person of the mighty: but in righteousness shalt thou judge. *Lev. 19:15*

2. All things come alike to all: there is one event to the righteous, and to the wicked; to the good and to the clean, and to the unclean. *Eccl. 9:2*

3. He maketh his sun to rise on the evil and on the good, and sendeth rain on the just and on the unjust. *Matt. 5:45*

4. God is no respecter of persons. *Acts 10:34*

5. There is no difference between the Jew and the Greek: for the same Lord over all is rich unto all that call upon him. *Rom. 10:12*

6. The Father, who without respect of persons judgeth according to every man's work. *1 Peter 1:17*

IMPATIENCE   (See also Patience.)

1. When the people saw that Moses delayed to come down out of the mount, the people gathered themselves together unto Aaron, and said unto him, Up, make us gods, which shall go before us. *Exod. 32:1*

2. O Lord, make haste to help me . . . make no tarrying, O my God. *Ps. 40:13,17*

3. O Lord . . . turn unto me . . . for I am in trouble: hear me speedily. *Ps. 69:16,17*

4. He that is hasty of spirit exalteth folly. *Prov. 14:29*

5. Lord, how long? *Isa. 6:11*

6. Ye have need of patience. *Heb. 10:36*

IMPERFECTION   (See also Mistake; Sin.)

1. Who can understand his errors? Cleanse thou me from secret faults. *Ps. 19:12*

2. There is not a just man upon earth, that doeth good, and sinneth not. *Eccl. 7:20*

3. If thy right eye offend thee, pluck it out, and cast it from thee: for it is profitable for thee that one of thy members should perish, and not that thy whole body should be cast into hell. *Matt. 5:29*

4. The spirit indeed is willing, but the flesh is weak. *Matt. 26:41*

5. Whosoever shall keep the whole law, and yet offend in one point, he is guilty of all. *James 2:10*

6. I have not found thy works perfect before God. *Rev. 3:2*

IMPERMANENCE   (See also Instability; Mortality; Permanence.)

1. His [man's] days are as a shadow that passeth away. *Ps. 144:4*

2. Heaven and earth shall pass away: but my words shall not pass away. *Luke 21:33*

3. Charity never faileth: but whether there be prophecies, they shall fail; whether there be tongues, they shall cease; whether there be knowledge, it shall vanish away. *1 Cor. 13:8*

4. The things which are seen are temporal; but the things which are not seen are eternal. *2 Cor. 4:18*

5. All flesh is as grass, and all the glory of man as the flower of grass. The grass withereth, and the flower thereof falleth away: but the word of the Lord endureth for ever. *1 Peter 1:24,25*

IMPORTANCE   See Fame; Reputation.

IMPRISONMENT (See also Captivity.)

1. Bring my soul out of prison. *Ps. 142:7*

2. The Lord looseth the prisoners. *Ps. 146:7*

3. I the Lord have called thee . . . to bring out the prisoners from the prison, and them that sit in darkness out of the prison house. *Isa. 42:6,7*

4. They are all of them snared in holes, and they are hid in prison houses. *Isa. 42:22*

5. He [the Lord] hath sent me . . . to proclaim liberty to the captives, and the opening of the prison to them that are bound. *Isa. 61:1*

6. I was in prison, and ye came unto me. . . . Inasmuch as ye have done it unto one of the least of these my brethren, ye have done it unto me. *Matt. 25:36,40*

7. [They] laid their hands on the apostles, and put them in the common prison. But the angel of the Lord by night opened the prison doors, and brought them forth. *Acts 5:18,19*

IMPROVEMENT See Growth; Self-Improvement.

IMPRUDENCE (See also Foolishness.)

1. Go to the ant, thou sluggard; consider her ways, and be wise. *Prov. 6:6*

2. He that is hasty of spirit exalteth folly. *Prov. 14:29*

3. The thoughts of the diligent tend only to plenteousness; but of every one that is hasty only to want. *Prov. 21:5*

4. Neither cast ye your pearls before swine, lest they trample them under their feet, and turn again and rend you. *Matt. 7:6*

5. Every one that heareth these sayings of mine, and doeth them not, shall be likened unto a foolish man, which built his house upon the sand: And the rain descended, and the floods came, and the winds blew, and beat upon that house; and it fell. *Matt. 7:26,27*

6. They that were foolish took their lamps, and took no oil with them. *Matt. 25:3*

7. Ye ought to be quiet, and to do nothing rashly. *Acts 19:36*

IMPURITY (See also Corruption; Evil; Pollution; Purity; Sin.)

1. Who can bring a clean thing out of an unclean? Not one. *Job 14:4*

2. How much more abominable and filthy is man, which drinketh iniquity like water? *Job 15:16*

3. Who can say, I have made my heart clean, I am pure from my sin? *Prov. 20:9*

4. That which cometh out of the man, that defileth the man. For from within, out of the heart of men, proceed evil thoughts, adulteries, fornications, murders, Thefts, covetousness, wickedness, deceit, lasciviousness, an evil eye, blasphemy, pride, foolishness. *Mark 7:20,22*

5. There is nothing unclean of itself: but to him that esteemeth any thing to be unclean, to him it is unclean. *Rom. 14:14*

6. No . . . unclean person . . . hath any inheritance in the kingdom of Christ and of God. *Eph. 5:5*

7. Unto them that are defiled and unbelieving is nothing pure; but even their mind and conscience is defiled. *Titus 1:15*

8. He which is filthy, let him be filthy still. *Rev. 22:11*

INCEST   See Sexual Perversion.

INCREASE   See Growth; Inflation.

INDECISION   (See also Choice; Decision.)

1. How long halt ye between two opinions? if the Lord be God follow him: but if Baal, then follow him. And the people answered him not a word. *1 Kings 18:21*

2. My heart was hot within me, while I was musing the fire burned. *Ps. 39:3*

3. Their heart is divided; now shall they be found faulty. *Hos. 10:2*

4. No man can serve two masters. *Matt. 6:24*

5. Lord, I will follow thee; but let me first go bid them farewell, which are at home at my house. And Jesus said unto him, No man, having put his hand to the plough, and looking back, is fit for the kingdom of God. *Luke 9:61, 62*

6. He that wavereth is like a wave of the sea driven with the wind and tossed . . . A double-minded man is unstable in all his ways. *James 1:6,8*

7. So then because thou art lukewarm, and neither cold nor hot, I will spue thee out of my mouth. *Rev. 3:16*

INDEPENDENCE   (See also Dependence; Liberty; Self-Centeredness.)

1. Thou shalt not follow a multitude to do evil. *Exod. 23:2*

2. Every man did that which was right in his own eyes. *Judg. 17:6*

3. I strived to preach the gospel, not where Christ was named, lest I should build upon another man's foundation. *Rom. 15:20*

4. Every man shall bear his own burden. *Gal. 6:5*

5. Laboring night and day, because we would not be chargeable unto any of you. *1 Thess. 2:9*

INDIFFERENCE (See also Apathy.)

1. How long are ye slack to go to possess the land, which the Lord God of your fathers hath given you? *Josh. 18:3*

2. There was no man that would know me . . . no man cared for my soul. *Ps. 142:4*

3. Let us not give heed to any of his words. *Jer. 18:18*

4. They considered not the miracle of the loaves. *Mark 6:52*

5. A judge, which feared not God, neither regarded man. *Luke 18:2*

6. When I have a convenient season, I will call for thee. *Acts 24:25*

7. Awake thou that sleepest, and arise from the dead, and Christ shall give thee light. *Eph. 5:14*

INDIGNATION See Anger.

INDOLENCE See Sloth.

INDUSTRY See Business; Work.

INEQUALITY (See also Equality; Favoritism; Injustice; Prejudice.)

1. The children of thy people say, The way of the Lord is not equal: but as for them, their way is not equal. *Ezek. 33:17*

2. [Ye] have been partial in the law. *Mal. 2:9*

3. Remember that thou in thy lifetime receivedst thy good things, and likewise Lazarus evil things: but now he is comforted, and thou art tormented. *Luke 16:25*

4. Be ye not unequally yoked together with unbelievers. *2 Cor. 6:14*

5. Are ye not then partial in yourselves? *James 2:4*

INEXPERIENCE See Immaturity.

INFALLIBILITY (See also God; God, Law of; Scripture.)

1. As for God, his way is perfect. *2 Sam. 22:31*

2. My words shall not be false: he that is perfect in knowledge is with thee. *Job 36:4*

3. The law of the Lord is perfect. *Ps. 19:7*

4. Whatsoever God doeth, it shall be for ever: nothing can be put to it, nor any thing taken from it. *Eccl. 3:14*

5. He showed himself alive after his passion by many infallible proofs. *Acts 1:3*

6. God, willing more abundantly to show unto the heirs of

promise the immutability of his counsel, confirmed it by an oath
. . . it was impossible for God to lie. *Heb. 6:17,18*

INFANT See Baby.

INFERIORITY (See also Humility; Priority; Superiority.)

1. I am the least in my father's house. *Judg. 6:15*

2. After thee shall arise another kingdom inferior to thee. *Dan. 2:39*

3. There cometh one mightier than I after me, the latchet of whose shoes I am not worthy to stoop down and unloose. *Mark 1:7*

4. I am the least of the apostles, that am not meet to be called an apostle, because I persecuted the church of God. *1 Cor. 15:9*

5. What is it wherein ye were inferior to other churches, except it be that I myself was not burdensome to you? *2 Cor. 12:13*

6. [I] am less than the least of all saints. *Eph. 3:8*

INFIDELITY See Adultery.

INFINITY See Eternity; God, Omnipresence of; God, Omniscience of; Immortality.

INFIRMITY See Handicap; Illness.

INFLATION (See also Consumerism; Wages.)

1. According to the multitude of years thou shalt increase the price thereof. *Lev. 25:16*

2. If he that sanctified it will redeem his house, then he shall add the fifth part of the money of thy estimation unto it, and it shall be his. *Lev. 27:15*

3. I pray you, let us leave off this usury. *Neh. 5:10*

4. These are the ungodly, who prosper in the world; they increase in riches. *Ps. 73:12*

5. There is that scattereth, and yet increaseth; and there is that withholdeth more than is meet, but it tendeth to poverty. *Prov. 11:24*

6. Ye have sown much, and bring in little; ye eat, but ye have not enough; ye drink, but ye are not filled with drink; ye clothe you, but there is none warm; and he that earneth wages earneth wages to put into a bag with holes. *Hag. 1:6*

INFLUENCE (See also Authority; Companions, Evil; Temptation.)

1. When Solomon was old . . . his wives turned away his heart after other gods. *1 Kings 11:4*

2. Manasseh made Judah and the inhabitants of Jerusalem to err, and to do worse than the heathen. *2 Chron. 33:9*

3. O house of Israel, cannot I do with you as this potter? saith the Lord. Behold, as the clay is in the potter's hand, so are ye in mine hand. *Jer. 18:6*

4. Take heed, beware of the leaven of the Pharisees, and of the leaven of Herod. *Mark 8:15*

5. Almost thou persuadest me to be a Christian. *Acts 26:28*

6. Know ye not that a little leaven leaveneth the whole lump? *1 Cor. 5:6*

7. Knowing therefore the terror of the Lord, we persuade men. *2 Cor. 5:11*

8. Hymenaeus and Philetus; Who concerning the truth have erred, saying that the resurrection is past already; and overthrow the faith of some. *2 Tim. 2:17,18*

INGRATITUDE **(See also Forgetfulness; Neglect; Thanksgiving.)**

1. Whoso rewardeth evil for good, evil shall not depart from his house. *Prov. 17:13*

2. A poor wise man . . . by his wisdom delivered the city; yet no man remembered that same poor man. *Eccl. 9:15*

3. I have nourished and brought up children, and they have rebelled against me. *Isa. 1:2*

4. I have redeemed them, yet they have spoken lies against me. *Hos. 7:13*

5. Many good works have I showed you from my Father; for which of those works do ye stone me? *John 10:32*

6. When they knew God, they glorified him not as God, neither were thankful. *Rom. 1:21*

INHERITANCE **(See also Genealogy.)**

1. He sold his birthright unto Jacob. *Gen. 25:33*

2. The Lord is the portion of mine inheritance and of my cup: thou maintainest my lot. The lines are fallen unto me in pleasant places; yea, I have a goodly heritage. *Ps. 16:5,6*

3. An inheritance may be gotten hastily at the beginning; but the end thereof shall not be blessed. *Prov. 20:21*

4. Blessed are the meek: for they shall inherit the earth. *Matt. 5:5*

5. We are the children of God: And if children, then heirs; heirs of God, and joint-heirs with Christ. *Rom. 8:16,17*

6. Hath not God chosen the poor of this world rich in faith, and heirs of the kingdom? *James 2:5*

7. An inheritance incorruptible, and undefiled, and that fadeth not away, reserved in heaven for you. *1 Peter 1:4*

8. He that overcometh shall inherit all things. *Rev. 21:7*

INIQUITY   See Evil; Sin.

INJUSTICE   (See also Bribery; Inequality; Judgment.)

1. Ye shall do no unrighteousness in judgment. *Lev. 19:15*

2. Thou shalt not wrest judgment; thou shalt not respect persons, neither take a gift: for a gift doth blind the eyes of the wise, and pervert the words of the righteous. *Deut. 16:19*

3. Cursed be he that perverteth the judgment of the stranger, fatherless, and widow. *Deut. 27:19*

4. How long will ye judge unjustly, and accept the persons of the wicked? *Ps. 82:2*

5. They gather themselves together against the soul of the righteous, and condemn the innocent blood. *Ps. 94:21*

6. An unjust man is an abomination to the just. *Prov. 29:27*

7. Wherefore doth the way of the wicked prosper? wherefore are all they happy that deal very treacherously? *Jer. 12:1*

8. Your treading is upon the poor . . . your manifold transgressions . . . afflict the just, they take a bribe, and they turn aside the poor in the gate from their right. *Amos 5:11,12*

9. He that is unjust in the least is unjust also in much. *Luke 16:10*

INNOCENCE   (See also Childlikeness; Guilt; Lamb; Purity; Simplicity.)

1. The innocent and righteous slay thou not. *Exod. 23:7*

2. Who ever perished, being innocent? *Job 4:7*

3. Blessed is the man unto whom the Lord imputeth not iniquity, and in whose spirit there is no guile. *Ps. 32:2*

4. Who can say, I have made my heart clean, I am pure from my sin? *Prov. 20:9*

5. How long will it be ere they attain to innocency? *Hos. 8:5*

6. Pilate . . . washed his hands before the multitude, saying, I am innocent of the blood of this just person. *Matt. 27:24*

7. Pilate [said] to the chief priests and to the people, I find no fault in this man. *Luke 23:4*

INSANITY

1. The Lord shall smite thee with madness. *Deut. 28:28*

2. He [David] changed his behavior before them, and feigned himself mad in their hands, and scrabbled on the doors of the gate, and let his spittle fall down upon his beard. *1 Sam. 21:13*

3. Surely oppression maketh a wise man mad. *Eccl. 7:7*

4. Lord, have mercy on my son: for he is a lunatic, and sore vexed: for ofttimes he falleth into the fire, and oft into the water. *Matt. 17:15*

5. They went out to lay hold on him: for they said, He is beside himself. *Mark 3:21*

6. He hath a devil, and is mad. *John 10:20*

7. Paul, thou art beside thyself; much learning doth make thee mad. But he said, I am not mad, most noble Festus; but speak forth the words of truth and soberness. *Acts 26:24,25*

8. If therefore the whole church be come together into one place, and all speak with tongues, and there come in those that are unlearned, or unbelievers, will they not say that ye are mad? *1 Cor. 14:23*

INSIGHT   See Knowledge; Understanding.

INSINCERITY   See Hypocrisy; Flattery.

INSPIRATION   (See also Holy Spirit; Prophet; Revelation; Scripture; Word.)

1. These are the words which thou shalt speak unto the children of Israel. *Exod. 19:6*

2. When the spirit rested upon them [the seventy elders], they prophesied, and did not cease. *Num. 11:25*

3. The inspiration of the Almighty giveth them understanding. *Job 32:8*

4. The Holy Ghost shall teach you in the same hour what ye ought to say. *Luke 12:12*

5. All scripture is given by inspiration of God. *2 Tim. 3:16*

6. Prophecy came not in old time by the will of man: but holy men of God spake as they were moved by the Holy Ghost. *2 Peter 1:21*

7. I [John] . . . heard behind me a great voice . . . Saying . . . What thou seest, write in a book. *Rev. 1:10,11*

INSTABILITY   (See also Impermanence; Unreliability.)

1. Her [a strange woman's] ways are movable, that thou canst not know them. *Prov. 5:6*

2. Meddle not with them that are given to change: for their calamity shall rise suddenly; and who knoweth the ruin of them both? *Prov. 24:21,22*

3. Why gaddest thou about so much to change thy way? *Jer. 2:36*

4. Every kingdom divided against itself is brought to desolation; and every city or house divided against itself shall not stand. *Matt. 12:25*

5. Be no more children, tossed to and fro, and carried about with every wind of doctrine. *Eph. 4:14*

6. He that wavereth is like a wave of the sea driven with the wind and tossed. *James 1:6*

7. A double-minded man is unstable in all his ways. *James 1:8*

INSTRUCTION   See Discipline; Education; Teaching.

INTEGRATION   (See also Equality; Race, Ethnic; Segregation; Unity.)

1. All things come alike to all: there is one event to the righteous, and to the wicked; to the good and to the clean, and to the unclean. *Eccl. 9:2*

2. All ye are brethren. *Matt. 23:8*

3. Ye know how that it is an unlawful thing for a man that is a Jew to keep company, or come unto one of another nation; but God hath showed me that I should not call any man common or unclean. *Acts 10:28*

4. Who maketh thee to differ from another? *1 Cor. 4:7*

5. There is neither Jew nor Greek, there is neither bond nor free, there is neither male nor female: for ye are all one in Christ Jesus. *Gal. 3:28*

6. There is neither Greek nor Jew, circumcision nor uncircumcision, Barbarian, Scythian, bond nor free: but Christ is all, and in all. *Col. 3:11*

INTEGRITY   See Honesty; Justice; Righteousness; Sincerity; Virtue.

INTELLIGENCE   See Knowledge; Understanding; Wisdom.

INTEMPERANCE   See Drunkenness; Gluttony; Promiscuity.

INTENTION   (See also Christ, Purpose of.)

1. They intended evil against thee. *Ps. 21:11*

2. He [the Lord] doth not afflict willingly nor grieve the children of men. *Lam. 3:33*

3. It is not the will of your Father which is in heaven, that one of these little ones should perish. *Matt. 18:14*

4. The spirit indeed is willing, but the flesh is weak. *Matt. 26:41*

5. I came down from heaven, not to do mine own will, but the will of him that sent me. *John 6:38*

6. [Ye] intend to bring this man's blood upon us. *Acts 5:28*

7. Every man according as he purposeth in his heart, so let him give. *2 Cor. 9:7*

8. The word of God is . . . a discerner of the thoughts and intents of the heart. *Heb. 4:12*

INTERCESSION   See Mediation.

INTERFERENCE   See Meddling; Obstacle.

INTERPRETATION   (See also Scripture; Tongues, Gift of; Understanding.)

1. We have dreamed a dream, and there is no interpreter of it. And Joseph said unto them, Do not interpretations belong to God? *Gen. 40:8*

2. They read in the book in the law of God distinctly, and gave the sense, and caused them to understand the reading. *Neh. 8:8*

3. Who knoweth the interpretation of a thing? *Eccl. 8:1*

4. It shall be a vexation only to understand the report. *Isa. 28:19*

5. I [Daniel] will read the writing unto the king, and make known to him the interpretation. *Dan. 5:17*

6. Beginning at Moses and all the prophets, he [Jesus] expounded unto them in all the scriptures the things concerning himself. *Luke 24:27*

7. To another [is given] the interpretation of tongues. *1 Cor. 12:10*

8. No prophecy of the scripture is of any private interpretation. *2 Peter 1:20*

INTERVENTION   See Meddling; Mediation.

INTOXICATION   See Drunkenness.

IRREVERENCE   See Blasphemy; Profanity.

ISRAEL   (See also Egypt; Middle East Conflict.)

1. If ye will obey my voice indeed and keep my covenant, then ye shall be a peculiar treasure unto me above all people. *Exod. 19:5*

2. Defile not therefore the land which ye shall inhabit, wherein I dwell: for I the Lord dwell among the children of Israel. *Num. 35:34*

3. Ye [Israel] shall be plucked from off the land whither thou goest to possess it. And the Lord shall scatter thee among all people, from the one end of the earth even unto the other. *Deut. 28:63,64*

4. Israel is a scattered sheep; the lions have driven him away. *Jer. 50:17*

5. Israel is an empty vine. *Hos. 10:1*

6. I am jealous for Jerusalem and for Zion with a great jealousy. *Zech. 1:14*

7. This is the covenant that I will make with the house of Israel . . . I will be to them a God, and they shall be to me a people. *Heb. 8:10*

J

JEALOUSY   (See also Envy; Resentment.)
1. When his brethren saw that their father loved him more than all his brethren, they hated him, and could not speak peaceably unto him. *Gen. 37:4*
2. I the Lord thy God am a jealous God. *Exod. 20:5*
3. They have moved me to jealousy with that which is not God . . . I will move them to jealousy with those which are not a people. *Deut. 32:21*
4. Jealousy is the rage of a man. *Prov. 6:34*
5. Jealousy is cruel as the grave. *Song of Sol. 8:6*
6. I am jealous over you with godly jealousy. *2 Cor. 11:2*

JERUSALEM   See Israel.

JESUS   See Christ.

JOURNEY   (See also Departure; Stranger.)
1. I am with thee, and will keep thee in all places whither thou goest. *Gen. 28:15*
2. Let us take our journey, and let us go. *Gen. 33:12*
3. All the congregation of the children of Israel journeyed from the wilderness of Sin, after their journeys . . . and pitched in Rephidim. *Exod. 17:1*
4. Your children shall wander in the wilderness forty years. *Num. 14:33*
5. I am a stranger with thee, and a sojourner, as all my fathers were. O spare me, that I may recover strength, before I go hence, and be no more. *Ps. 39:12,13*
6. As a bird that wandereth from her nest, so is a man that wandereth from his place. *Prov. 27:8*

7. They shall wander from sea to sea, and from the north even to the east, they shall run to and fro to seek the word of the Lord. *Amos 8:12*

8. [Joseph] took the young child and his mother by night, and departed into Egypt. *Matt. 2:14*

9. Go your ways: behold, I send you forth as lambs among wolves. *Luke 10:3*

JOY   See Happiness.

JUDGMENT   (See also Bribery; Decision; Impartiality; Injustice; Trial.)

1. The judgments of the Lord are true and righteous altogether. *Ps. 19:9*

2. God shall bring every work into judgment, with every secret thing, whether it be good, or whether it be evil. *Eccl. 12:14*

3. Judge not, that ye be not judged. For with what judgment ye judge, ye shall be judged. *Matt. 7:1,2*

4. Out of thine own mouth will I judge thee. *Luke 19:22*

5. Judge not according to the appearance, but judge righteous judgment. *John 7:24*

6. He hath appointed a day, in the which he will judge the world in righteousness by that man whom he hath ordained. *Acts 17:31*

7. Whosoever thou art that . . . judgest another, thou condemnest thyself; for thou that judgest doest the same things. *Rom. 2:1*

8. It is a very small thing that I should be judged of you, or of man's judgment: yea, I judge not mine own self . . . he that judgeth me is the Lord. *1 Cor. 4:3,4*

9. Fear God . . . for the hour of his judgment is come. *Rev. 14:7*

JUSTICE   (See also Equality; Impartiality; Righteousness; Judgment.)

1. That which is altogether just shalt thou follow. *Deut. 16:20*

2. He that ruleth over men must be just. *2 Sam. 23:3*

3. The path of the just is as the shining light, that shineth more and more unto the perfect day. *Prov. 4:18*

4. There shall no evil happen to the just. *Prov. 12:21*

5. The way of the just is uprightness: thou, most upright, dost weigh the path of the just. *Isa. 26:7*

6. He [that] is just, he shall surely live. *Ezek. 18:9*

7. What doth the Lord require of thee, but to do justly, and to love mercy, and to walk humbly with thy God? *Mic. 6:8*

8. The just shall live by faith. *Rom. 1:17*

JUSTIFICATION   (See also Reason; Self-Centeredness.)
1. [Adam] said, The woman who thou gavest to be with me, she gave me of the tree, and I did eat. *Gen. 3:12*
2. In the Lord shall all the seed of Israel be justified, and shall glory. *Isa. 45:25*
3. They all with one consent began to make excuse. *Luke 14:18*
4. And by him [Jesus] all that believe are justified from all things, from which ye could not be justified by the law of Moses. *Acts 13:39*
5. Knowing that a man is not justified by the works of the law, but by the faith of Jesus Christ, even we have believed in Jesus Christ, that we might be justified by the faith of Christ, and not by works of the law: for by works of the law shall no flesh be justified. *Gal. 3:16*

K

KIDNAPPING
1. He that stealeth a man, and selleth him, or if he be found in his hand, he shall surely be put to death. *Exod. 21:16*
2. If a man be found stealing any of his brethren of the children of Israel, and maketh merchandise of him, or selleth him; then that thief shall die. *Deut. 24:7*
3. Go and lie in wait in the vineyards . . . if the daughters of Shiloh come out to dance in dances, then come ye out of the vineyards, and catch you every man his wife of the daughters of Shiloh, and go to the land of Benjamin. *Judg. 21:20,21*

KILLING   See Abortion; Assassination; Cannibalism; Capital Punishment; Christ, Crucifixion of; Euthanasia; Martyr; Murder; Suicide.

KINDNESS   (See also Benevolence; Generosity; God, Goodness of; Mercy; Sympathy; Unselfishness.)
1. I have showed you kindness, that ye will also show kindness. *Josh. 2:12*
2. Thou shalt not only while yet I live show me the kindness of the Lord . . . But also thou shalt not cut off thy kindness from my house for ever. *1 Sam. 20:14,15*
3. With everlasting kindness will I have mercy on thee. . . . my kindness shall not depart from thee. *Isa. 54:8,10*
4. Show mercy and compassions every man to his brother. *Zech. 7:9*
5. I was ahungered, and ye gave me meat: I was thirsty, and ye gave me drink: I was a stranger, and ye took me in: Naked, and ye clothed me: I was sick, and ye visited me: I was in prison, and ye came unto me. *Matt. 25:35,36*

6. He [God] is kind unto the unthankful and to the evil. *Luke 6:35*

7. Be ye kind one to another, tenderhearted, forgiving one another. *Eph. 4:32*

KING **(See also Christ; God; Lord.)**

1. God save the king. *1 Sam. 10:24*

2. Who is this King of glory? The Lord of hosts, he is the King of glory. *Ps. 24:10*

3. The king that faithfully judgeth the poor, his throne shall be established for ever. *Prov. 29:14*

4. The Lord is . . . an everlasting king. *Jer. 10:10*

5. Thy King cometh unto thee . . . lowly, and riding upon an ass. *Zech. 9:9*

6. THIS IS JESUS THE KING OF THE JEWS. *Matt. 27:37*

7. Shall I crucify your King? The chief priests answered, We have no king but Caesar. *John 19:15*

8. Jesus Christ . . . the prince of the kings of the earth. *Rev. 1:5*

9. The Lamb . . . is Lord of lords, and King of kings. *Rev. 17:14*

KINGDOM **(See also Earth; Heaven; Nation.)**

1. Blessed are the poor in spirit: for theirs is the kingdom of heaven. *Matt. 5:3*

2. Blessed are they which are persecuted for righteousness' sake: for theirs is the kingdom of heaven. *Matt. 5:10*

3. Whosoever therefore shall break one of these least commandments, and shall teach men so, he shall be called the least in the kingdom of heaven: but whosoever shall do and teach them, the same shall be called great in the kingdom of heaven. *Matt. 5:19*

4. Thy kingdom come. Thy will be done in earth, as it is in heaven. *Matt. 6:10*

5. Not every one that saith unto me, Lord, Lord, shall enter into the kingdom of heaven; but he that doeth the will of my Father which is in heaven. *Matt. 7:21*

6. The kingdom of heaven is like to a grain of mustard seed, which a man took, and sowed in his field: Which indeed is the least of all seeds: but when it is grown, it is the greatest among herbs, and becometh a tree. *Matt. 13:31,32*

7. The kingdom of heaven is like unto leaven, which a woman took, and hid in three measures of meal, till the whole was leavened. *Matt. 13:33*

8. The kingdom of God is at hand. *Mark 1:15*

9. Suffer the little children to come unto me, and forbid them not: for of such is the kingdom of God. *Mark 10:14*

10. My kingdom is not of this world. *John 18:36*

11. The kingdom of God is not in word, but in power. *1 Cor. 4:20*

12. The kingdoms of this world are become the kingdoms of our Lord, and of his Christ. *Rev. 11:15*

KNOWLEDGE (See also God, Omniscience of; Ignorance; Teaching; Understanding; Wisdom.)

1. Such knowledge is too wonderful for me; it is high, I cannot attain unto it. *Ps. 139:6*

2. A wise man is strong; yea, a man of knowledge increaseth strength. *Prov. 24:5*

3. The earth shall be full of the knowledge of the Lord, as the waters cover the sea. *Isa. 11:9*

4. My people are destroyed for lack of knowledge: because thou hast rejected knowledge, I will also reject thee. *Hos. 4:6*

5. All that heard him were astonished at his understanding and answers. *Luke 2:47*

6. Knowledge puffeth up. . . . And if any man think that he knoweth any thing, he knoweth nothing yet as he ought to know. *1 Cor. 8:1,2*

7. Be filled with the knowledge of his will in all wisdom and spiritual understanding . . . increasing in the knowledge of God. *Col. 1:9,10*

8. God, and of the Father, and of Christ; In whom are hid all the treasures of wisdom and knowledge. *Col. 2:2,3*

L

LABOR See Work.

LACK See Need.

LAMB (See also Christ; Innocence; Shepherd.)

1. He is our God; and we are the people of his pasture, and the sheep of his hand. *Ps. 95:7*

2. The wolf also shall dwell with the lamb. *Isa. 11:6*

3. He is brought as a lamb to the slaughter. *Isa. 53:7*

4. They shall no more be a prey to the heathen, neither shall the beast of the land devour them; but they shall dwell safely, and none shall make them afraid . . . ye my flock, the flock of my pasture, are men, and I am your God, saith the Lord God. *Ezek. 34:28,31*

5. What man of you, having a hundred sheep, if he lose one of them, doth not leave the ninety and nine in the wilderness, and go after that which is lost, until he find it? *Luke 15:4*

6. Behold the Lamb of God, which taketh away the sin of the world. *John 1:29*

7. Other sheep I have, which are not of this fold: them also I must bring, and they shall hear my voice; and there shall be one fold, and one shepherd. *John 10:16*

8. Feed my lambs. *John 21:15*

9. The Lamb shall overcome them: for he is Lord of lords, and King of kings. *Rev. 17:14*

LAND (See also Earth; Exploration.)

1. Let the dry land appear. *Gen. 1:9*

2. All the land which thou seest, to thee will I give it. *Gen. 13:15*

3. A land flowing with milk and honey. *Exod. 3:8*

4. The field of the suburbs of their cities may not be sold; for it is their perpetual possession. *Lev. 25:34*

5. The Lord thy God bringeth thee into a good land, a land of brooks of water, of fountains and depths that spring out of valleys and hills. *Deut. 8:7*

6. The land is as the garden of Eden before them, and behind them a desolate wilderness. *Joel 2:3*

LANGUAGE (See also Speaking; Tongues, Gift of.)

1. The whole earth was of one language, and of one speech. *Gen. 11:1*

2. Let us go down, and there confound their language, that they may not understand one another's speech. . . . Therefore is the name of it [the tower] called Babel; because the Lord did there confound the language of all the earth. *Gen. 11:7,9*

3. Death and life are in the power of the tongue. *Prov. 18:21*

4. Surely thou [Peter] also art one of them; for thy speech betrayeth thee. *Matt. 26:73*

5. The multitude came together, and were confounded, because that every man heard them speak in his own language. *Acts 2:6*

LAST JUDGMENT See Christ, Second Coming of; Judgment; Resurrection of the Dead.

LAST SUPPER See Eucharist.

LATENESS See Procrastination; Tardiness.

LAW (See also God, Law of; Lawyer; Trial.)

1. They that forsake the law praise the wicked: but such as keep the law contend with them. *Prov. 28:4*

2. He that keepeth the law, happy is he. *Prov. 29:18*

3. As many as have sinned without law shall also perish without law: and as many as have sinned in the law shall be judged by the law. *Rom. 2:12*

4. When the Gentiles, which have not the law, do by nature the things contained in the law, these, having not the law, are a law unto themselves: Which show the work of the law written in their hearts. *Rom. 2:14,15*

5. Love is the fulfilling of the law. *Rom. 13:10*

6. All things are lawful for me, but all things are not expedient: all things are lawful for me, but all things edify not. *1 Cor. 10:23*

7. The letter killeth, but the spirit giveth life. *2 Cor. 3:6*

8. No man is justified by the law in the sight of God. *Gal. 3:11*

9. The law was our schoolmaster to bring us unto Christ, that we might be justified by faith. But after that faith is come, we are no longer under a schoolmaster. *Gal. 3:24,25*

10. The law is good, if a man use it lawfully. *1 Tim. 1:8*

LAWYER   (See also Law; Trial.)

1. One of them, which was a lawyer, asked him a question, tempting him, and saying, Master, which is the great commandment in the law? *Matt. 22:35,36*

2. Woe unto you also, ye lawyers! for ye lade men with burdens grievous to be borne, and ye yourselves touch not the burdens with one of your fingers . . . ye have taken away the key of knowledge. *Luke 11:46,52*

LAZINESS   See Sloth.

LEADER   See Christ, Leadership of; King; Leadership.

LEADERSHIP   (See also Bishop; Christ, Leadership of; Deacon; Elder; Follower; Guidance; Ministry; Shepherd.)

1. The Lord is my shepherd . . . he leadeth me in the paths of righteousness. *Ps. 23:1,3*

2. He led them forth by the right way, that they might go to a city of habitation. *Ps. 107:7*

3. A man's heart deviseth his way: but the Lord directeth his steps. *Prov. 16:9*

4. A little child shall lead them. *Isa. 11:6*

5. I have given him for a witness to the people, a leader and commander to the people. *Isa. 55:4*

6. If the blind lead the blind, both shall fall into the ditch. *Matt. 15:14*

LEARNING   See Education; Knowledge; Teaching.

LEGAL PROCESS   See Trial.

LENDING   See Borrowing and Lending.

LIBEL   See Falsehood; Perjury; Slander.

LIBERATION   See Deliverance; Escape; Liberty; Release.

LIBERALISM   (See also Conservatism.)

1. Why do thy disciples transgress the tradition of the elders? . . . Why do ye also transgress the commandment of God by your tradition? *Matt. 15:2,3*

2. No man putteth a piece of a new garment upon an old . . . And no man putteth new wine into old bottles . . . But new wine must be put into new bottles. *Luke 5:36–38*

3. I have yet many things to say unto you, but ye cannot bear them now. *John 16:12*

4. Jesus of Nazareth shall destroy this place, and shall change the customs which Moses delivered us. *Acts 6:14*

5. Be not conformed to this world: but be ye transformed by the renewing of your mind. *Rom. 12:2*

LIBERTY   (See also Captivity; Deliverance; Escape.)

1. Let my people go. *Exod. 5:1*

2. Remember this day, in which ye came out from Egypt, out of the house of bondage. *Exod. 13:3*

3. Proclaim liberty throughout all the land unto all the inhabitants thereof. *Lev. 25:10*

4. The Lord [hath] brought you out with a mighty hand, and redeemed you out of the house of bondmen, from the hand of Pharaoh king of Egypt. *Deut. 7:8*

5. I will walk at liberty: for I seek thy precepts. *Ps. 119:45*

6. Thou mayest say to the prisoners, Go forth. *Isa. 49:9*

7. Ye shall know the truth, and the truth shall make you free. *John 8:32*

8. If the Son therefore shall make you free, ye shall be free indeed. *John 8:36*

9. The chief captain answered, With a great sum obtained I this freedom. And Paul said, But I was free born. *Acts 22:28*

10. He that is called in the Lord, being a servant, is the Lord's freeman: likewise also he that is called, being free, is Christ's servant. *1 Cor. 7:22*

11. Stand fast therefore in the liberty wherewith Christ hath made us free, and be not entangled again with the yoke of bondage. *Gal. 5:1*

LIE   See Deceit; Falsehood; Perjury.

LIFE   (See also Creation; Death; Mortality.)

1. The Lord God formed man of the dust of the ground, and breathed into his nostrils the breath of life; and man became a living soul. *Gen. 2:7*

2. No man is sure of life. *Job 24:22*

3. We spend our years as a tale that is told . . . yet is their strength labor and sorrow; for it is soon cut off, and we fly away. *Ps. 90:9,10*

4. To him that is joined to all the living there is hope: for a living dog is better than a dead lion. *Eccl. 9:4*

5. Take no thought for your life . . . Is not the life more than meat? *Matt. 6:25*

6. Strait is the gate, and narrow is the way, which leadeth unto life. *Matt. 7:14*

7. I am the bread of life. *John 6:35*

8. I am the way, the truth, and the life. *John 14:6*

9. To live is Christ. *Phil. 1:21*

10. What is your life? It is even a vapor, that appeareth for a little time, and then vanisheth away. *James 4:14*

11. He that hath the Son hath life; and he that hath not the Son of God hath not life. *1 John 5:12*

LIFE, BOOK OF   See Book.

LIFE, EVERLASTING   See Immortality.

LIGHT   (See also Darkness; Example; Guidance; Realization.)

1. God said, Let there be light: and there was light . . . And God called the light Day. *Gen. 1:3–5*

2. The path of the just is as the shining light, that shineth more and more unto the perfect day. *Prov. 4:18*

3. The people that walked in darkness have seen a great light: they that dwell in the land of the shadow of death, upon them hath the light shined. *Isa. 9:2*

4. Ye are the light of the world . . . Let your light so shine before men, that they may see your good works, and glorify your Father which is in heaven. *Matt. 5:14,16*

5. The light of the body is the eye: if therefore thine eye be single, thy whole body shall be full of light. *Matt. 6:22*

6. The light shineth in darkness; and the darkness comprehended it not . . . He [John] was not that Light, but was sent to bear witness of that Light. That was the true Light, which lighteth every man that cometh into the world. *John 1:5,8,9*

7. I am the light of the world: he that followeth me shall not walk in darkness, but shall have the light of life. *John 8:12*

8. While ye have light, believe in the light, that ye may be the children of light. *John 12:36*

9. God is light, and in him is no darkness at all. *1 John 1:5*

LINEAGE   See Genealogy.

LISTENING   (See also Acceptance.)

1. They [the heathen] have ears, but they hear not. *Ps. 115:6*

2. The ear of the wise seeketh knowledge. *Prov. 18:15*

3. Thou heardest not . . . that time that thine ear was not opened. *Isa. 48:8*

F

4. Incline your ear, and come unto me: hear, and your soul shall live. *Isa. 55:3*

5. He that hath ears to hear, let him hear. *Matt. 11:15*

6. Let every man be swift to hear . . . But be ye doers of the word, and not hearers only. *James 1:19,22*

LONELINESS   (See also Exile; Independence; Solitude.)

1. It is not good that the man should be alone; I will make him a help meet for him. *Gen. 2:18*

2. I, even I only, am left. *1 Kings 19:10*

3. My lovers and my friends stand aloof from my sore; and my kinsmen stand afar off. *Ps. 38:11*

4. I looked for some to take pity, but there was none; and for comforters, but I found none. *Ps. 69:20*

5. I watch, and am as a sparrow alone upon the housetop. *Ps. 102:7*

6. There was no man that would know me: refuge failed me; no man cared for my soul. *Ps. 142:4*

7. I was left alone. *Isa. 49:21*

8. I have trodden the winepress alone; and of the people there was none with me. *Isa. 63:3*

9. My God, my God, why hast thou forsaken me? *Matt. 27:46*

10. No man stood with me, but all men forsook me. *2 Tim. 4:16*

LORD   (See also Christ; God; King.)

1. Know ye that the Lord he is God. *Ps. 100:3*

2. O Lord our God, other lords beside thee have had dominion over us; but by thee only will we make mention of thy name. *Isa. 26:13*

3. The Son of man is Lord even of the sabbath day. *Matt. 12:8*

4. Ye call me Master and Lord: and ye say well; for so I am. *John 13:13*

5. The servant is not greater than his lord. *John 15:20*

6. Christ both died, and rose, and revived, that he might be Lord both of the dead and living. *Rom. 14:9*

7. The Lamb . . . is Lord of lords, and King of kings. *Rev. 17:14*

LORD, FEAR OF   See Fear of the Lord.

LORD'S PRAYER   (See also Prayer.)

1. After this manner therefore pray ye: Our Father which art in heaven, Hallowed by thy name. Thy kingdom come. Thy will be done in earth, as it is in heaven. Give us this day our daily bread. And forgive us our debts, as we forgive our debtors. And lead us not into temptation, but deliver us from evil: For thine is the kingdom, and the power, and the glory, for ever. Amen. *Matt. 6:9–13*

LORD'S SUPPER   See Eucharist.

LOSS   (See also Failure.)

1. The Lord gave, and the Lord hath taken away; blessed be the name of the Lord. *Job 1:21*

2. Ye are the salt of the earth: but if the salt have lost his savor . . . it is thenceforth good for nothing. *Matt. 5:13*

3. He that findeth his life shall lose it: and he that loseth his life for my sake shall find it. *Matt. 10:39*

4. Take therefore the talent from him, and give it unto him which hath ten talents. For unto every one that hath shall be given, and he shall have abundance: but from him that hath not shall be taken away even that which he hath. *Matt. 25:28,29*

5. What shall it profit a man, if he shall gain the whole world, and lose his own soul? *Mark 8:36*

6. If any man's work shall be burned, he shall suffer loss. *1 Cor. 3:15*

LOVE   (See also Affection; Brotherhood; Charity; Christ, Love of; Friendship; Neighbor.)

1. Thou shalt love thy neighbor as thyself. *Lev. 19:18*

2. Thou shalt love the Lord thy God with all thine heart, and with all thy soul, and with all thy might. *Deut. 6:5*

3. Love covereth all sins. *Prov. 10:12*

4. A time to love, and a time to hate. *Eccl. 3:8*

5. Many waters cannot quench love, neither can the floods drown it. *Song of Sol. 8:7*

6. Love your enemies. *Matt. 5:44*

7. Love one another; as I have loved you, that ye also love one another. *John 13:34*

8. Greater love hath no man than this, that a man lay down his life for his friends. *John 15:13*

9. Love one another: for he that loveth another hath fulfilled the law . . . love is the fulfilling of the law. *Rom. 13:8,10*

10. Let us love one another: for love is of God; and every one that loveth is born of God, and knoweth God. He that loveth not knoweth not God; for God is love. *1 John 4:7,8*

11. God is love; and he that dwelleth in love dwelleth in God, and God in him. *1 John 4:16*

12. There is no fear in love; but perfect love casteth out fear. *1 John 4:18*

LOYALTY (See also Constancy; Faithfulness; God, Faithfulness of; Patriotism; Trust.)

1. For whither thou goest, I will go; and where thou lodgest, I will lodge: thy people shall be my people, and thy God my God. *Ruth 1:16*

2. Thine are we, David, and on thy side. *1 Chron. 12:18*

3. A friend loveth at all times. *Prov. 17:17*

4. A man that hath friends must show himself friendly: and there is a friend that sticketh closer than a brother. *Prov. 18:24*

5. Faithful are the wounds of a friend. *Prov. 27:6*

6. Thine own friend, and thy father's friend, forsake not. *Prov. 27:10*

7. Greater love hath no man than this, that a man lay down his life for his friends. *John 15:13*

LUST (See also Adultery; Covetousness; Depravity; Desire; Gluttony; Greed; Promiscuity.)

1. Thou shalt not covet thy neighbor's wife. *Exod. 20:17*

2. Lust not after her beauty in thine heart. *Prov. 6:25*

3. They were as fed horses in the morning: every one neighed after his neighbor's wife. *Jer. 5:8*

4. Whosoever looketh on a woman to lust after her hath committed adultery with her already in his heart. *Matt. 5:28*

5. Walk in the Spirit, and ye shall not fulfill the lust of the flesh. For the flesh lusteth against the Spirit, and the Spirit against the flesh . . . so that ye cannot do the things that ye would. *Gal. 5:16,17*

6. Flee also youthful lusts. *2 Tim. 2:22*

7. When lust hath conceived, it bringeth forth sin: and sin, when it is finished, bringeth forth death. *James 1:15*

8. Abstain from fleshly lusts. *1 Peter 2:11*

9. All that is in the world, the lust of the flesh, and the lust of the eyes, and the pride of life, is not of the Father, but is of the world. And the world passeth away, and the lust thereof. *1 John 2:16,17*

LUXURY (See also Grandeur; Wealth; Worldliness.)

1. In the court of the garden of the king's palace; Where were white, green, and blue, hangings, fastened with cords of fine linen and purple to silver rings and pillars of marble; the beds were of gold and silver, upon a pavement of red, and blue, and white, and black, marble. And they gave them drink in vessels of gold, (the vessels being diverse one from another,) and royal wine in abundance. *Esth. 1:5–7*

2. All thy garments smell of myrrh, and aloes, and cassia, out of the ivory palaces. *Ps. 45:8*

3. The king's daughter is all glorious within: her clothing is of wrought gold. *Ps. 45:13*

4. I have decked my bed with coverings of tapestry, with carved works, with fine linen of Egypt. I have perfumed my bed with myrrh, aloes, and cinnamon. *Prov. 7:16,17*

5. All her household are clothed with scarlet. She maketh herself coverings of tapestry; her clothing is silk and purple. *Prov. 31:21,22*

6. There was a certain rich man, which was clothed in purple and fine linen, and fared sumptuously every day. *Luke 16:19*

7. [I will] that women adorn themselves . . . not with braided hair, or gold, or pearls, or costly array; But . . . with good works. *1 Tim. 2:9,10*

LYING   See Falsehood; Perjury.

MADNESS   See Insanity.

MAGIC   See Fortunetelling; Occult.

MAGNIFICENCE   See Glory; Grandeur.

MAJESTY   See Authority; Glory; Grandeur.

MALE   See Man; Sex.

MALICE   (See also Cruelty; Hatred; Hostility.)

1. Let none of you imagine evil in your hearts against his neighbor. *Zech. 8:17*

2. Let us keep the feast, not with the old leaven, neither with the leaven of malice and wickedness; but with the unleavened bread of sincerity and truth. *1 Cor. 5:8*

3. In malice be ye children, but in understanding be men. *1 Cor. 14:20*

4. Let all bitterness, and wrath, and anger, and clamor, and evil speaking, be put away from you, with all malice. *Eph. 4:31*

5. We ourselves also were sometimes . . . living in malice and envy, hateful, and hating one another. *Titus 3:3*

6. Laying aside all malice . . . desire the sincere milk of the word. *1 Peter 2:1,2*

7. [Submit yourselves] As free, and not using your liberty for a cloak of maliciousness, but as the servants of God. *1 Peter 2:16*

MAN   (See also Sex; Woman.)

1. God created man in his own image, in the image of God created he him. *Gen. 1:27*

2. The man is become as one of us, to know good and evil . . . Therefore the Lord God sent him forth from the garden of Eden, to till the ground from whence he was taken. *Gen. 3:22,23*

3. Man that is born of a woman is of few days, and full of trouble. *Job 14:1*

4. What manner of man is this, that even the wine and the sea obey him? *Mark 4:41*

5. The head of every man is Christ; and the head of the woman is the man. *1 Cor. 11:3*

6. Put on the new man, which is renewed in knowledge after the image of him that created him. *Col. 3:10*

7. What is man, that thou art mindful of him? *Heb. 2:6*

MANIFESTATION   See Miracle; Revelation; Sign.

MANKIND   See Man; Woman.

MAN, SPIRIT OF   See Spirit, Human.

MARRIAGE   (See also Betrothal; Celibacy; Divorce; Virginity.)

1. Therefore shall a man leave his father and his mother, and shall cleave unto his wife: and they shall be one flesh. *Gen. 2:24*

2. Rejoice with the wife of thy youth. Let her be as the loving hind and pleasant roe; let her breasts satisfy thee at all times; and be thou ravished always with her love. *Prov. 5:18,19*

3. Whoso findeth a wife findeth a good thing, and obtaineth favor of the Lord. *Prov. 18:22*

4. They are no more twain, but one flesh. What therefore God hath joined together, let not man put asunder. *Matt. 19:6*

5. Let every man have his own wife, and let every woman have her own husband . . . The wife hath not power of her own body, but the husband: and likewise also the husband hath not power of his own body, but the wife. *1 Cor. 7:2,4*

6. It is better to marry than to burn. *1 Cor. 7:9*

7. Wives, submit yourselves unto your own husbands . . . For the husband is the head of the wife . . . so let the wives be [subject] to their own husbands in every thing. Husbands, love your wives . . . He that loveth his wife loveth himself. *Eph. 5:22,28*

8. Husbands, dwell with them according to knowledge, giving honor unto the wife, as unto the weaker vessel, and as being heirs together of the grace of life. *1 Peter 3:7*

MARTYR   (See also Death; Persecution; Sacrifice; Scapegoat.)

1. The dead bodies of thy servants have they given to be meat unto the fowls of the heaven, the flesh of thy saints unto the beasts of the earth. Their blood have they shed like water round about Jerusalem; and there was none to bury them. *Ps. 79:2,3*

2. He that loseth his life for my sake shall find it. *Matt. 10:39*

3. Give me here John Baptist's head in a charger. *Matt. 14:8*

4. And they stoned Stephen, calling upon God and saying, Lord Jesus receive my spirit. *Acts 7:59*

5. I saw the woman drunken with the blood of the saints, and with the blood of the martyrs of Jesus. *Rev. 17:6*

6. I saw the souls of them that were beheaded for the witness of Jesus, and for the word of God . . . and they lived and reigned with Christ a thousand years. *Rev. 20:4*

MASTER   See Christ; God; Lord.

MASTURBATION   See Sexual Perversion.

MATERIALISM   See Commercialism; Greed; Wealth; Worldliness.

MATURITY   (See also Growth.)

1. It is thou, O king, that art grown and become strong. *Dan. 4:22*

2. When it is grown, it is the greatest among herbs, and becometh a tree. *Matt. 13:32*

3. When the fruit is brought forth, immediately he putteth in the sickle, because the harvest is come. *Mark 4:29*

4. Jesus increased in wisdom and stature, and in favor with God and man. *Luke 2:52*

5. Look on the fields; for they are white already to harvest. *John 4:35*

6. When I became a man, I put away childish things. *1 Cor. 13:11*

7. Thrust in thy sickle, and reap: for the time is come for thee to reap; for the harvest of the earth is ripe. *Rev. 14:15*

MEANING   See Interpretation; Understanding.

MEDDLING   (See also Gossip.)

1. Why shouldest thou meddle to thy hurt? *2 Kings 14:10*

2. Forbear thee from meddling with God. *2 Chron. 35:21*

3. It is an honor for a man to cease from strife: but every fool will be meddling. *Prov. 20:3*

4. He that passeth by, and meddleth with strife belonging not to him, is like one that taketh a dog by the ears. *Prov. 26:17*

5. We hear that there are some which walk among you disorderly, working not at all, but are busybodies. *2 Thess. 3:11*

6. Let none of you suffer . . . as a busybody in other men's matters. *1 Peter 4:15*

MEDIATION **(See also Atonement; Diplomacy; Peacemaking.)**

1. I stood between the Lord and you at that time, to show you the word of the Lord. *Deut. 5:5*

2. He bare the sin of many, and made intercession for the transgressors. *Isa. 53:12*

3. The Spirit itself maketh intercession for us with groanings which cannot be uttered. *Rom. 8:26*

4. It is Christ . . . who also maketh intercession for us. *Rom. 8:34*

5. There is one God, and one mediator between God and men, the man Christ Jesus. *1 Tim. 2:5*

6. He is able also to save them to the uttermost that come unto God by him, seeing he ever liveth to make intercession for them. *Heb. 7:25*

7. Jesus the mediator of the new covenant. *Heb. 12:24*

8. If any man sin, we have an advocate with the Father, Jesus Christ. *1 John 2:1*

MEDICINE **See Healing; Physician.**

MEDITATION **(See also Prayer; Thought.)**

1. Isaac went out to meditate in the field at the eventide. *Gen. 24:63*

2. This book of the law shall not depart out of thy mouth; but thou shalt meditate therein day and night. *Josh. 1:8*

3. In his [the Lord's] law doth he meditate day and night. *Ps. 1:2*

4. Commune with your own heart upon your bed, and be still. *Ps. 4:4*

5. Let the words of my mouth, and the meditation of my heart, be acceptable in thy sight, O Lord. *Ps. 19:14*

6. My soul shall be satisfied . . . When I remember thee upon my bed, and meditate on thee in the night watches. *Ps. 63:5,6*

7. I remember the days of old; I meditate on all thy works; I muse on the work of thy hands. *Ps. 143:5*

8. Meditate upon these things; give thyself wholly to them; that thy profiting may appear to all. *1 Tim. 4:15*

MEMORY **(See also Forgetfulness.)**

1. All the ends of the world shall remember and turn unto the Lord. *Ps. 22:27*

2. The righteous shall be in everlasting remembrance. *Ps. 112:6*

3. There is no remembrance of former things; neither shall there be any remembrance of things that are to come with those that shall come after. *Eccl. 1:11*

4. Remember ye not the former things, neither consider the things of old. *Isa. 43:18*

5. They may forget, yet will I not forget thee. *Isa. 49:15*

6. This is my body which is given for you: this do in remembrance of me. *Luke 22:19*

7. Lord, remember me when thou comest into thy kingdom. *Luke 23:42*

8. This second epistle, beloved, I now write unto you; in both which I stir up your pure minds by way of remembrance. *2 Peter 3:1*

9. Remember ye the words which were spoken . . . of our Lord Jesus Christ. *Jude 1:17*

MENTAL ILLNESS   See Insanity.

MERCY   (See also Benevolence; God, Mercy of; Goodness; Pity.)

1. Surely goodness and mercy shall follow me all the days of my life. *Ps. 23:6*

2. Thy mercy, O Lord, is in the heavens. *Ps. 36:5*

3. Unto thee, O Lord, belongeth mercy: for thou renderest to every man according to his work. *Ps. 62:12*

4. The Lord is merciful and gracious, slow to anger, and plenteous in mercy. *Ps. 103:8*

5. Blessed are the merciful: for they shall obtain mercy. *Matt. 5:7*

6. God be merciful to me a sinner. *Luke 18:13*

7. Mercy rejoiceth against judgment. *James 2:13*

MERCY KILLING   See Euthanasia.

MESSENGER   See Angel; Forerunner; Prophet.

MESSIAH   See Christ; Savior.

MIDDLE EAST CONFLICT   (See also Egypt; Israel.)

1. The Egyptians said, Let us flee from the face of Israel; for the Lord fighteth for them against the Egyptians. *Exod. 14:25*

2. I will set thy bounds from the Red sea even unto the sea of the Philistines, and from the desert unto the river: for I will deliver the inhabitants of the land into your hand; and thou shalt drive them out before thee. *Exod. 23:31*

3. This is the land that shall fall unto you [children of Israel] for an inheritance, even the land of Canaan with the coasts thereof. *Num. 34:2*

4. The Lord thy God hath cut off the nations, whose land the Lord thy God giveth thee [Israel], and thou succeedest them, and dwellest in their cities, and in their houses. *Deut. 19:1*

5. Thou shalt not remove thy neighbor's landmark, which they of old time have set in thine inheritance, which thou shalt inherit in the land that the Lord thy God giveth thee to possess it. *Deut. 19:14*

6. The land of Judah shall be a terror unto Egypt. *Isa. 19:17*

7. Egypt shall be a desolation, and Edom shall be a desolate wilderness . . . But Judah shall dwell for ever, and Jerusalem from generation to generation. *Joel 3:19,20*

8. I will make Jerusalem a cup of trembling unto all the people round about, when they shall be in the siege both against Judah and against Jerusalem. And in that day will I make Jerusalem a burdensome stone for all people: all that burden themselves with it shall be cut in pieces, though all the people of the earth be gathered together against it. *Zech. 12:2,3*

MIGHT **See God, The Almighty; God, Power of; Power; Strength.**

MILITARY **See Army, Christian; Draft, Military; War.**

MIND **(See also Conscience; Heart; Spirit, Human.)**

1. Thou wilt keep him in perfect peace, whose mind is stayed on thee. *Isa. 26:3*

2. Thou shalt love the Lord thy God . . . with all thy mind. *Mark 12:30*

3. They received the word with all readiness of mind. *Acts 17:11*

4. With the mind I myself serve the law of God; but with the flesh the law of sin. *Rom. 7:25*

5. Be ye transformed by the renewing of your mind. *Rom. 12:2*

6. Who hath known the mind of the Lord, that he may instruct him? But we have the mind of Christ. *1 Cor. 2:16*

7. Gird up the loins of your mind. *1 Peter 1:13*

MINISTRY **(See also Bishop; Church; Church, Mission of; Deacon; Elder; Evangelism; Missionary; Ordination.)**

1. Whosoever will be great among you, let him be your minister . . . Even as the Son of man came not to be ministered unto, but to minister. *Matt. 20:26,28*

2. He ordained twelve . . . that he might send them forth to preach. *Mark 3:14*

3. I [Jesus] have appeared unto thee for this purpose, to make thee a minister. *Acts 26:16*

4. Though I preach the gospel, I have nothing to glory of: for necessity is laid upon me; yea, woe is unto me, if I preach not the gospel! . . . What is my reward then? Verily that, when I preach the gospel, I may make the gospel of Christ without charge, that I abuse not my power in the gospel. *1 Cor. 9:16,18*

5. Preach the word; be instant in season, out of season; reprove, rebuke, exhort with all long-suffering and doctrine. *2 Tim. 4:2*

6. Minister the same one to another, as good stewards of the manifold grace of God. *1 Peter 4:10*

MIRACLE   (See also Healing; Sign; Tongues, Gift of; Wonder.)

1. Many believed in his name, when they saw the miracles which he did. *John 2:23*

2. No man can do these miracles that thou doest, except God be with him. *John 3:2*

3. A great multitude followed him, because they saw his miracles. *John 6:2*

4. The Father that dwelleth in me, he doeth the works. *John 14:10*

5. He that believeth on me, the works that I do shall he do also; and greater works than these shall he do. *John 14:12*

6. Jesus of Nazareth, a man approved of God among you by miracles and wonders and signs, which God did by him in the midst of you. *Acts 2:22*

7. He therefore that ministereth to you the Spirit, and worketh miracles among you, doeth he it by the works of the law, or by the hearing of faith? *Gal. 3:5*

8. God also bearing them witness, both with signs and wonders, and with divers miracles, and gifts of the Holy Ghost. *Heb. 2:4*

MISERLINESS   See Stinginess.

MISERY   See Depression; Distress; Sorrow; Suffering.

MISSION   See Christ, Purpose of; Church, Mission of; Evangelism; Ministry; Missionary.

MISSIONARY   (See also Evangelism; Ministry.)

1. Declare his glory among the heathen, his wonders among all people. *Ps. 96:3*

2. Whom shall I send, and who will go for us? Then said I, Here am I; send me. *Isa. 6:8*

3. Go ye therefore, and teach all nations, baptizing them in the name of the Father, and of the Son, and of the Holy Ghost: Teaching them to observe all things whatsoever I have commanded you. *Matt. 28:19,20*

4. Go ye into all the world, and preach the gospel to every creature. *Mark 16:15*

5. The Lord appointed other seventy also, and sent them two and two before his face into every city and place. *Luke 10:1*

6. As thou hast sent me into the world, even so have I also sent them into the world. *John 17:18*

MISTAKE   (See also Imperfection; Sin.)

1. I have played the fool, and have erred exceedingly. *1 Sam. 26:21*

2. Be it indeed that I have erred, mine error remaineth with myself. *Job 19:4*

3. Suffer not thy mouth to cause thy flesh to sin; neither say thou before the angel, that it was an error. *Eccl. 5:6*

4. They err in vision, they stumble in judgment. *Isa. 28:7*

5. Ye do err, not knowing the scriptures, nor the power of God. *Matt. 22:29*

6. He is not the God of the dead, but the God of the living: ye therefore do greatly err. *Mark 12:27*

7. If any of you do err from the truth, and one convert him; Let him know, that he which converteth the sinner from the error of his way shall save a soul from death. *James 5:19,20*

MOCKERY   See Scorn.

MODEL   See Example.

MODERATION   (See also Self-Control; Sobriety.)

1. Give me neither poverty nor riches. *Prov. 30:8*

2. Every man that striveth for the mastery is temperate in all things. *1 Cor. 9:25*

3. The fruit of the Spirit is . . . temperance. *Gal. 5:22,23*

4. Let your moderation be known unto all men. *Phil. 4:5*

5. Add to your faith virtue; and to virtue knowledge; And to knowledge temperance. *2 Peter 1:5,6*

MODESTY   (See also Dress; Nakedness; Virtue.)

1. The eyes of them both were opened, and they knew that they were naked; and they sewed fig leaves together, and made themselves aprons. *Gen. 3:7*

2. She took a veil, and covered herself. *Gen. 24:65*

3. Every woman that prayeth or prophesieth with her head uncovered dishonoreth her head . . . let her be covered. *1 Cor. 11:5,6*

4. [I will therefore] that women adorn themselves in modest apparel, with shamefacedness and sobriety. *1 Tim. 2:9*

MONARCH   See King.

MONEY   (See also Greed; Luxury; Wealth; Worldliness.)

1. Money answereth all things. *Eccl. 10:19*

2. Buy wine and milk without money and without price. Wherefore do ye spend money for that which is not bread? *Isa. 55:1,2*

3. Provide neither gold, nor silver, nor brass in your purses. *Matt. 10:9*

4. When he had found one pearl of great price, [he] went and sold all that he had, and bought it. *Matt. 13:46*

5. Thy money perish with thee, because thou hast thought that the gift of God may be purchased with money. *Acts 8:20*

6. [Be] not greedy of filthy lucre. *1 Tim. 3:8*

7. The love of money is the root of all evil. *1 Tim. 6:10*

MORALITY   See Justice; Purity; Righteousness; Virtue.

MORTALITY   (See also Death; Impermanence; Life.)

1. We must needs die, and are as water spilt on the ground, which cannot be gathered up again. *2 Sam. 14:14*

2. What man is he that liveth, and shall not see death? Shall he deliver his soul from the hand of the grave? *Ps. 89:48*

3. As for man, his days are as grass . . . For the wind passeth over it, and it is gone; and the place thereof shall know it no more. *Ps. 103:15,16*

4. This mortal must put on immortality. *1 Cor. 15:53*

5. We have this treasure in earthen vessels . . . For we which live are alway delivered unto death for Jesus' sake, that the life also of Jesus might be made manifest in our mortal flesh. *2 Cor. 4:7,11*

6. It is appointed unto men once to die. *Heb. 9:27*

MOTHER   (See also Children; Family; Father; Parent.)

1. Adam called his wife's name Eve; because she was the mother of all living. *Gen. 3:20*

2. Honor thy father and thy mother. *Exod. 20:12*

3. He maketh the barren woman to keep house, and to be a joyful mother of children. *Ps. 113:9*

4. A foolish son is the heaviness of his mother. *Prov. 10:1*

5. Despise not thy mother when she is old. *Prov. 23:22*

6. [A virtuous woman] looketh well to the ways of her household, and eateth not the bread of idleness. Her children arise up, and call her blessed; her husband also, and he praiseth her. *Prov. 31:27,28*

7. She [Mary] brought forth her firstborn son, and wrapped him in swaddling clothes, and laid him in a manger. *Luke 2:7*

MOURNING   See Sorrow.

MURDER   (See also Assassination; Cannibalism; Capital Punishment; Euthanasia; Martyr; Suicide.)

1. Cain rose up against Abel his brother, and slew him. *Gen. 4:8*

2. Whoso sheddeth man's blood, by man shall his blood be shed. *Gen. 9:6*

3. Thou shalt not kill. *Exod. 20:13*

4. Will ye steal, murder, and commit adultery, and swear falsely? *Jer. 7:9*

5. Fear not them which kill the body, but are not able to kill the soul. *Matt. 10:28*

6. Jesus said, Thou shalt do no murder. *Matt. 19:18*

7. Whosoever hateth his brother is a murderer: and ye know that no murderer hath eternal life abiding in him. *1 John 3:15*

MURMURING   See Complaint; Discontent.

MUSIC   (See also Praise; Song.)

1. David and all the house of Israel played before the Lord on all manner of instruments made of fir wood, even on harps, and on psalteries, and on timbrels, and on cornets, and on cymbals. *2 Sam. 6:5*

2. Praise him with the sound of the trumpet: praise him with the psaltery and harp. Praise him with the timbrel and dance: praise him with stringed instruments and organs. *Ps. 150:3,4*

3. Take a harp, go about the city . . . make sweet melody, sing many songs, that thou mayest be remembered. *Isa. 23:16*

4. We will sing my songs to the stringed instruments all the days of our life in the house of the Lord. *Isa. 38:20*

5. I am their music. *Lam. 3:63*

6. Take thou away from me the noise of thy songs; for I will not hear the melody of thy viols. *Amos 5:23*

MYSTERY (See also Revelation; Secrecy; Trinity, Holy.)
1. No man can find out the work that God maketh from the beginning to the end. *Eccl. 3:11*
2. Unto you it is given to know the mystery of the kingdom of God: but unto them that are without, all these things are done in parables: that seeing they may see, and not perceive; and hearing they may hear, and not understand. *Mark 4:11,12*
3. O the depth of the riches both of the wisdom and knowledge of God! how unsearchable are his judgments, and his ways past finding out! *Rom. 11:33*
4. I show you a mystery; We shall not all sleep, but we shall all be changed. *1 Cor. 15:51*
5. By revelation . . . by the Spirit . . . I should preach among the Gentiles the unsearchable riches of Christ . . . to make all men see what is the fellowship of the mystery, which from the beginning of the world hath been hid in God. *Eph. 3:3–9*
6. We are members of his body, of his flesh, and of his bones . . . This is a great mystery: but I speak concerning Christ and the church. *Eph. 5:30,32*
7. [Praying] that I may open my mouth boldly, to make known the mystery of the gospel. *Eph. 6:19*
8. Without controversy great is the mystery of godliness: God was manifest in the flesh, justified in the Spirit. *1 Tim. 3:16*

N

NAÏVETÉ See Childlikeness; Innocence; Simplicity.

NAKEDNESS (See also Dress; Modesty; Shame.)

1. They were both naked, the man and his wife, and were not ashamed. *Gen. 2:25*

2. Naked came I out of my mother's womb, and naked shall I return thither. *Job 1:21*

3. They shall strip thee also of thy clothes, and shall take thy fair jewels, and leave thee naked and bare. *Ezek. 16:39*

4. He that is courageous among the mighty shall flee away naked in that day, saith the Lord. *Amos 2:16*

5. I will discover thy skirts upon thy face, and I will show the nations thy nakedness. *Nah. 3:5*

6. [I was] Naked, and ye clothed me. *Matt. 25:36*

7. Even unto this present hour we . . . are naked. *1 Cor. 4:11*

8. Being clothed we shall not be found naked. *2 Cor. 5:3*

NAME See Fame; Reputation.

NATION (See also Kingdom; Patriotism.)

1. These are the families of the sons of Noah, after their generations, in their nations: and by these were the nations divided in the earth after the flood. *Gen. 10:32*

2. I will make of thee a great nation . . . in thee shall all families of the earth be blessed. *Gen. 12:2,3*

3. Righteousness exalteth a nation: but sin is a reproach to any people. *Prov. 14:34*

4. He shall judge among the nations, and shall rebuke many people: and they shall beat their swords into plowshares, and their spears into pruninghooks: nation shall not lift up sword against nation, neither shall they learn war any more. *Isa. 2:4*

5. The nations shall rush like the rushing of many waters: but God shall rebuke them, and they shall flee far off, and shall be chased . . . like a rolling thing before the whirlwind. *Isa. 17:13*

6. The nations are as a drop of a bucket, and are counted as the small dust of the balance. *Isa. 40:15*

7. A little one shall become a thousand, and a small one a strong nation. *Isa. 60:22*

8. I will make them one nation . . . and one king shall be king to them all: and they shall be no more two nations. *Ezek. 37:22*

9. Before him shall be gathered all nations: and he shall separate them one from another, as a shepherd divideth his sheep from the goats. *Matt. 25:32*

10. [God] hath made of one blood all nations of men for to dwell on all the face of the earth. *Acts 17:26*

   NATIONALITY   See Race, Ethnic.

   NATIVITY   See Birth.

   NATURAL RELIGION   (See also Animal; God, Existence of .)

1. Ask now the beasts, and they shall teach thee; and the fowls of the air, and they shall tell thee: or speak to the earth, and it shall teach thee: and the fishes of the sea shall declare unto thee. Who knoweth not in all these that the hand of the Lord hath wrought this? in whose hand is the soul of every living thing, and the breath of all mankind. *Job 12:7–10*

2. When I consider the heavens, the work of thy fingers, the moon and the stars, which thou hast ordained; what is man, that thou art mindful of him? and the son of man, that thou visitest him? For thou hast made him a little lower than the angels, and hast crowned him with glory and honor. Thou madest him to have dominion over the works of thy hands; thou hast put all things under his feet. *Ps. 8:3–6*

3. The heavens declare the glory of God; and the firmament showeth his handiwork . . . His going forth is from the end of the heaven, and his circuit unto the ends of it: and there is nothing hid from the heat thereof. *Ps. 19:1,6*

4. In him [God] we live, and move, and have our being . . . For we are also his offspring. *Acts 17:28*

5. The invisible things of him from the creation of the world are clearly seen, being understood by the things that are made. *Rom. 1:20*

NATURE   See Animal; Environment; Natural Religion; Pollution.

NEED   (See also Desire; Hunger.)

1. Whence should I have flesh to give unto all this people? for they weep unto me, saying, Give us flesh, that we may eat. *Num. 11:13*

2. Who provideth for the raven his food? When his young ones cry unto God, they wander for lack of meat. *Job 38:41*

3. There is no want to them that fear him. The young lions do lack, and suffer hunger: but they that seek the Lord shall not want any good thing. *Ps. 34:9,10*

4. Your Father knoweth what things ye have need of, before ye ask him. *Matt. 6:8*

5. One thing thou lackest: go thy way, sell whatsoever thou hast, and give to the poor, and thou shalt have treasure in heaven: and come, take up the cross, and follow me. *Mark 10:21*

6. We have no more but five loaves and two fishes; except we should go and buy meat for all this people. For they were about five thousand men. *Luke 9:13,14*

7. Walk honestly toward them that are without . . . that ye may have lack of nothing. *1 Thess. 4:12*

NEGLECT   (See also Forgetfulness; Ingratitude.)

1. Be not now negligent: for the Lord hath chosen you . . . to serve him. *2 Chron. 29:11*

2. Let us not give heed to any of his words. *Jer. 18:18*

3. The diseased have ye not strengthened, neither have ye healed that which was sick, neither have ye bound up that which was broken, neither have ye brought again that which was driven away, neither have ye sought that which was lost. *Ezek. 34:4*

4. That servant, which knew his lord's will, and prepared not himself, neither did according to his will, shall be beaten with many stripes . . . For unto whomsoever much is given, of him shall be much required. *Luke 12:47,48*

5. Their widows were neglected in the daily ministration. *Acts 6:1*

6. Neglect not the gift that is in thee. *1 Tim. 4:14*

7. How shall we escape, if we neglect so great salvation? *Heb. 2:3*

8. To him that knoweth to do good, and doeth it not, to him it is sin. *James 4:17*

NEGLIGENCE   See Forgetfulness; Neglect.

NEIGHBOR (See also Brotherhood; Friendship; Love.)

1. Thou shalt not bear false witness against thy neighbor. Thou shalt not covet thy neighbor's house, thou shalt not covet thy neighbor's wife, nor his manservant, nor his maidservant, nor his ox, nor his ass, nor any thing that is thy neighbor's. *Exod. 20:16,17*

2. Thou shalt love thy neighbor as thyself. *Lev. 19:18*

3. Better is a neighbor that is near than a brother far off. *Prov. 27:10*

4. They helped every one his neighbor. *Isa. 41:6*

5. Speak ye every man the truth to his neighbor . . . And let none of you imagine evil in your hearts against his neighbor. *Zech. 8:16,17*

6. Which now of these three, thinkest thou, was neighbor unto him that fell among the thieves? And he said, He that showeth mercy on him. *Luke 10:36,37*

7. Love worketh no ill to his neighbor: therefore love is the fulfilling of the law. *Rom. 13:10*

8. Let every one of us please his neighbor for his good to edification. *Rom. 15:2*

NUDITY See Nakedness.

OATH   See Blasphemy; Profanity; Vow.

OBEDIENCE   (See also Christian Obligation; Disobedience; Duty; God, Law of; Law; Surrender.)

1. Ye shall observe to do therefore as the Lord your God hath commanded you: ye shall not turn aside to the right hand or to the left. *Deut. 5:32*

2. To obey is better than sacrifice. *1 Sam. 15:22*

3. Fear God, and keep his commandments: for this is the whole duty of man. *Eccl. 12:13*

4. Obey my voice, and I will be your God, and ye shall be my people: and walk ye in all the ways that I have commanded you, that it may be well unto you. *Jer. 7:23*

5. Thy will be done in earth, as it is in heaven. *Matt. 6:10*

6. Not as I will, but as thou wilt. *Matt. 26:39*

7. Children, obey your parents . . . Servants, be obedient to them that are your masters. *Eph. 6:1,5*

8. Obey them that have the rule over you, and submit yourselves: for they watch for your souls. *Heb. 13:17*

9. Be ye doers of the word, and not hearers only, deceiving your own selves. *James 1:22*

10. Submit yourselves to every ordinance of man for the Lord's sake. . . . For so is the will of God. *1 Peter 2:13,15*

11. Blessed are they that do his commandments, that they may have right to the tree of life, and may enter in through the gates into the city. *Rev. 22:14*

OBLIGATION   See Christian Obligation; Duty; Responsibility.

OBSCENITY   See Blasphemy; Profanity.

OBSTACLE   (See also Companions, Evil; Temptation.)

1. They shall be as thorns in your sides, and their gods shall be a snare unto you. *Judg. 2:3*

2. He shall be . . . a stone of stumbling and for a rock of offense . . . And many among them shall stumble, and fall, and be broken, and be snared, and be taken. *Isa. 8:14,15*

3. To subvert a man in his cause, the Lord approveth not. *Lam. 3:36*

4. Ye blind guides, which strain at a gnat, and swallow a camel. *Matt. 23:24*

5. Some fell among thorns; and the thorns sprang up with it, and choked it. *Luke 8:7*

6. If a man walk in the night, he stumbleth, because there is no light in him. *John 11:10*

7. Who shall separate us from the love of Christ? shall tribulation, or distress, or persecution, or famine, or nakedness, or peril, or sword? *Rom. 8:35*

8. Take heed lest by any means this liberty of yours become a stumbling block to them that are weak. *1 Cor. 8:9*

OCCULT   (See also Astrology; Cults, Religious; Demons; Fortunetelling; Idolatry; Paganism.)

1. Thou shalt not suffer a witch to live. *Exod. 22:18*

2. A man also or woman that hath a familiar spirit, or that is a wizard, shall surely be put to death. *Lev. 20:27*

3. There shall not be found among you any one . . . that useth divination, or an observer of times, or an enchanter, or a witch, Or a charmer, or a consulter with familiar spirits, or a wizard, or a necromancer. For all that do these things are an abomination unto the Lord. *Deut. 18:10–12*

4. I will cut off witchcrafts out of thine hand; and thou shalt have no more soothsayers. *Mic. 5:12*

5. I will be a swift witness against the sorcerers. *Mal. 3:5*

6. There was a certain man, called Simon, which beforetime in the same city used sorcery, and bewitched the people of Samaria. *Acts 8:9*

7. By thy sorceries were all nations deceived. *Rev. 18:23*

8. Sorcerers . . . shall have their part in the lake which burneth with fire and brimstone: which is the second death. *Rev. 21:8*

OCCUPATION   See Business; Vocation; Work.

OFFENSE   See Sin.

OFFERING   See Giving; Sacrifice; Tithe.

OMNIPOTENCE   See God, The Almighty; God, Power of.

OMNIPRESENCE   See God, Omnipresence of.

OMNISCIENCE   See God, Omniscience of.

ONENESS   See Trinity, Holy; Unity.

OPEN-MINDEDNESS   See Liberalism.

OPPORTUNITY   (See also Procrastination.)

1. To every thing there is a season, and a time to every purpose under the heaven. *Eccl. 3:1*

2. They that were ready went in with him . . . and the door was shut. *Matt. 25:10*

3. Look on the fields; for they are white already to harvest. *John 4:35*

4. Now is the accepted time; behold, now is the day of salvation. *2 Cor. 6:2*

5. As we have therefore opportunity, let us do good unto all men. *Gal. 6:10*

6. Ye were also careful, but ye lacked opportunity. *Phil. 4:10*

OPPOSITION   See Argument; Enemy; Fighting; Heresy; Protest.

OPPRESSION   (See also Captivity; Persecution.)

1. The cry of the children of Israel is come unto me: and I have also seen the oppression wherewith the Egyptians oppress them. *Exod. 3:9*

2. Ye shall not oppress one another. *Lev. 25:14*

3. Lord, thou hast heard the desire of the humble . . . to judge the fatherless and the oppressed, that the man of the earth may no more oppress. *Ps. 10:17,18*

4. He [God] . . . shall break in pieces the oppressor. *Ps. 72:4*

5. Envy thou not the oppressor, and choose none of his ways. *Prov. 3:31*

6. [I] considered all the oppressions that are done under the sun: and behold the tears of such as were oppressed, and they had no comforter; and on the side of their oppressors there was power; but they had no comforter. *Eccl. 4:1*

7. They shall take them captives, whose captives they were; and they shall rule over their oppressors. *Isa. 14:2*

8. I [the Lord] will be a swift witness against . . . those that oppress. *Mal. 3:5*

OPTIMISM   See Hope.

ORDINATION   (See also Ministry.)

1. I ordained thee a prophet unto the nations. *Jer. 1:5*

2. He ordained twelve, that they should be with him, and that he might send them forth to preach, And to have power to heal sicknesses, and to cast out devils. *Mark 3:14,15*

3. We speak the wisdom of God in a mystery, even the hidden wisdom, which God ordained before the world unto our glory. *1 Cor. 2:7*

4. The Lord ordained that they which preach the gospel should live of the gospel. *1 Cor. 9:14*

5. I am ordained a preacher, and an apostle . . . a teacher of the Gentiles in faith and verity. *1 Tim. 2:7*

6. Ordain elders in every city, as I had appointed thee. *Titus 1:5*

7. Every high priest taken from among men is ordained for men in things pertaining to God. *Heb. 5:1*

ORIGIN   See Beginning; Creation.

ORPHAN   (See also Adoption; Children; God, Family of; God, Fatherhood of; Widow.)

1. Ye shall not afflict any . . . fatherless child. *Exod. 22:22*

2. I delivered . . . the fatherless, and him that had none to help him. *Job 29:12*

3. If I have lifted up my hand against the fatherless . . . then let mine arm fall from my shoulder blade. *Job 31:21,22*

4. When my father and my mother forsake me, then the Lord will take me up. *Ps. 27:10*

5. A father of the fatherless . . . is God. *Ps. 68:5*

6. I will be a swift witness against . . . those that oppress . . . the fatherless . . . saith the Lord. *Mal. 3:5*

7. Pure religion and undefiled before God and the Father is this, To visit the fatherless and widows in their affliction, and to keep himself unspotted from the world. *James 1:27*

P

PACIFISM   See Peace; Peacemaking.

PACT   See Covenant.

PAGANISM   (See also Cults, Religious; Fortunetelling; Idolatry; Ignorance; Occult.)

1. Why do the heathen rage? *Ps. 2:1*

2. O God, the heathen are come into thine inheritance; thy holy temple have they defiled; they have laid Jerusalem on heaps. *Ps. 79:1*

3. The heathen shall fear the name of the Lord. *Ps. 102:15*

4. I the Lord have called thee . . . and give thee for a covenant of the people, for a light of the Gentiles. *Isa. 42:6*

5. Learn not the way of the heathen, and be not dismayed at the signs of heaven; for the heathen are dismayed at them. *Jer. 10:2*

6. Men shall worship him . . . even all the isles of the heathen. *Zeph. 2:11*

7. Then Paul stood in the midst of Mar's hill, and said, Ye men of Athens, I perceive that in all things ye are too superstitious. *Acts 17:22*

8. But I say, that the things which the Gentiles sacrifice, they sacrifice to devils, and not to God: and I would not that ye should have fellowship with devils. *1 Cor. 10:20*

9. The Gentiles should be fellow heirs, and of the same body, and partakers of his promise in Christ by the gospel. *Eph. 3:6*

10. Walk not as other Gentiles walk . . . Having the understanding darkened, being alienated from the life of God through the ignorance that is in them, because of the blindness of their heart. *Eph. 4:17,18*

PAIN   See Suffering.

PARABLE (See also Gospel.)

1. Incline your ears . . . I will open my mouth in a parable. *Ps. 78:1,2*

2. The legs of the lame are not equal: so is a parable in the mouth of fools. *Prov. 26:7*

3. All these things spake Jesus unto the multitude in parables; and without a parable spake he not unto them: That it might be fulfilled which was spoken by the prophet, saying, I will open my mouth in parables; I will utter things which have been kept secret from the foundation of the world. *Matt. 13:34,35*

4. He taught them many things by parables . . . Unto you it is given to know the mystery of the kingdom of God: but unto them that are without, all these things are done in parables: that seeing they may see, and not perceive; and hearing they may hear, and not understand. *Mark 4:2,11,12*

PARADISE (See also Heaven; Kingdom; Salvation.)

1. God planted a garden eastward in Eden; and there he put the man whom he had formed. And out of the ground made the Lord God to grow every tree that is pleasant to the sight, and good for food; the tree of life . . . and the tree of knowledge. *Gen. 2:8,9*

2. Today shalt thou be with me in paradise. *Luke 23:43*

3. He was caught up into paradise, and heard unspeakable words, which it is not lawful for a man to utter. *2 Cor. 12:4*

4. To him that overcometh will I give to eat of the tree of life, which is in the midst of the paradise of God. *Rev. 2:7*

PARDON See Forgiveness; Remission of Sins.

PARENT (See also Family; Father; God, Fatherhood of; Mother.)

1. Honor thy father and thy mother. *Exod. 20:12*

2. When my father and my mother forsake me, then the Lord will take me up. *Ps. 27:10*

3. A wise son maketh a glad father: but a foolish son is the heaviness of his mother. *Prov. 10:1*

4. Whoso curseth his father or his mother, his lamp shall be put out in obscure darkness. *Prov. 20:20*

5. The children shall rise up against their parents, and cause them to be put to death. *Matt. 10:21*

6. He that loveth father or mother more than me is not worthy of me: and he that loveth son or daughter more than me is not worthy of me. *Matt. 10:37*

7. There is no man that hath left . . . parents . . . for the kingdom of God's sake, Who shall not receive manifold more. *Luke 18:29,30*

8. The children ought not to lay up for the parents, but the parents for the children. *2 Cor. 12:14*

PARSIMONY   See Stinginess.

PARTIALITY   See Favoritism; Prejudice.

PASSION, SEXUAL   See Lust.

PASSOVER   (See also Protection.)

1. In the tenth day of this month they shall take to them every man a lamb . . . without blemish, a male of the first year . . . And ye shall keep it up until the fourteenth day of the same month: and the whole assembly of the congregation of Israel shall kill it in the evening. And they shall take of the blood, and strike it on the two side posts and on the upper door posts of the houses, wherein they shall eat . . . the flesh in that night, roast with fire, and unleavened bread . . . and that which remaineth of it until the morning ye shall burn with fire . . . it is the Lord's passover . . . and when I see the blood, I will pass over you, and the plague shall not be upon you to destroy you, when I smite the land of Egypt. And this day shall be unto you for a memorial . . . ye shall keep it a feast by an ordinance for ever. *Exod. 12:3–14*

2. The first day of the feast of unleavened bread the disciples . . . did as Jesus had appointed them; and they made ready the passover. *Matt. 26:17,19*

3. [Jesus] said unto them, With desire I have desired to eat this passover with you before I suffer. *Luke 22:15*

4. Christ our passover is sacrificed for us: Therefore let us keep the feast, not with old leaven, neither with the leaven of malice and wickedness; but with the unleavened bread of sincerity and truth. *1 Cor. 5:7,8*

PASTOR   See Ministry; Shepherd.

PATIENCE   (See also Impatience; Self-Control; Tolerance.)

1. I have waited for thy salvation, O Lord. *Gen. 49:18*

2. My soul waiteth for the Lord more than they that watch for the morning. *Ps. 130:6*

3. The patient in spirit is better than the proud in spirit. *Eccl. 7:8*

4. In your patience possess ye your souls. *Luke 21:19*

5. We glory in tribulations also: knowing that tribulation worketh patience; And patience, experience; and experience, hope. *Rom. 5:3,4*

6. Let us not be weary in well doing: for in due season we shall reap. *Gal. 6:9*

7. Be patient toward all men. *1 Thess. 5:14*

8. Ye have need of patience, that, after ye have done the will of God, ye might receive the promise. *Heb. 10:36*

9. Let us run with patience the race that is set before us. *Heb. 12:1*

10. The trying of your faith worketh patience. But let patience have her perfect work, that ye may be perfect and entire, wanting nothing. *James 1:3,4*

11. Be ye also patient; stablish your hearts: for the coming of the Lord draweth nigh. *James 5:8*

12. Ye have heard of the patience of Job. *James 5:11*

13. Here is the patience of the saints: here are they that keep the commandments of God, and the faith of Jesus. *Rev. 14:12*

PATRIOTISM   (See also Nation.)

1. Let me depart, that I may go to mine own country. *1 Kings 11:21*

2. If I forget thee, O Jerusalem, let my right hand forget her cunning, . . . let my tongue cleave to the roof of my mouth. *Ps. 137:5,6*

3. For Zion's sake will I not hold my peace, and for Jerusalem's sake I will not rest, until the righteousness thereof go forth as brightness, and the salvation thereof as a lamp that burneth. *Isa. 62:1*

4. Render therefore to all their dues: tribute to whom tribute is due, custom to whom custom; fear to whom fear; honor to whom honor. *Rom. 13:7*

PAYMENT   See Reward; Wages.

PEACE   (See also Peacemaking; Silence; War.)

1. Mark the perfect man, and behold the upright: for the end of that man is peace. *Ps. 37:37*

2. Great peace have they which love the law: and nothing shall offend them. *Ps. 119:165*

3. Her ways are ways of pleasantness, and all her paths are peace. *Prov. 3:17*

4. A time of war, and a time of peace. *Eccl. 3:8*

5. His name shall be called . . . The Prince of Peace. *Isa. 9:6*

6. The wolf also shall dwell with the lamb, and the leopard shall lie down with the kid. . . . And the suckling child shall play on the hole of the asp. *Isa. 11:6,8*

7. The work of righteousness shall be peace. *Isa. 32:17*

8. Peace to him that is far off, and to him that is near. *Isa. 57:19*

9. Glory to God in the highest, and on earth peace, good will toward men. *Luke 2:14*

10. Peace be to this house. *Luke 10:5*

11. Peace I leave you, my peace I give unto you. *John 14:27*

12. If it be possible, as much as lieth in you, live peaceably with all men. *Rom. 12:18*

13. God is not the author of confusion, but of peace. *1 Cor. 14:33*

14. The peace of God, which passeth all understanding, shall keep your hearts and minds through Christ Jesus. *Phil. 4:7*

15. Follow peace with all men, and holiness, without which no man shall see the Lord. *Heb. 12:14*

PEACE OF MIND   See Contentment.

PEACEMAKING   (See also Diplomacy; Peace; War.)

1. Ye shall not go up, nor fight against your brethren. *2 Chron. 11:4*

2. He maketh wars to cease unto the end of the earth; he breaketh the bow, and cutteth the spear in sunder; he burneth the chariot in the fire. *Ps. 46:9*

3. It is an honor for a man to cease from strife: but every fool will be meddling. *Prov. 20:3*

4. They shall beat their swords into plowshares, and their spears into pruninghooks: nation shall not lift up sword against nation, neither shall they learn war anymore. *Isa. 2:4*

5. I will make a covenant of peace with them; it shall be an everlasting covenant. *Ezek. 37:26*

6. The counsel of peace shall be between them both. *Zech. 6:13*

7. Blessed are the peacemakers: for they shall be called the children of God. *Matt. 5:9*

8. Put up again thy sword into his place: for all they that take the sword shall perish with the sword. *Matt. 26:52*

9. He sendeth an ambassage, and desireth conditions of peace. *Luke 14:32*

10. Let us therefore follow after the things which make for peace, and things wherewith one may edify another. *Rom. 14:19*

11. Let not the sun go down upon your wrath. *Eph. 4:26*

PENALTY   See Punishment; Result.

PENANCE   See Confession of Sins; Repentance.
PENITENCE   See Repentance.
PERCEPTION   See Understanding.
PERFECTION   See Infallibility.
PERFORMANCE   (See also Work.)
1. Thou hast done well in executing that which is right in mine eyes. *2 Kings 10:30*
2. God . . . performeth all things for me. *Ps. 57:2*
3. Commit thy works unto the Lord, and thy thoughts shall be established. *Prov. 16:3*
4. He is strong that executeth his word. *Joel 2:11*
5. What he had promised, he was able also to perform. *Rom. 4:21*
6. He which hath begun a good work in you will perform it until the day of Jesus Christ. *Phil. 1:6*
7. Whatsoever ye do in word or deed, do all in the name of the Lord Jesus, giving thanks to God. *Col. 3:17*
8. He that doeth the will of God abideth for ever. *1 John 2:17*
PERJURY   (See also Falsehood; Vow; Witness.)
1. Thou shalt not bear false witness against thy neighbor. *Exod. 20:16*
2. Thou shalt not raise a false report: put not thine hand with the wicked to be an unrighteous witness. *Exod. 23:1*
3. A false witness shall not be unpunished; and he that speaketh lies shall perish. *Prov. 19:9*
4. A man that beareth false witness against his neighbor is a maul, and a sword, and a sharp arrow. *Prov. 25:18*
5. They have spoken words, swearing falsely in making a covenant: thus judgment springeth up as hemlock in the furrows of the field. *Hos. 10:4*
6. Love no false oath: for all these are things that I hate, saith the Lord. *Zech. 8:17*
7. I will be a swift witness against . . . false swearers. *Mal. 3:5*
8. Many bear false witness against him, but their witness agreed not together. *Mark 14:56*
PERMANENCE   (See also Constancy; Eternity; Immortality; Impermanence.)
1. I will abide in thy tabernacle for ever. *Ps. 61:4*
2. Before the mountains were brought forth, or ever thou hadst formed the earth and the world, even from everlasting to everlasting, thou art God. *Ps. 90:2*

3. The grass withereth, the flower fadeth: but the word of our God shall stand for ever. *Isa. 40:8*

4. The foundation of God standeth sure. *2 Tim. 2:19*

5. Jesus Christ the same yesterday and today, and for ever. *Heb. 13:8*

6. The word of the Lord endureth for ever. *1 Peter 1:25*

PERSECUTION   (See also Martyr; Oppression; Suffering.)

1. For thy sake I have borne reproach. *Ps. 69:7*

2. He was wounded for our transgressions, he was bruised for our iniquities: the chastisement of our peace was upon him; and with his stripes we are healed. *Isa. 53:5*

3. He was oppressed, and he was afflicted, yet he opened not his mouth: he is brought as a lamb to the slaughter. *Isa. 53:7*

4. Blessed are they which are persecuted for righteousness' sake: for theirs is the kingdom of heaven. Blessed are ye, when men shall revile you, and persecute you, and say all manner of evil against you falsely, for my sake. *Matt. 5:10,11*

5. Ye shall be hated of all men for my name's sake: but he that endureth to the end shall be saved. *Matt. 10:22*

6. If they have persecuted me, they will also persecute you. *John 15:20*

7. Which of the prophets have not your fathers persecuted? *Acts 7:52*

8. Saul, Saul, why persecutest thou me? . . . I am Jesus whom thou persecutest: it is hard for thee to kick against the pricks. *Acts 9:4,5*

9. I take pleasure in . . . persecutions, in distresses for Christ's sake: for when I am weak, then am I strong. *2 Cor. 12:10*

10. All that live godly in Christ Jesus shall suffer persecution. *2 Tim. 3:12*

PERSEVERANCE   See Determination.

PERSUASION   See Influence.

PERVERSION   (See also Corruption; Depravity; Evil; Sexual Perversion.)

1. The imagination of man's heart is evil from his youth. *Gen. 8:21*

2. The wicked walk on every side, when the vilest men are exalted. *Ps. 12:8*

3. Better is the poor that walketh in his uprightness, than he that is perverse in his ways, though he be rich. *Prov. 28:6*

4. Woe unto them that call evil good, and good evil; that put darkness for light, and light for darkness. *Isa. 5:20*

5. [Thou] didst debase thyself even unto hell. *Isa. 57:9*

PESSIMISM See Despair; Discouragement; Hopelessness.

PHYSICAL APPEARANCE See Appearance; Beauty; Transfiguration.

PHYSICIAN (See also Healing; Health; Illness.)

1. In his disease he sought not to the Lord, but to the physicians. *2 Chron. 16:12*

2. Ye are all physicians of no value. *Job 13:4*

3. They that be whole need not a physician, but they that are sick. *Matt. 9:12*

4. [She] had suffered many things of many physicians, and had spent all that she had, and was nothing bettered, but rather grew worse. *Mark 5:26*

5. They shall lay hands on the sick, and they shall recover. *Mark 16:18*

6. Physician, heal thyself. *Luke 4:23*

7. Luke, the beloved physician. *Col. 4:14*

PIETY See Holiness.

PITY (See also God, Mercy of; Mercy; Sympathy.)

1. Have pity upon me. *Job 19:21*

2. Like as a father pitieth his children, so the Lord pitieth them that fear him. *Ps. 103:13*

3. He that hath pity upon the poor lendeth unto the Lord; and that which he hath given will he pay him again. *Prov. 19:17*

4. Blessed are the merciful: for they shall obtain mercy. *Matt. 5:7*

5. Shouldest not thou also have had compassion on thy fellow-servant, even as I had pity on thee? *Matt. 18:33*

6. The Lord is very pitiful, and of tender mercy. *James 5:11*

PLEASURE (See also Amusement.)

1. He that loveth pleasure shall be a poor man. *Prov. 21:17*

2. I commended mirth, because a man hath no better thing under the sun, than to eat, and to drink, and to be merry; for that shall abide with him of his labor the days of his life. *Eccl. 8:15*

3. Go thy way, eat thy bread with joy, and drink thy wine with a merry heart; for God now accepteth thy works. *Eccl. 9:7*

4. Let us eat and drink; for tomorrow we shall die. *Isa. 22:13*

5. That which fell among thorns are they, which, when they have heard, go forth, and are choked with cares and riches and

pleasures of this life, and bring no fruit to perfection. *Luke 8:14*
6. Soul, thou hast much goods laid up for many years; take thine ease, eat, drink, and be merry. *Luke 12:19*
7. Lovers of pleasures more than lovers of God. *2 Tim. 3:4*
8. Choosing rather to suffer affliction with the people of God, than to enjoy the pleasures of sin for a season. *Heb. 11:25*
9. [They] shall receive the reward of unrighteousness, as they that count it pleasure to riot in the day time. *2 Peter 2:13*

PLEDGE   See Covenant; Vow.

PLENTIFULNESS   See Abundance; Fertility.

PLOT   See Conspiracy.

POLITENESS   See Courtesy.

POLITICS   See Diplomacy; Nation; Patriotism; Peacemaking.

POLLUTION   (See also Corruption; Drug Abuse; Earth; Environment.)
1. Ye shall not pollute the land wherein ye are. *Num. 35:33*
2. Thou shalt die in a polluted land. *Amos 7:17*
3. Because it is polluted, it shall destroy you, even with a sore destruction. *Mic. 2:10*
4. If after they have escaped the pollutions of the world . . . they are again entangled therein, and overcome, the latter end is worse with them than the beginning. *2 Peter 2:20*
5. Many men died of the waters, because they were made bitter. *Rev. 8:11*
6. There arose a great smoke . . . as the smoke of a great furnace; and the sun and the air were darkened by reason of the smoke. *Rev. 9:2*

POSSESSION, SATANIC   See Demons; Exorcism.

POSTPONEMENT   See Procrastination.

POVERTY   (See also Beggar; Need.)
1. The poor shall never cease out of the land . . . open thine hand wide unto thy brother, to thy poor, and to thy needy. *Deut. 15:11*
2. Blessed is he that considereth the poor: the Lord will deliver him in time of trouble. *Ps. 41:1*
3. I am poor and needy, and my heart is wounded within me. *Ps. 109:22*
4. He raiseth up the poor out of the dust, and lifteth the needy out of the dunghill; that he may set him with princes. *Ps. 113:7,8*
5. The poor is hated even of his own neighbor . . . He that

despiseth his neighbor sinneth: but he that hath mercy on the poor, happy is he. *Prov. 14:20,21*

6. Better is the poor that walketh in his uprightness, than he that is perverse in his ways, though he be rich. *Prov. 28:6*

7. Give me neither poverty nor riches. *Prov. 30:8*

8. The poor shall feed, and the needy shall lie down in safety. *Isa. 14:30*

9. Ye have the poor with you always, and whensoever ye will ye may do them good. *Mark 14:7*

10. Blessed be ye poor: for yours is the kingdom of God. *Luke 6:20*

11. As poor, yet making many rich; as having nothing, and yet possessing all things. *2 Cor. 6:10*

12. Hath not God chosen the poor of this world rich in faith, and heirs of the kingdom? *James 2:5*

POWER   (See also Authority; God, The Almighty; God, Power of; Strength.)

1. As a prince hast thou power with God and with men, and hast prevailed. *Gen. 32:28*

2. Thy right hand, O Lord, is become glorious in power: thy right hand, O Lord, hath dashed in pieces the enemy. *Exod. 15:6*

3. He giveth power to the faint; and to them that have no might he increaseth strength. *Isa. 40:29*

4. Thou, O king, art a king of kings: for the God of heaven hath given thee a kingdom, power, and strength, and glory. *Dan. 2:37*

5. For thine is the kingdom, and the power, and the glory. *Matt. 6:13*

6. Thou hast given him power over all flesh, that he should give eternal life to as many as thou hast given him. *John 17:2*

7. Ye shall receive power, after that the Holy Ghost is come upon you. *Acts 1:8*

8. Let every soul be subject unto the higher powers. For there is no power but of God: the powers that be are ordained of God. *Rom. 13:1*

9. He is able even to subdue all things unto himself. *Phil. 3:21*

PRAISE   (See also Glory; Music; Prayer; Song; Thanksgiving; Worship.)

1. Whoso offereth praise glorifieth me. *Ps. 50:23*

2. O Lord, open thou my lips; and my mouth shall show forth thy praise. *Ps. 51:15*

3. From the rising of the sun unto the going down of the same the Lord's name is to be praised. *Ps. 113:3*

4. Let everything that hath breath praise the Lord. *Ps. 150:6*

5. My soul doth magnify the Lord, and my spirit hath rejoiced in God my Savior . . . all generations shall call me blessed. For he that is mighty hath done to me great things; and holy is his name. *Luke 1:46,49*

6. There was with the angel a multitude of the heavenly host praising God, and saying, Glory to God in the highest. *Luke 2:13,14*

PRAYER   (See also Answer; Lord's Prayer; Meditation.)

1. Let the words of my mouth, and the meditation of my heart, be acceptable in thy sight, O Lord. *Ps. 19:14*

2. Hear the voice of my supplications when as I cry unto thee, when I lift up my hands toward thy holy oracle. *Ps. 28:2*

3. I have called daily upon thee, I have stretched out my hands unto thee. *Ps. 88:9*

4. The Lord is nigh unto all them that call upon him . . . in truth. *Ps. 145:18*

5. Incline thine ear, O Lord, and hear. *Isa. 37:17*

6. Ye shall seek me, and find me, when ye shall search for me with all your heart. *Jer. 29:13*

7. Ask, and it shall be given you; seek, and ye shall find; knock, and it shall be opened unto you. *Matt. 7:7*

8. If two of you shall agree on earth as touching any thing that they shall ask, it shall be done for them of my Father which is in heaven. *Matt. 18:19*

9. What things soever ye desire, when ye pray, believe that ye receive them, and ye shall have them. *Mark 11:24*

10. When ye pray, say, Our Father which art in heaven . . . *Luke 11:2*

11. Whatsoever ye shall ask in my name, that will I do, that the Father may be glorified in the Son. *John 14:13*

12. If ye abide in me, and my words abide in you, ye shall ask what ye will, and it shall be done unto you. *John 15:7*

13. Pray without ceasing. *1 Thess. 5:17*

14. Ye ask, and receive not, because ye ask amiss. *James 4:3*

15. Pray one for another, that ye may be healed. The effectual fervent prayer of a righteous man availeth much. *James 5:16*

PREACHER   See Ministry.

PREACHING   See Evangelism.

PREDESTINATION   (See also Election.)

1. Truly the Son of man goeth, as it was determined. *Luke 22:22*

2. It is not for you to know the times or the seasons, which the Father hath put in his own power. *Acts 1:7*

3. Do whatsoever thy hand and thy counsel determined before to be done. *Acts 4:28*

4. [God] hath determined the times before appointed. *Acts 17:26*

5. For whom he did foreknow, he [God] also did predestinate to be conformed to the image of his Son. *Rom. 8:29*

6. Having predestinated us unto the adoption of children by Jesus Christ to himself. *Eph. 1:5*

PREFERENCE   See Favoritism.

PREJUDICE   (See also Favoritism; Inequality; Race, Ethnic; Segregation.)

1. Stand by thyself, come not near to me; for I am holier than thou. These [that say this] are a smoke in my nose. *Isa. 65:5*

2. Why eateth your Master with publicans and sinners? *Matt. 9:11*

3. Ye blind guides, which strain at a gnat, and swallow a camel. *Matt. 23:24*

4. Master, we saw one casting out devils in thy name; and we forbad him, because he followeth not with us. And Jesus said unto him, Forbid him not: for he that is not against us is for us. *Luke 9:49,50*

5. I am not as other men are. *Luke 18:11*

6. They all murmured, saying, That he was gone to be guest with a man that is a sinner. *Luke 19:7*

7. Can there any good thing come out of Nazareth? *John 1:46*

8. The Jews have no dealings with the Samaritans. *John 4:9*

9. Saul, yet breathing out threatenings and slaughter against the disciples of the Lord. *Acts 9:1*

10. Are we better than they? *Rom. 3:9*

PREPARATION   (See also Willingness.)

1. Set thine house in order; for thou shalt die. *2 Kings 20:1*

2. Thou preparest a table before me in the presence of mine enemies: thou anointest my head with oil; my cup runneth over. *Ps. 23:5*

3. The preparations of the heart in man, and the answer of the tongue, is from the Lord. *Prov. 16:1*

4. Prepare ye the way of the Lord, make straight in the desert a highway for our God. *Isa. 40:3*

5. Since the beginning of the world men have not heard, nor perceived by the ear, neither hath the eye seen, O God, beside thee, what he hath prepared for him that waiteth for him. *Isa. 64:4*

6. Be ye also ready: for in such an hour as ye think not the Son of man cometh. *Matt. 24:44*

7. If I go and prepare a place for you, I will come again, and receive you unto myself; that where I am, there ye may be also. *John 14:3*

8. Your feet shod with the preparation of the gospel of peace. *Eph. 6:15*

9. Be ready always to give an answer to every man that asketh you a reason of the hope that is in you. *1 Peter 3:15*

PRESENT   See Gift.

PRESERVATION   See Protection.

PRIDE   (See also Boasting; Self-Centeredness; Vanity.)

1. Pride compasseth them about as a chain. *Ps. 73:6*

2. Only by pride cometh contention. *Prov. 13:10*

3. Every one that is proud in heart is an abomination . . . he shall not be unpunished. *Prov. 16:5*

4. Pride goeth before destruction, and an haughty spirit before a fall. *Prov. 16:18*

5. A man's pride shall bring him low. *Prov. 29:23*

6. The lofty looks of man shall be humbled, and the haughtiness of men shall be bowed down. *Isa. 2:11*

7. Because thou hast lifted up thyself in height . . . I have therefore delivered him into the hand of the mighty one of the heathen. *Ezek. 31:10,11*

8. Though thou exalt thyself as the eagle, and though thou set thy nest among the stars, thence will I bring thee down. *Obad. 1:4*

9. All the proud . . . shall be stubble: and the day that cometh shall burn them up. *Mal. 4:1*

10. If any man desire to be first, the same shall be last of all, and servant of all. *Mark 9:35*

11. He hath scattered the proud in the imagination of their hearts. *Luke 1:51*

12. Be not wise in your own conceits. *Rom. 12:16*

13. He is proud, knowing nothing. *1 Tim. 6:4*

14. God resisteth the proud, but giveth grace unto the humble. *James 4:6*

PRIEST   See Ministry.

PRIORITY   (See also Inferiority; Superiority.)

1. And thou shalt not go aside from any of the words which I command thee this day, to the right hand, or to the left, to go after other gods to serve them. *Deut. 28:14*

2. A day in thy courts is better than a thousand. I had rather be a doorkeeper in the house of my God, than to dwell in the tents of wickedness. *Ps. 84:10*

3. I will make him my first-born higher than the kings of the earth. *Ps. 89:27*

4. Seek ye first the kingdom of God, and his righteousness. *Matt. 6:33*

5. Many that are first shall be last; and the last shall be first. *Matt. 19:30*

6. The dead in Christ shall rise first. *1 Thess. 4:16*

7. I am Alpha and Omega, the beginning and the ending. *Rev. 1:8*

PRISON   See Imprisonment.

PRIVACY   See Solitude.

PROCRASTINATION   (See also Backsliding; Sloth; Tardiness.)

1. I will do tomorrow as the king hath said. *Esth. 5:8*

2. Boast not thyself of tomorrow; for thou knowest not what a day may bring forth. *Prov. 27:1*

3. Lord, suffer me first to go and bury my father. But Jesus said unto him, Follow me; and let the dead bury their dead. *Matt. 8:21,22*

4. Lord, I will follow thee; but let me first go bid them farewell, which are at home at my house. And Jesus said unto him, No man, having put his hand to the plough, and looking back, is fit for the kingdom of God. *Luke 9:61,62*

5. Why tarriest thou? arise, and be baptized. *Acts 22:16*

6. And as he [Paul] reasoned of righteousness, temperance, and judgment to come, Felix trembled, and answered, Go thy way for this time; when I have a convenient season, I will call for thee. *Acts 24:25*

PROFANITY   (See also Blasphemy.)
1. Thou shalt not take the name of the Lord thy God in vain. *Exod. 20:7*
2. He will curse thee to thy face. *Job 1:11*
3. As he clothed himself with cursing like as with his garment, so let it come into his bowels like water, and like oil into his bones. *Ps. 109:18*
4. Bless them that curse you. *Matt. 5:44*
5. Not that which goeth into the mouth defileth a man; but that which cometh out of the mouth. *Matt. 15:11*
6. Avoiding profane and vain babblings. *1 Tim. 6:20*

PROFESSION   See Vocation; Work.

PROGRESS   See Growth; Improvement; Self-Improvement.

PROMISCUITY   (See also Adultery; Lust; Prostitution; Seduction; Sex.)
1. His master's wife cast her eyes upon Joseph; and said, Lie with me. *Gen. 39:7*
2. King Solomon loved many strange women. . . . he had seven hundred wives, princesses, and three hundred concubines. *1 Kings 11:1,3*
3. No whoremonger . . . hath any inheritance in the kingdom of Christ and of God. *Eph. 5:5*
4. Abstain from fleshly lusts, which war against the soul. *1 Peter 2:11*
5. Giving themselves over to fornication, and going after strange flesh, [they] are set forth for an example, suffering the vengeance of eternal fire. *Jude 1:7*

PROMISE   See Covenant; Vow.

PROOF   See God, Existence of; Miracle; Reason; Sign.

PROPHECY   See Prophet; Tongues, Gift of.

PROPHETS   (See also False Prophet; Forerunner; Inspiration.)
1. The Lord God . . . revealeth his secret unto his servants the prophets. *Amos 3:7*
2. The prophets, do they live for ever? *Zech. 1:5*
3. It is not ye that speak, but the Spirit of your Father which speaketh in you. *Matt. 10:20*

4. A prophet is not without honor, save in his own country. *Matt. 13:57*

5. I send unto you prophets . . . and some of them ye shall kill and crucify. *Matt. 23:34*

6. Thou, child, shalt be called the prophet of the Highest: for thou shalt go before the face of the Lord to prepare his ways. *Luke 1:76*

7. Which of the prophets have not your fathers persecuted? *Acts 7:52*

8. Though I have the gift of prophecy . . . and have not charity, I am nothing. *1 Cor. 13:2*

9. We know in part, and we prophesy in part. *1 Cor. 13:9*

10. He that prophesieth speaketh unto men to edification, and exhortation, and comfort. . . . [he] edifieth the church. *1 Cor. 14:3,4*

11. God, who at sundry times and in divers manners spake in time past unto the fathers by the prophets. *Heb. 1:1*

12. Prophecy came not . . . by the will of man: but . . . by the Holy Ghost. *2 Peter 1:21*

PROSPERITY   See Success; Wealth.

PROSTITUTION   (See also Adultery; Promiscuity.)

1. Do not prostitute thy daughter, to cause her to be a whore; lest the land fall to whoredom, and the land become full of wickedness. *Lev. 19:29*

2. Thou shalt not bring the hire of a whore, or the price of a dog [a male prostitute] . . . these are abomination unto the Lord. *Deut. 23:18*

3. The lips of a strange woman drop as a honeycomb, and her mouth is smoother than oil: but her end is bitter as wormwood, sharp as a two-edged sword. Her feet go down to death; her steps take hold on hell. . . . Remove thy way far from her, and come not nigh the door of her house. *Prov. 5:3–8*

4. Keep thee from the strange woman . . . which flattereth with her words. . . . Now is she without, now in the streets, and lieth in wait at every corner. *Prov. 7:5,12*

5. The mouth of strange women is a deep pit. *Prov. 22:14*

6. He that keepeth company with harlots spendeth his substance. *Prov. 29:3*

7. Know ye not that your bodies are the members of Christ? shall I then take the members of Christ, and make them the members of a harlot? God forbid. *1 Cor. 6:15*

PROTECTION (See also God, Help of; Passover; Refuge.)
1. Two of every sort shalt thou bring into the ark, to keep them alive with thee. *Gen. 6:19*
2. The Lord watch between me and thee, when we are absent one from another. *Gen. 31:49*
3. Keep me as the apple of the eye; hide me under the shadow of thy wings. *Ps. 17:8*
4. The Lord is my shepherd; I shall not want. . . . though I walk through the valley of the shadow of death, I will fear no evil: for thou art with me. *Ps. 23:1,4*
5. The Lord is my light and my salvation; whom shall I fear? The Lord is the strength of my life; of whom shall I be afraid? *Ps. 27:1*
6. He shall cover thee with his feathers, and under his wings shall thou trust: his truth shall be thy shield and buckler. *Ps. 91:4*
7. The Lord is thy keeper. . . . [He] shall preserve thee from all evil. *Ps. 121:5–7*
8. Sparrows . . . shall not fall on the ground without your Father. But the very hairs of your head are all numbered. Fear ye not therefore, ye are of more value than many sparrows. *Matt. 10:29–31*
9. I give unto you power to tread on serpents and scorpions, and over all the power of the enemy: and nothing shall by any means hurt you. *Luke 10:19*
10. Put on the whole armor of God, that ye may be able to stand against the wiles of the devil. *Eph. 6:11*

PROTEST (See also Church, Criticism of; Rebellion; Rejection.)
1. They agreed not among themselves. *Acts 28:35*

PRUDENCE See Carefulness; Caution; Discretion.

PSALM See Music; Praise; Song.

PUNISHMENT (See also Capital Punishment; Chastisement; Discipline; Hell; Result; Retaliation.)
1. [I] will smite all the first-born in the land of Egypt . . . and against all the gods of Egypt I will execute judgment. *Exod. 12:12*
2. If ye . . . will not do all my commandments, but that ye break my covenant: I also will do this unto you; I will even appoint over you terror, consumption. . . . And I will set my face against you. *Lev. 26:15–17*
3. My father hath chastised you with whips, but I will chastise you with scorpions. *1 Kings 12:11*

4. The wicked shall not be unpunished. *Prov. 11:21*

5. I will punish the world for their evil, and the wicked for their iniquity. *Isa. 13:11*

6. Ye serpents, ye generation of vipers, how can ye escape the damnation of hell? *Matt. 23:33*

7. Depart from me, ye cursed, into everlasting fire, prepared for the devil. *Matt. 25:41*

9. [He] will gather the wheat into his garner; but the chaff he will burn with fire unquenchable. *Luke 3:17*

10. He that believeth not is condemned. *John 3:18*

11. He that doeth wrong shall receive for the wrong which he hath done: and there is no respect of persons. *Col. 3:25*

PURITY (See also Celibacy; Holiness; Impurity; Innocence; Virginity; Virtue.)

1. Shall a man be more pure than his Maker? *Job 4:17*

2. The commandment of the Lord is pure, enlightening the eyes. *Ps. 19:8*

3. The words of the pure are pleasant. *Prov. 15:26*

4. Blessed are the pure in heart: for they shall see God. *Matt. 5:8*

5. Whatsoever things are pure . . . think on these things. *Phil. 4:8*

6. Keep thyself pure. *1 Tim. 5:22*

7. Unto the pure all things are pure. *Titus 1:15*

8. Every man that hath this hope in him purifieth himself, even as he is pure. *1 John 3:3*

PURPOSE See Christ, Purpose of; Church, Mission of; Intention; Reason.

PYROMANIA See Arson.

QUARREL   See Argument; Fighting.

QUESTION   (See also Curiosity; Doubt.)

1. The queen of Sheba . . . came to prove him [Solomon] with hard questions. *1 Kings 10:1*

2. If a man die, shall he live again? *Job 14:14*

3. Why reason ye these things in your hearts? *Mark 2:8*

4. What manner of man is this, that even the wind and the sea obey him. *Mark 4:41*

5. After three days they found him in the temple, sitting in the midst of the doctors, both hearing them, and asking them questions. *Luke 2:46*

6. [Herod] questioned with him in many words; but he answered him nothing. *Luke 23:9*

7. How can these things be? *John 3:9*

8. Why asketh thou me? ask them which heard me. *John 18:21*

9. Do all things without murmurings and disputings. *Phil. 2:14*

10. Foolish and unlearned questions avoid. *1 Tim. 2:23*

QUIETNESS   See Peace; Silence.

RACE, ETHNIC   (See also Integration; Prejudice; Segregation.)
1. Eve . . . was the mother of all living. *Gen.* 3:20
2. Therefore is the name of it called Babel; because the Lord did there confound the language of all the earth: and from thence did the Lord scatter them abroad upon the face of all the earth. *Gen.* 11:9
3. Can the Ethiopian change his skin? *Jer.* 13:23
4. It is an unlawful thing for a man that is a Jew to keep company, or come unto one of another nation. *Acts* 10:28
5. [God] hath made of one blood all nations of men for to dwell on all the face of the earth. *Acts* 17:26
6. There is neither Greek nor Jew, circumcision nor uncircumcision, Barbarian, Scythian, bond nor free: but Christ is all, and in all. *Col.* 3:11

RAIN   See Weather.

RAPE
1. If a man find a betrothed damsel in the field, and the man force her, and lie with her: then the man . . . shall die. *Deut.* 22:25
2. The man took his concubine, and brought her forth unto them; and they knew her, and abused her all the night until morning: and when the day began to spring, they let her go. *Judges* 19:25

RASHNESS   See Imprudence.

READINESS   See Preparation; Willingness.

READING   (See also Book; Scripture; Writing.)
1. Of making many books there is no end; and much study is a weariness of the flesh. *Eccl.* 12:12

2. Seek ye out of the book of the Lord, and read. *Isa. 34:16*

3. As his [Christ's] custom was, he went into the synagogue on the sabbath day, and stood up for to read. *Luke 4:16*

4. Understandest thou what thou readest? *Acts 8:30*

5. Ye are our epistle written in our hearts, known and read of all men. *2 Cor. 3:2*

6. Blessed is he that readeth. *Rev. 1:3*

7. No man was found worthy to open and to read the book. *Rev. 5:4*

REALIZATION   (See also Light; Revelation; Understanding.)

1. I have heard of thee by the hearing of the ear: but now mine eye seeth thee. *Job 42:5*

2. Lord, make me to know mine end, and the measure of my days, what it is; that I may know how frail I am. *Ps. 39:4*

3. In that day shall the deaf hear the words of the book, and the eyes of the blind shall see out of obscurity, and out of darkness. *Isa. 29:18*

4. To open their eyes, and to turn them from darkness to light, and from the power of Satan unto God, that they may receive forgiveness of sins, and inheritance among them which are sanctified by faith that is in me. *Acts 26:18*

5. Now we see through a glass, darkly; but then face to face: now I know in part; but then shall I know even as also I am known. *1 Cor. 13:12*

6. Awake thou that sleepest, and arise from the dead, and Christ shall give thee light. *Eph. 5:14*

REASON   (See also Justification.)

1. To every thing there is a season and a time to every purpose under the heaven. *Eccl. 3:1*

2. Produce your cause, saith the Lord; bring forth your strong reasons. *Isa. 41:21*

3. All things work together for good to them that love God. *Rom 8:28*

4. All things are for your sakes. *2 Cor. 4:15*

5. [God] hath saved us, and called us with a holy calling, not according to our works, but according to his own purpose and grace. *2 Tim. 1:9*

6. Be ready always to give an answer to every man that asketh you a reason of the hope that is in you. *1 Peter 3:15*

REBELLION   (See also Defiance; Protest; Sin.)

1. God forbid that we should rebel against the Lord, and turn this day from following the Lord. *Josh. 22:29*

2. Rebellion is as the sin of witchcraft. *1 Sam. 15:23*

3. They are of those that rebel against the light. *Job 24:13*

4. Why do the heathen rage . . . The kings of the earth set themselves, and the rulers take counsel together, against the Lord. *Ps. 2:1,2*

5. An evil man seeketh only rebellion. *Prov. 17:11*

6. Woe to the rebellious children. *Isa. 30:1*

7. They rebelled, and vexed his holy Spirit: therefore he was turned to be their enemy, and he fought against them. *Isa. 63:10*

8. This people hath a revolting and a rebellious heart; they are revolted and gone. *Jer. 5:23*

9. I will cast thee from off the face of the earth: this year thou shalt die, because thou hast taught rebellion against the Lord. *Jer. 28:16*

REBIRTH   See Baptism; Born Again; Reincarnation.

REBUKE   See Chastisement.

RECONCILIATION   See Atonement; Christ, Purpose of; Forgiveness.

RECREATION   See Amusement; Pleasure.

REDEEMER   See Christ; Redemption; Savior.

REDEMPTION   (See also Atonement; Christ, Purpose of; Deliverance; Release; Remission of Sins; Salvation; Savior.)

1. God will redeem my soul from the power of the grave. *Ps. 49:15*

2. Let Israel hope in the Lord: for with the Lord there is mercy, and with him is plenteous redemption. *Ps. 130:7*

3. I have redeemed thee, I have called thee by thy name; thou art mine. *Isa. 43:1*

4. The redeemed of the Lord shall return . . . and everlasting joy shall be upon their head: they shall obtain gladness and joy; and sorrow and mourning shall flee away. *Isa. 51:11*

5. Blessed be the Lord God of Israel; for he hath visited and redeemed his people. *Luke 1:68*

6. God sent forth his Son . . . To redeem them that were under the law, that we might receive the adoption of sons. *Gal. 4:4,5*

7. Ye were not redeemed with corruptible things, as silver and gold . . . But with the precious blood of Christ. *1 Peter 1:18,19*

REFORM (See also **Conversion; Repentance; Self-Improvement.**

1. If ye will not be reformed by me by these things, but will walk contrary unto me; Then will I also walk contrary unto you. *Lev. 26:23,24*

2. They cleansed the chambers: and thither brought I again the vessels of the House of God. *Neh. 13:9*

3. Amend your ways and your doings, and I will cause you to dwell in this place. *Jer. 7:3*

4. Jesus went into the temple of God, and cast out all them that sold and bought in the temple, and overthrew the tables of the moneychangers, and the seats of them that sold doves. *Matt. 21:12*

5. No man putteth new wine into old bottles: else the new wine doth burst the bottles, and the wine is spilled, and the bottles will be marred: but new wine must be put into new bottles. *Mark 2:22*

6. Go, and sin no more. *John 8:11*

7. We shall not all sleep, but we shall all be changed. *1 Cor. 15:51*

8. Put on the new man. *Eph. 4:24*

9. Forgetting those things which are behind, and reaching forth unto those things which are before, I press toward the mark for the prize of the high calling of God in Christ Jesus. *Phil: 3:13,14*

10. Change our vile body, that it may be fashioned like unto his glorious body. *Phil. 3:21*

11. I saw a new heaven and a new earth. *Rev. 21:1*

REFUGE (See also **God, Help of; Help; Protection.**)

1. The eternal God is thy refuge, and underneath are the everlasting arms. *Deut. 33:27*

2. Abide thou with me, fear not: for he that seeketh my life seeketh thy life: but with me thou shalt be in safeguard. *1 Sam. 22:23*

3. They . . . embrace the rock for want of a shelter. *Job 24:8*

4. The Lord also will be a refuge for the oppressed, a refuge in times of trouble. *Ps. 9:9*

5. He that dwelleth in the secret place of the Most High shall abide under the shadow of the Almighty. . . . He is my refuge and my fortress. *Ps. 91:1,2*

6. In the multitude of counselors there is safety. *Prov. 11:14*

7. The fear of man bringeth a snare: but whoso putteth his trust in the Lord shall be safe. *Prov. 29:25*

8. My people shall dwell in a peaceable habitation, and in sure dwellings, and in quiet resting places. *Isa. 32:18*

REFUSAL   See Defiance; Rejection.

REGRESSION   See Backsliding.

REGRET   (See also Repentance.)

1. Let the day perish wherein I was born. *Job 3:3*

2. I abhor myself, and repent in dust and ashes. *Job 42:6*

3. Judas, which had betrayed him, when he saw that he was condemned, repented himself, and brought again the thirty pieces of silver to the chief priests and elders, Saying, I have sinned in that I have betrayed the innocent blood. *Matt. 27:3,4*

4. Peter went out, and wept bitterly. *Luke 22:62*

5. If ye through the Spirit do mortify the deeds of the body, ye shall live. *Rom. 8:13*

REJECTION   (See also Agnosticism; Atheism; Desertion; Faithlessness; Rebellion.)

1. They have not rejected thee, but they have rejected me. *1 Sam. 8:7*

2. The stone which the builders refused is become the head stone of the corner. *Ps. 118:22*

3. He is despised and rejected of men. *Isa. 53:3*

4. Your burnt offerings are not acceptable, nor your sacrifices sweet unto me. *Jer. 6:20*

5. The wise men . . . have rejected the word of the Lord; and what wisdom is in them? *Jer. 8:9*

6. Because thou hast rejected knowledge, I will also reject thee. *Hos. 4:6*

7. Whosoever shall deny me before men, him will I also deny before my Father which is in heaven. *Matt. 10:33*

8. Get thee behind me, Satan. *Matt. 16:23*

9. No prophet is accepted in his own country. *Luke 4:24*

10. Because thou art lukewarm, and neither cold nor hot, I will spew thee out of my mouth. *Rev. 3:16*

REJOICING   See Happiness.

RELAXATION   See Amusement; Pleasure; Rest.

RELEASE   (See also Deliverance.)

1. Weeping may endure for a night, but joy cometh in the morning. *Ps. 30:5*

2. Thou hast taken away all thy wrath. *Ps. 85:3*

3. [The Lord has chosen] to undo the heavy burdens, and to let

the oppressed go free, and that ye break every yoke. *Isa. 58:6*

4. The Spirit of the Lord God is upon me; because the Lord hath anointed me to preach good tidings unto the meek; he hath sent me to bind up the brokenhearted, to proclaim liberty to the captives, and the opening of the prison to them that are bound! *Isa. 61:1*

5. Father, into thy hands I commend my spirit. *Luke 23:46*

6. Knowest thou not that I have the power to crucify thee, and have power to release thee? *John 19:10*

RELIABILITY   See Faithfulness; God, Faithfulness of; Loyalty.

RELIANCE   See Dependence.

RELIEF   (See also Help.)

1. If thy brother be waxen poor, and fallen in decay with thee; then thou shalt relieve him: yea, though he be a stranger, or a sojourner; that he may live with thee. *Lev. 25:35*

2. Learn to do well . . . relieve the oppressed. *Isa. 1:17*

3. I will seek that which was lost and bring again that which was driven away, and will bind up that which was broken, and will strengthen that which was sick. *Ezek. 34:16*

4. Then the disciples, every man according to his ability, determined to send relief unto the brethren. *Acts 11:29*

5. She have relieved the afflicted. *1 Tim. 5:10*

RELIGION   See Belief; Cults, Religious; Faith; Idolatry; Natural Religion; Occult; Paganism.

RELIGIOUS CULTS   See Cults, Religious.

REMEMBRANCE   See Memory.

REMISSION OF SINS   (See also Atonement; Christ, Purpose of; Confession of Sins; Forgiveness; Redemption.)

1. Thou hast forgiven the iniquity of thy people, thou hast covered all their sin. *Ps. 85:2*

2. Though your sins be as scarlet, they shall be as white as snow. *Isa. 1:18*

3. This is my blood of the new testament, which is shed for many for the remission of sins. *Matt. 26:28*

4. Behold the Lamb of God, which taketh away the sin of the world. *John 1:29*

5. Repent, and be baptized every one of you in the name of Jesus Christ for the remission of sins. *Acts 2:38*

6. Being justified freely by his grace through the redemption that is in Christ Jesus . . . through faith in his blood . . . for the remission of sins that are past, through the forbearance of God. *Rom. 3:24,25*

REMORSE   See Regret; Repentance.

RENEWAL   See Born Again; Revival.

REPARATION   See Restitution.

REPAYMENT   See Restitution.

REPENTANCE   (See also Confession of Sins; Regret.)

1. Woe is me! for I am undone. *Isa. 6:5*

2. Let the wicked forsake his way, and the unrighteous man his thoughts: and let him return unto the Lord, and he will have mercy upon him; and to our God, for he will abundantly pardon. *Isa. 55:7*

3. If the wicked will turn from all his sins that he hath committed, and keep all my statues, and do that which is lawful and right, he shall surely live, he shall not die. *Ezek. 18:21*

4. Turn ye even to me with all your heart, and with fasting, and with weeping, and with mourning: And rend your heart, and not your garments. *Joel 2:12,13*

5. Repent ye: for the kingdom of heaven is at hand. *Matt. 3:2*

6. I am not come to call the righteous, but sinners to repentance. *Matt. 9:13*

7. Father, I have sinned against heaven, and in thy sight, and am no more worthy to be called thy son. *Luke 15:21*

8. Repent ye therefore, and be converted, that your sins may be blotted out, when the times of refreshing shall come from the presence of the Lord. *Acts 3:19*

9. I rejoice, not that ye were made sorry, but that ye sorrowed to repentance. . . . For godly sorrow worketh repentance to salvation not to be repented of. *2 Cor. 7:9,10*

REPRESSION   See Oppression.

REPRODUCTION   See Fertility; Marriage.

REPROOF   See Chastisement.

REPUTATION   (See also Fame.)

1. O Lord our Lord, how excellent is thy name in all the earth! *Ps. 8:9*

2. His name shall endure for ever: his name shall be continued as long as the sun: and men shall be blessed in him: all nations shall call him blessed. *Ps. 72:17*

3. A good name is rather to be chosen than great riches. *Prov. 22:1*

4. Her husband is known in the gates, when he sitteth among the elders of the land. *Prov. 31:33*

5. A good name is better than precious ointment. *Eccl. 7:1*

6. A prophet is not without honor, save in his own country, and in his own house. *Matt. 13:57*

7. Your names are written in heaven. *Luke 10:20*

8. [Christ Jesus] made himself of no reputation, and took upon him the form of a servant, and was made in the likeness of men. *Phil. 2:7*

9. Whose names are in the book of life. *Phil. 4:3*

REQUIREMENT   See Christian Obligation; Duty.

RESENTMENT   See Anger; Bitterness; Envy; Hatred; Jealousy; Malice.

RESIGNATION   See Acceptance; Tolerance.

RESOLUTION   See Decision; Determination; Intention.

RESPECT   (See also Courtesy; Fear of the Lord.)

1. Honor thy father and thy mother. *Exod. 20:12*

2. Honor the face of the old man. *Lev. 19:32*

3. [God] respecteth not any that are wise of heart. *Job 37:24*

4. I will meditate in thy precepts, and have respect unto thy ways. *Ps. 119:15*

5. God is no respecter of persons: But in every nation he that feareth him, and worketh righteousness, is accepted with him *Acts 10:34,35*

6. Render therefore to all their dues . . . honor to whom honor [is due]. *Rom. 13:7*

7. In lowliness of mind let each esteem other better than themselves. *Phil. 2:3*

8. Honor all men. Love the brotherhood. Fear God. Honor the king. *1 Peter 2:17*

RESPONSE   See Answer.

RESPONSIBILITY   (See also Blame; Christian Obligation; Duty.)

1. The fathers shall not be put to death for the children, neither shall the children be put to death for the fathers: every man shall be put to death for his own sin. *Deut. 24:16*

2. And be it indeed that I have erred, mine error remaineth with myself. *Job 19:4*

3. The soul that sinneth, it shall die . . . the righteousness of the righteous shall be upon him, and the wickedness of the wicked shall be upon him. *Ezek. 18:20*

4. I must be about my Father's business. *Luke 2:49*

5. Render therefore unto Caesar the things which be Caesar's, and unto God the things which be God's. *Luke 20:25*

6. Owe no man any thing, but to love one another: for he that loveth another hath fulfilled the law. *Rom. 13:8*

7. Every one of us shall give account of himself to God. *Rom. 14:12*

8. If God so loved us, we ought also to love one another. *1 John 4:11*

REST   (See also Sabbath.)

1. Six days thou shalt do thy work, and on the seventh day thou shalt rest. *Exod. 23:12*

2. It is vain for you to rise up early, to sit up late, to eat the bread of sorrows: for so he giveth his beloved sleep. *Ps. 127:2*

3. I will not give sleep to mine eyes, or slumber to mine eyelids, until I find out a place for the Lord. *Ps. 132:4,5*

4. Come unto me, all ye that labor and are heavy laden, and I will give you rest. *Matt. 11:28*

5. And he said to them, Come ye yourselves apart into a desert place, and rest a while. *Mark 6:31*

6. Watch ye therefore . . . Lest coming suddenly he find you sleeping. *Mark 13:35,36*

7. There remaineth therefore a rest to the people of God. For he that is entered into his rest, he also hath ceased from his own works, as God did from his. Let us labor therefore to enter into that rest, lest any man fall after . . . unbelief. *Heb. 4:9–11*

RESTITUTION   (See also Borrowing and Lending.)

1. He should make full restitution. *Exod. 22:3*

2. He shall make amends for the harm that he hath done. *Lev. 5:16*

3. He shall recompense his trespass with the principal thereof, and add unto it the fifth part thereof, and give it unto him against whom he hath trespassed. *Num. 5:7*

4. According to his substance shall the restitution be. *Job 20:18*

5. When I come again, I will repay thee. *Luke 10:35*

6. If I have taken any thing from any man by false accusation, I restore him fourfold. *Luke 19:8*

7. Recompense to no man evil for evil. *Rom. 12:17*

RESTORATION   See Healing; Reunion; Revival.

RESTRAINT   See Moderation; Self-Control.

RESULT   (See also Excommunication; Punishment; Reward.)

1. His mischief shall return upon his own head. *Ps. 7:16*

2. Thou renderest to every man according to his work. *Ps. 62:12*

3. Whoso rewardeth evil for good, evil shall not depart from his house. *Prov. 17:13*

4. Whoso diggeth a pit shall fall therein: and he that rolleth a stone, it will return upon him. *Prov. 26:27*

5. They have sown the wind, and they shall reap the whirlwind. *Hos. 8:7*

6. Ye have plowed wickedness, ye have reaped iniquity. *Hos. 10:13*

7. As thou hast done, it shall be done unto thee: thy reward shall return upon thine own head. *Obad. 1:15*

8. Some fell among the thorns; and the thorns sprung up, and choked them: But other fell into good ground, and brought forth fruit, some an hundredfold. *Matt. 13:7,8*

9. Unto every one that hath [used his talents] shall be given, and he shall have abundance: but from him that hath not shall be taken away even that which he hath. *Matt. 25:29*

10. Whatsoever a man soweth, that shall he also reap. *Gal. 6:7*

RESURRECTION OF THE DEAD   (See also Christ, Resurrection of; Death; Immortality; Millennium.)

1. If a man die, shall he live again? *Job 14:14*

2. God will redeem my soul from the power of the grave: for he shall receive me. *Ps. 49:15*

3. And many of them that sleep in the dust of the earth shall awake, some to everlasting life, and some to shame and everlasting contempt. *Dan. 12:2*

4. Thou shalt be recompensed at the resurrection of the just. *Luke 14:14*

5. The dead shall hear the voice of the Son of God. . . . And shall come forth; they that have done good, unto the resurrection of life; and they that have done evil, unto the resurrection of damnation. *John 5:25,29*

6. I am the resurrection, and the life: he that believeth in me, though he were dead, yet shall he live. *John 11:25*

7. We are buried with him by baptism into death: that like as Christ was raised up from the dead by the glory of the Father, even so we also should walk in newness of life. *Rom. 6:4*

8. As in Adam all die, even so in Christ shall all be made alive. *1 Cor. 15:22*

9. The resurrection of the dead . . . is sown in corruption; it is raised in incorruption: It is sown in dishonor; it is raised in glory: it is sown in weakness; it is raised in power: It is sown a natural body; it is raised a spiritual body. *1 Cor. 15:42–44*

RETALIATION   (See also God, Wrath of; Punishment; Result.)

1. Eye for eye, tooth for tooth. *Exod. 21:24*

2. To me belongeth vengeance . . . I will make mine arrows drunk with blood, and my sword shall devour flesh. *Deut. 32:35,42*

3. The sword shall never depart from thine house; because thou hast despised me. *2 Sam. 12:10*

4. I will recompense their iniquity and their sin double. *Jer. 16:18*

5. It hath been said, An eye for an eye, and a tooth for a tooth: But I say unto you . . . whosoever shall smite thee on thy right cheek, turn to him the other also. *Matt. 5:38,39*

6. Avenge not yourselves . . . Vengeance is mine; I will repay, saith the Lord. *Rom. 12:19*

7. If thine enemy hunger, feed him; if he thirst, give him drink: for in so doing thou shalt heap coals of fire on his head. *Rom. 12:20*

8. Jesus shall be revealed from heaven with his mighty angels, In flaming fire taking vengeance on them that know not God, and that obey not the gospel. *2 Thess. 1:7,8*

RETRIBUTION   See Punishment; Result; Retaliation.

RETURN   See Christ, Second Coming of; Reunion.

REUNION   (See also Atonement; God, Family of; Unity.)

1. God setteth the solitary in families. *Ps. 68:6*

2. The ransomed of the Lord shall return . . . they shall obtain joy and gladness, and sorrow and sighing shall flee away. *Isa. 35:10*

3. He that scattered Israel will gather him, and keep him, as a shepherd doth his flock. *Jer. 31:10*

4. Rejoice with me; for I have found my sheep which was lost. *Luke 15:6*

5. There is joy in the presence of the angels of God over one sinner that repenteth. *Luke 15:10*

6. This my son was dead, and is alive again; he was lost, and is found. *Luke 15:24*

REVELATION   (See also Discovery; Dream; God; God, Existence of; Mystery; Realization.)

1. There is a God in heaven that revealeth secrets. *Dan. 2:28*

2. Thou hast hid these things from the wise and prudent, and hast revealed them unto babes. *Matt. 11:25*

3. Nothing is secret, that shall not be made manifest; neither any thing hid, that shall not be known. *Luke 8:17*

4. What I do thou knowest not now; but thou shalt know hereafter. *John 13:7*

5. All things that I have heard of my Father I have made known unto you. *John 15:15*

6. We have received . . . the spirit which is of God; that we might know the things that are freely given to us of God. *1 Cor. 2:12*

7. I neither received it [the gospel] of man, neither was I taught it, but by the revelation of Jesus Christ. *Gal. 1:12*

REVENGE   See Retaliation.

REVERENCE   See Fear of the Lord; Respect.

REVIVAL   (See also Baptism; Born Again.)

1. The Lord is my shepherd. . . . He restoreth my soul. *Ps. 23:1,3*

2. Create in me a clean heart, O God; and renew a right spirit within me. *Ps. 51:10*

3. The spirit be poured upon us from on high, and the wilderness be a fruitful field. *Isa. 32:15*

4. They that wait upon the Lord shall renew their strength; they shall mount up with wings as eagles; they shall run, and not be weary; and they shall walk, and not faint. *Isa. 40:31*

5. They that dwell under his shadow shall . . . revive as the corn, and grow as the vine. *Hos. 14:7*

6. O Lord, revive thy work in the midst of the years. *Hab. 3:2*

7. Though our outward man perish, yet the inward man is renewed day by day. *2 Cor. 4:16*

8. Put on the new man, which is renewed in knowledge after the image of him that created him. *Col. 3:10*

REVOLUTION   See Rebellion.

REWARD   **(See also Crown; Punishment; Result; Salvation; Wages.)**

1. Have ye rewarded evil for good? *Gen. 44:4*

2. The Lord gave Job twice as much as he had before. *Job 42:10*

3. In keeping of them [commandments] there is great reward. *Ps. 19:11*

4. Because he hath set his love upon me, therefore will I deliver him: I will set him on high. *Ps. 91:14*

5. He that hath a bountiful eye shall be blessed; for he giveth of his bread to the poor. *Prov. 22:9*

6. God giveth to a man that is good in his sight wisdom, and knowledge, and joy. *Eccl. 11:1*

7. Cast thy bread upon the waters: for thou shalt find it after many days. *Eccl. 11:1*

8. Since the beginning of the world men have not heard, nor perceived by the ear, neither hath the eye seen, O God, beside thee, what he hath prepared for him that waiteth for him. *Isa. 64:4*

9. Great is your reward in heaven. *Matt. 5:12*

10. They which run in a race run all, but one receiveth the prize. *1 Cor. 9:24*

11. Whatsoever good thing any man doeth, the same shall he receive of the Lord. *Eph. 6:8*

12. I press toward the mark for the prize of the high calling of God in Christ Jesus. *Phil. 3:14*

RICHES   See Money; Wealth; Worldliness.

RIDICULE   See Scorn.

RIGHTEOUSNESS   (See also Goodness; Holiness; Impartiality; Virtue.)

1. And he [Abram] believed in the Lord; and he counted it to him for righteousness. *Gen. 15:6*

2. The righteous Lord loveth rightousness; his countenance doth behold the upright. *Ps. 11:7*

3. The righteous shall flourish like the palm tree: he shall grow like a cedar in Lebanon. *Ps. 92:12*

4. Better is a little with righteousness, than great revenues without right. *Prov. 16:8*

5. The wicked flee when no man pursueth: but the righteous are bold as a lion. *Prov. 28:1*

6. The work of righteousness shall be peace; and the effect of righteousness quietness and assurance for ever. *Isa. 32:17*

7. Blessed are they which do hunger and thirst after righteousness: for they shall be filled. *Matt. 5:6*

8. Blessed are they which are persecuted for righteousness' sake: for theirs is the kingdom of heaven. *Matt. 5:10*

9. But seek ye first the kingdom of God, and his righteousness; and all these things shall be added unto you. *Matt. 6:33*

10. Put on the whole armor of God . . . having your loins girt about with truth, and having on the breastplate of righteousness. *Eph. 6:11,14*

RISK See Danger.

RITUAL (See also Baptism; Celebration; Circumcision; Eucharist; Passover.)

1. Put off thy shoes from off thy feet, for the place whereon thou standest is holy ground. *Exod. 3:5*

2. Take of the blood, and strike it on the two side posts and on the upper door post of the houses. . . . it is the Lord's passover. *Exod. 12:7,11*

3. Ye shall keep it [Passover] in his appointed season: according to the rites of it, and according to all the ceremonies thereof. *Num. 9:3*

4. Man looketh on the outward appearance, but the Lord looketh on the heart. *1 Sam. 16:7*

5. I hate, I despise your feast days, and I will not smell in your solemn assemblies. Though you offer me burnt offerings and your meat offerings, I will not accept them . . . Take thou away from me the noise of thy songs . . . But let judgment run down as waters, and righteousness as a mighty stream. *Amos 5:21–24*

6. He took bread, and gave thanks, and brake it, and gave unto them, saying, This is my body which is given for you: this do in remembrance of me. *Luke 22:19*

7. Go ye therefore, and teach all nations, baptizing them in the name of the Father, and of the Son, and of the Holy Ghost. *Matt. 28:20*

RIVALRY See Competition.

ROBBERY See Thief.

ROCK

1. He is the Rock, his work is perfect. *Deut. 32:4*

2. The Lord is my rock, and my fortress, and my deliverer; . . . blessed be my rock; and exalted be the God of the rock of my salvation. *2 Sam. 22:2,47*

3. He brought me up also out of an horrible pit, out of the miry clay, and set my feet upon a rock, and established my goings. *Ps. 40:2*

4. Lead me to the rock that is higher than I. *Ps. 61:2*

5. A man shall be . . . as the shadow of a great rock in a weary land. *Isa. 32:2*

6. Whosoever heareth these sayings of mine, and doeth them, I will liken him unto a wise man, which built his house upon a rock . . . it fell not: for it was founded upon a rock. *Matt. 7:24,25*

7. Thou art Peter, and upon this rock I will build my church. *Matt. 16:18*

8. What is this then that is written, The stone which the builders rejected, the same is become the head of the corner? Whosoever shall fall upon that stone shall be broken; but on whomsoever it shall fall, it will grind him to powder. *Luke 20:17,18*

9. They drank of that spiritual Rock that followed them: and that Rock was Christ. *1 Cor. 10:4*

RUFFIAN   (See also Companions, Evil.)

1. The fool and the brutish person perish. *Ps. 49:10*

2. Deliver me, O my God, out of the hand of the wicked, out of the hand of the unrighteous and cruel man. *Ps. 71:4*

3. A brutish man knoweth not; neither doth a fool understand this. *Ps. 92:6*

4. I will . . . deliver thee into the hand of brutish men. *Ezek. 21:31*

5. With force and with cruelty have ye ruled them. *Ezek. 34:4*

RULE   See God, Law of; Golden Rule; Law.

RULER   See King.

RUMOR   See Gossip.

S

SABBATH   (See also Church, Attendance at; Rest.)

1. God blessed the seventh day, and sanctified it: because that in it he had rested from all his work. *Gen. 2:3*

2. Remember the sabbath day, to keep it holy. . . . in it thou shalt not do any work. *Exod. 20:8,10*

3. Bear no burden on the sabbath day. *Jer. 17:21*

4. The sabbath was made for man, and not man for the sabbath: Therefore the Son of man is Lord also of the sabbath. *Mark 2:27,28*

5. And he came to Nazareth, . . . and as his custom was, he went into the synagogue on the sabbath day, and stood up for to read. *Luke 4:16*

6. One man esteemeth one day above another: another esteemeth every day alike. . . . He that regardeth the day, regardeth it unto the Lord. *Rom. 14:5,6*

SACRIFICE   (See also Christ, Crucifixion of; Christ, Purpose of; Fasting; Lamb; Martyr; Scapegoat.)

1. To do justice and judgment is more acceptable to the Lord than sacrifice. *Prov. 21:3*

2. Bring no more vain oblations; incense is an abomination unto me. *Isa. 1:13*

3. I desired mercy, and not sacrifice; and the knowledge of God more than burnt offerings. *Hos. 6:6*

4. To love him with all the heart, and with all the understanding, and with all the soul, and with all the strength, and to love his neighbor as himself, is more than all whole burnt offerings and sacrifices. *Mark 12:33*

5. If any man will come after me, let him deny himself, and take up his cross daily, and follow me. *Luke 9:23*

6. The good shepherd giveth his life for the sheep. *John 10:11*

7. Present your bodies a living sacrifice, holy, acceptable unto God. *Rom. 12:1*

8. Christ also hath loved us, and hath given himself for us an offering and sacrifice to God. *Eph. 5:2*

SACRILEGE   See Blasphemy; Sin.

SADNESS   (See also Sorrow.)

1. Why is thy countenance sad, seeing thou art not sick? this is nothing else but sorrow of the heart. *Neh. 2:2*

2. I am weary with my groaning; all the night make I my bed to swim; I water my couch with my tears. Mine eye is consumed because of grief. *Ps. 6:6,7*

3. Weeping may endure for a night, but joy cometh in the morning. *Ps. 30:5*

4. They that sow in tears shall reap in joy. *Ps. 126:5*

5. A time to weep, and a time to laugh. *Eccl. 3:4*

6. She weepeth sore in the night . . . she hath none to comfort her: all her friends have dealt treacherously with her, they are become her enemies. *Lam. 1:2*

7. There shall be weeping and gnashing of teeth. *Matt. 8:12*

8. Blessed are ye that weep now: for ye shall laugh. *Luke 6:21*

9. Jesus wept. *John 11:35*

10. Ye shall weep and lament, but the world shall rejoice: and ye shall be sorrowful, but your sorrow shall be turned into joy. *John 16:20*

11. For godly sorrow worketh repentance to salvation not to be repented of: but the sorrow of the world worketh death. *2 Cor. 7:10*

12. God shall wipe away all tears from their eyes. *Rev. 7:17*

SAFETY   See Passover; Protection; Refuge.

SAINT   See Apostle; Disciple; Martyr.

SALARY   See Wages.

SALVATION   (See also Atonement; Born Again; Christ, Purpose of; Deliverance; Paradise; Protection; Redemption; Reward; Savior; Victory.)

1. I have seen God face to face, and my life is preserved. *Gen. 32:30*

2. God is my salvation; I will trust, and not be afraid. . . . with joy shall ye draw water out of the wells of salvation. *Isa. 12:2,3*

3. [John the Baptist shall] give knowledge of salvation unto his people by the remission of their sins. *Luke 1:77*

4. Whosoever shall call on the name of the Lord shall be saved. *Acts 2:21*

5. Now is the accepted time; behold, now is the day of salvation. *2 Cor. 6:2*

6. By grace are ye saved through faith; and that not of yourselves: it is the gift of God. *Eph. 2:8*

7. In my absence, work out your own salvation with fear and trembling. For it is God which worketh in you both to will and to do of his good pleasure. *Phil. 2:12,13*

8. Be sober, putting on the breastplate of faith and love; and for an helmet, the hope of salvation. *1 Thess. 5:8*

9. He that overcometh, the same shall be clothed in white raiment; and I will not blot out his name out of the book of life, but I will confess his name before my Father. *Rev. 3:5*

SANCTION   See Approval.

SANCTITY   See Holiness.

SATAN   See Demons.

SATISFACTION   See Contentment.

SAVIOR   (See also Christ; Christ, Purpose of; Deliverance; Redemption; Salvation.)

1. They shall cry unto the Lord because of the oppressors, and he shall send them a savior, and a great one, and he shall deliver them. *Isa. 19:20*

2. I, am the Lord; and beside me there is no savior. *Isa. 43:11*

3. He saved others; himself he cannot save. *Matt. 27:42*

4. Unto you is born this day . . . a Savior, which is Christ the Lord. *Luke 2:11*

5. The Son of man is not come to destroy men's lives, but to save them. *Luke 9:56*

6. We trust in the living God, who is the Savior of all men, specially of those that believe. *1 Tim. 4:10*

7. The Father sent the Son to be the Savior of the world. *1 John 4:14*

SCAPEGOAT   (See also Christ, Purpose of; Lamb; Martyr; Sacrifice.)

1. The scapegoat, shall be presented alive before the Lord, to make an atonement with him. . . . the goat shall bear upon him all their iniquities. *Lev. 16:10,22*

2. He was wounded for our transgressions, he was bruised for our iniquities: the chastisement of our peace was upon him; and with his stripes we are healed. *Isa. 53:5*

3. Behold the Lamb of God, which taketh away the sin of the world. *John 1:29*

4. It is expedient for us, that one man should die for the people, and that the whole nation perish not. *John 11:50*

5. Christ was once offered to bear the sins of many. *Heb. 9:28*

SCHISM   See Division.

SCORN   (See also Contempt; Hatred.)

1. They mocked the messengers of God, and despised his words, and misused his prophets. *2 Chron. 36:16*

2. I am as one mocked of his neighbor . . . the just upright man is laughed to scorn. *Job 12:4*

3. Our soul is exceedingly filled with the scorning of those that are at ease, and with the contempt of the proud. *Ps. 123:4*

4. He scorneth the scorners. *Prov. 3:34*

5. A scorner seeketh wisdom, and findeth it not. *Prov. 14:6*

6. Cast out the scorner, and contention shall go out; yea, strife and reproach shall cease. *Prov. 22:10*

7. They [the Chaldeans] shall scoff at the kings, and the princes shall be a scorn unto them. *Hab. 1:10*

8. They shall mock him, and shall scourge him, and shall spit upon him, and shall kill him. *Mark 10:34*

SCRIPTURE   (See also Book; Doctrine; God, Law of; Gospel; Infallibility; Inspiration; Interpretation; Reading; Writing.)

1. The writing was the writing of God. *Exod. 32:16*

2. [The Lord said] Take thee a roll of a book, and write therein all the words that I have spoken. *Jer. 36:2*

3. Search the scriptures; for in them ye think ye have eternal life. *John 5:39*

4. The scripture cannot be broken. *John 10:35*

5. These are written, that ye might believe that Jesus is the Christ, the Son of God; and that believing ye might have life through his name. *John 20:31*

6. All scripture is given by inspiration of God, and is profitable for doctrine, for reproof, for correction, for instruction in righ-

teousness: That the man of God may be perfect. *2 Tim. 3:16,17*
7. The grass withereth, and the flower thereof falleth away: but the word of the Lord endureth for ever. *1 Peter 1:24,25*
8. Seal not the sayings of the prophecy of this book. *Rev. 22:10*
9. If any man shall add unto these things [writings], God shall add unto him the plagues that are written in this book: And if any man shall take away from the words of the book of this prophecy, God shall take away his part out of the book of life, and out of the holy city, and from the things which are written in this book. *Rev. 22:18,19*

SEARCH   See Exploration.
SEASON   See Time.
SECLUSION   See Hiding; Solitude.
SECRECY   (See also Hiding; Mystery; Revelation.)
1. The secret things belong unto the Lord our God: but those things which are revealed belong unto us and to our children. *Deut. 29:29*
2. Tell it not in Gath, publish it not in the streets. *2 Sam. 1:20*
3. He [the wicked] lieth in wait secretly as a lion in his den. *Ps. 10:9*
4. Stolen waters are sweet, and bread eaten in secret is pleasant. *Prov. 9:17*
5. God shall bring every work into judgment, with every secret thing, whether it be good, or whether it be evil. *Eccl. 12:14*
6. Nothing is secret, that shall not be made manifest; neither any thing hid, that shall not be known. *Luke 8:17*
7. Every one that doeth evil hateth the light . . . lest his deeds should be reproved. *John 3:20*

SECURITY   See Protection; Trust.
SEDUCTION   (See also Promiscuity; Temptation.)
1. Entice him, and see wherein his great strength lieth. *Judg. 16:5*
2. With her much fair speech she caused him to yield. *Prov. 7:21*
3. In the latter times some shall depart from the faith, giving heed to seducing spirits, and doctrines of devils. *1 Tim. 4:1*
4. Evil men and seducers shall wax worse and worse, deceiving, and being deceived. *2 Tim. 3:13*
5. Every man is tempted, when he is drawn away of his own lust, and enticed. *James 1:14*
6. They allure through the lusts of the flesh, through much wantonness. *2 Peter 2:18*

SEGREGATION   See Division; Prejudice; Race, Ethnic.

SELF-CENTEREDNESS   (See also Pride; Selfishness; Vanity.)

1. If I justify myself, mine own mouth shall condemn me: if I say, I am perfect, it shall also prove me perverse. *Job 9:20*

2. The backslider in heart shall be filled with his own ways: and a good man shall be satisfied from himself. *Prov. 14:14*

3. He that trusteth in his own heart is a fool. *Prov. 28:26*

4. And I will say to my soul, Soul, thou hast much goods laid up for many years; take thine ease, eat, drink, and be merry. *Luke 12:19*

5. He that loveth his life shall lose it; and he that hateth his life in this world shall keep it unto life eternal. *John 12:25*

6. Who maketh thee to differ from another? and what hast thou that thou didst not receive? *1 Cor. 4:7*

7. Let him that thinketh he standeth take heed lest he fall. *1 Cor. 10:12*

8. If a man think himself to be something, when he is nothing, he deceiveth himself. *Gal. 6:3*

SELF-CONTROL   (See also Celibacy; Moderation; Patience; Silence; Sobriety; Tolerance.)

1. The spirit within me constraineth me. *Job 32:18*

2. He that is slow to anger is better than the mighty; and he that ruleth his spirit than he that taketh a city. *Prov. 16:32*

3. He that hath knowledge spareth his words. . . . Even a fool, when he holdeth his peace, is counted wise: and he that shutteth his lips is esteemed a man of understanding. *Prov. 17:27,28*

4. He that hath no rule over his own spirit is like a city that is broken down, and without walls. *Prov. 25:28*

5. Every man that striveth for the mastery is temperate in all things. . . . I keep under my body, and bring it into subjection: lest that by any means, when I have preached to others, I myself should be a castaway. *1 Cor. 9:25,27*

SELF-DENIAL   See Celibacy; Fasting; Sacrifice; Virginity.

SELF-IMPROVEMENT   (See also Growth; Improvement; Reform.)

1. The righteous also shall hold on his way, and he that hath clean hands shall be stronger and stronger. *Job 17:9*

2. The path of the just is as the shining light, that shineth more and more unto the perfect day. *Prov. 4:18*

3. The power which the Lord hath given me to edification, and not to destruction. *2 Cor. 13:10*

4. Put on the new man. *Eph. 4:24*

5. Therefore leaving the principles of the doctrine of Christ, let us go on unto perfection; not laying again the foundation of repentance from dead works and of faith toward God. *Heb. 6:1*

6. As newborn babes, desire the sincere milk of the word, that ye may grow thereby. *1 Peter 2:2*

SELF-INDULGENCE See Drunkenness; Gluttony; Pleasure; promiscuity; Selfishness.

SELFISHNESS (See also Greed; Self-Centeredness; Stinginess; Vanity.)

1. He that withholdeth corn, the people shall curse him. *Prov. 11:26*

2. For men to search their own glory is not glory. *Prov. 25:27*

3. Seekest thou great things for thyself? seek them not: for, behold, I will bring evil upon all flesh. *Jer. 45:5*

4. Let no man seek his own. *1 Cor. 10:24*

5. Whoso hath this world's good, and seeth his brother have need, and shutteth up his bowels of compassion from him, how dwelleth the love of God in him? *1 John 3:17*

SELF-RESTRAINT See Moderation; Self-Control.

SELF-RIGHTEOUSNESS See Hypocrisy; Self-Centeredness.

SELF-SATISFACTION See Contentment; Self-Centeredness.

SENSUALITY See Adultery; Lust; Promiscuity; Prostitution.

SEPARATION (See also Division; Divorce; Race, Ethnic.)

1. The Lord hath utterly separated me from his people. *Isa. 56:3*

2. He shall separate them one from another, as a shepherd divideth his sheep from the goats. *Matt. 25:32*

3. Blessed are ye, when men shall hate you, and when they shall separate you from their company, and shall reproach you, and cast out your name as evil. *Luke 6:22*

4. Between us and you there is a great gulf fixed: so that they which would pass from hence to you cannot; neither can they pass to us, that would come from hence. *Luke 16:26*

5. Who shall separate us from the love of Christ? shall tribulation, or distress, or persecution, or famine, or nakedness, or peril, or sword? *Rom. 8:35*

6. Ye have respect to him that weareth the gay clothing, and say unto him, Sit thou here in a good place; and say to the poor, Stand thou there, or sit here under my footstool: Are ye not then partial in yourselves, and are become judges of evil thoughts? *James 2:3,4*

SERVICE   (See also Christian Obligation; Obedience.)

1. We are the servants of the God of heaven and earth. *Ezra 5:11*

2. Serve the Lord with gladness: come before his presence with singing. *Ps. 100:2*

3. Thou shalt worship the Lord thy God, and him only shalt thou serve. *Matt. 4:10*

4. No man can serve two masters: for either he will hate the one, and love the other; or else he will hold to the one, and despise the other. Ye cannot serve God and mammon. *Matt. 6:24*

5. These many years do I serve thee, neither transgressed I at any time thy commandment. *Luke 15:29*

6. By love serve one another. *Gal. 5:13*

SEVEN DEADLY SINS   See Anger; Covetousness; Envy; Gluttony; Lust; Pride; Sloth.

SEX   (See also Adultery; Lust; Promiscuity; Prostitution; Sexual Perversion.)

1. He which made them at the beginning made them male and female. *Matt. 19:4*

2. To be carnally minded is death; but to be spiritually minded is life and peace. . . . the carnal mind is enmity against God. *Rom. 8:6,7*

3. The body is not for fornication, but for the Lord; and the Lord for the body. . . . therefore glorify God in your body, and in your spirit, which are God's. *1 Cor. 6:13,20*

4. There is neither male nor female: for ye are all one in Christ Jesus. *Gal. 3:28*

SEXUAL ASSAULT   See Rape; Seduction.

SEXUAL PERVERSION   (See also Homosexuality; Perversion.)

1. Whosoever lieth with a beast shall surely be put to death. *Exod. 22:19*

2. None of you shall approach to any that is near of kin to him, to uncover their nakedness. . . . it is wickedness. *Lev. 18:6,17*

3. Neither shalt thou lie with any beast to defile thyself therewith: neither shall any woman stand before a beast to lie down thereto: it is confusion. *Lev. 18:23*

4. Cursed be he that lieth with his father's wife . . . with his sister . . . with his mother-in-law. *Deut. 27:20–23*

5. Another hath lewdly defiled his daughter-in-law; and another in thee hath humbled his sister, his father's daughter. *Ezek. 22:11*

6. There is fornication among you, and such fornication . . . that one should have his father's wife. *1 Cor. 5:1*

7. These filthy dreamers defile the flesh. *Jude 1:8*

SHAME   (See also Cowardice; Guilt; Nakedness.)

1. I was afraid, because I was naked; and I hid myself. *Gen. 3:10*

2. I am ashamed and blush to lift up my face to thee, my God: for our iniquities are increased over our head, and our trespass is grown up unto the heavens. *Ezra 9:6*

3. Behold, I am vile; what shall I answer thee? I will lay mine hand upon my mouth. *Job 40:4*

4. My confusion is continually before me, and the shame of my face hath covered me. *Ps. 44:15*

5. As they were increased, so they sinned against me: therefore will I change their glory into shame. *Hos. 4:7*

6. The unjust knoweth no shame. *Zeph. 3:5*

7. Whosoever shall be ashamed of me and of my words, of him shall the Son of man be ashamed. *Luke 9:26*

8. They crucify to themselves the Son of God afresh, and put him to an open shame. *Heb. 6:6*

SHARING   See Charity; Evangelism; Fellowship; Generosity.

SHEEP   See Lamb; Shepherd.

SHELTER   See Refuge.

SHEPHERD   (See also Bishop; Elder; Lamb; Ministry.)

1. The Lord is my shepherd; I shall not want. *Ps. 23:1*

2. He shall feed his flock like a shepherd: he shall gather the lambs with his arm, and carry them in his bosom. *Isa. 40:11*

3. Woe be unto the pastors that destroy and scatter the sheep of my pasture. . . . I will gather the remnant of my flock. . . . And I will set up shepherds over them which shall feed them: and they shall fear no more, nor be dismayed, neither shall they be lacking. *Jer. 23:1–4*

4. Smite the shepherd, and the sheep shall be scattered. *Zech. 13:7*

5. Rejoice with me; for I have found my sheep which was lost. *Luke 15:6*

6. He that entereth in by the door is the shepherd of the sheep. . . . I am the door: by me if any man enter in, he shall be saved, and shall go in and out, and find pasture. *John 10:2,9*

7. I am the good shepherd. . . . I lay down my life for the sheep. *John 10:11,15*

SICKNESS See Illness.

SIGN (See also Miracle; Warning; Wonder.)

1. Let there be lights in the firmament of the heaven . . . and let them be for signs. *Gen. 1:14*

2. I do set my bow in the cloud, and it shall be for a token of a covenant between me and the earth. *Gen. 9:13*

3. My sabbaths ye shall keep: for it is a sign between me and you throughout your generations. *Exod. 31:13*

4. Be not dismayed at the signs of heaven. *Jer. 10:2*

5. The star, which they saw in the east, went before them, till it came and stood over where the young child was. *Matt. 2:9*

6. Can ye not discern the signs of the times? *Matt. 16:3*

7. What shall be the sign of thy coming, and of the end of the world? *Matt. 24:3*

8. This shall be a sign unto you; Ye shall find the babe wrapped in swaddling clothes, lying in a manger. *Luke 2:12*

9. This is an evil generation: they seek a sign; and there shall no sign be given it, but the sign of Jonah the prophet. *Luke 11:29*

SILENCE (See also Peace; Speaking.)

1. Even a fool, when he holdeth his peace, is counted wise: and he that shutteth his lips is esteemed a man of understanding. *Prov. 17:28*

2. A time to keep silence, and a time to speak. *Eccl. 3:7*

3. Better is a handful with quietness, than both the hands full with travail and vexation of spirit. *Eccl. 4:6*

4. The Lord is in his holy temple: let all the earth keep silence before him. *Hab. 2:20*

5. If these [disciples] should hold their peace, the stones would immediately cry out. *Luke 19:40*

6. He was led as a sheep to the slaughter; and like a lamb dumb before his shearer, so opened he not his mouth. *Acts 8:32*

7. Study to be quiet, and to do your own business. *1 Thess. 4:11*

SIMPLICITY   (See also Childlikeness; Innocence.)

1. The Lord preserveth the simple. *Ps. 116:6*

2. The entrance of thy words giveth light; it giveth understanding unto the simple. *Ps. 119:130*

3. How long, ye simple ones, will ye love simplicity? *Prov. 1:22*

4. In simplicity and godly sincerity, not with fleshly wisdom, but by the grace of God, we have had our conversation in the world, and more abundantly to you-ward. *2 Cor. 1:12*

5. I fear, lest by any means, as the serpent beguiled Eve through his subtlety, so you minds should be corrupted from the simplicity that is in Christ. *2 Cor. 11:3*

SIN   (See also Corruption; Crime; Decadence; Depravity; Evil; Impurity; Neglect.)

1. Ye shall not eat of it, neither shall ye touch it, lest ye die. . . . she took of the fruit thereof, and did eat, and gave also unto her husband with her; and he did eat. *Gen. 3:3,6*

2. Ye have sinned against the Lord: and be sure your sin will find you out. *Num. 32:23*

3. There is not a just man upon earth, that doeth good, and sinneth not. *Eccl. 7:20*

4. One sinner destroyeth much good. *Eccl. 9:18*

5. All manner of sin and blasphemy shall be forgiven unto men: but the blasphemy against the Holy Ghost shall not be forgiven unto men. *Matt. 12:31*

6. As by one man's disobedience many were made sinners, so by the obedience of one shall many be made righteous. *Rom. 5:19*

7. The wages of sin is death. *Rom. 6:23*

8. To him that knoweth to do good, and doeth it not, to him it is sin. *James 4:17*

9. If we say that we have no sin, we deceive ourselves. *1 John 1:8*

10. Sin is the transgression of the law. *1 John 3:4*

SINCERITY   (See also Honesty; Truth.)

1. Blessed is the man . . . in whose spirit there is no guile. *Ps. 32:2*

2. Let love be without dissimulation. *Rom. 12:9*

3. Not with eyeservice, as menpleasers; but as the servants of Christ, doing the will of God from the heart. *Eph. 6:6*

4. Grace be with all them that love our Lord Jesus Christ in sincerity. *Eph. 6:24*

5. Be sincere and without offense till the day of Christ. *Phil. 1:10*

SIN, CONFESSION OF   See Confession of Sins.

SIN, DEADLY   See Anger; Covetousness; Envy; Gluttony; Lust; Pride; Sloth.

SIN, REMISSION OF   See Remission of Sins.

SKEPTICISM   See Agnosticism; Doubt.

SLANDER   (See also Accusation; Blasphemy; Falsehood; Gossip.)

1. Whoso privily slandereth his neighbor, him will I cut off. *Ps. 101:5*

2. The mouth of the wicked and the mouth of the deceitful are opened against me: they have spoken against me with a lying tongue. *Ps. 109:2*

3. He that hideth hatred with lying lips, and he that uttereth a slander, is a fool. *Prov. 10:18*

4. Not that which goeth into the mouth defileth a man; but that which cometh out. *Matt. 15:11*

5. Be not deceived: evil communications corrupt good manners. *1 Cor. 15:33*

6. The tongue can no man tame; it is an unruly evil, full of deadly poison. *James 3:8*

7. Speak not evil one of another. *James 4:11*

SLAVERY   See Captivity; Imprisonment.

SLEEP   See Rest.

SLOTH   (See also Procrastination; Unemployment.)

1. Go to the ant . . . consider her ways, and be wise. . . . How long wilt thou sleep, O sluggard? when wilt thou arise out of thy sleep? *Prov. 6:6,9*

2. He that gathereth in summer is a wise son: but he that sleepeth in harvest is a son that causeth shame. *Prov. 10:5*

3. The soul of the sluggard desireth, and hath nothing: but the soul of the diligent shall be made fat. *Prov. 13:4*

4. He also that is slothful in his work is brother to him that is a great waster. *Prov. 18:9*

5. Slothfulness casteth into a deep sleep; and an idle soul shall suffer hunger. *Prov. 19:15*

6. By much slothfulness the building decayeth; and through idleness of the hands the house droppeth through. *Eccl. 10:18*

7. He that observeth the wind shall not sow; and he that regardeth the clouds shall not reap. *Eccl. 11:4*

8. [Be] Not slothful in business. *Rom. 12:11*

SLYNESS   See Cunning.

SMUGNESS   See Pride; Self-Centeredness.

SOBERNESS   See Sobriety.

SOBRIETY   (See also Drunkenness; Moderation; Self-Control.)

1. Every man that striveth for the mastery is temperate in all things. *1 Cor. 9:25*

2. Let us, who are of the day, be sober. *1 Thess. 5:8*

3. Aged men be sober. . . . aged women likewise, that they . . . may teach the young women to be sober. . . . Young men likewise exhort to be sober-minded. *Titus 2:2–6*

4. Be ye therefore sober, and watch unto prayer. *1 Peter 4:7*

SODOMY   See Homosexuality; Sexual Perversion.

SOLDIER   See Army, Christian; War.

SOLITUDE   (See also Loneliness.)

1. He himself went a day's journey into the wilderness. *1 Kings 19:4*

2. I watch, and am as a sparrow alone upon the housetop. *Ps. 102:7*

3. Two are better than one . . . if two lie together, then they have heat: but how can one be warm alone? *Eccl. 4:9,11*

4. Sit ye here, while I go and pray yonder. *Matt. 26:36*

5. He went out, and departed into a solitary place, and there prayed. *Mark 1:35*

SONG   (See also Celebration; Dancing; Music; Praise.)

1. The morning stars sang together, and all the sons of God shouted for joy. *Job 38:7*

2. Sing unto him a new song; play skilfully with a loud noise. *Ps. 33:3*

3. Make a joyful noise unto God, all ye lands: sing forth the honor of his name. *Ps. 66:1,2*

4. As he that taketh away a garment in cold weather, and as vinegar upon nitre, so is he that singeth songs to a heavy heart. *Prov. 25:20*

5. The Song of songs, which is Solomon's. *Song of Sol. 1:1*

6. The Lord JEHOVAH is my strength and my song. *Isa. 12:2*

7. Let the word of Christ dwell in you richly in all wisdom; teaching and admonishing one another in psalms and hymns and spiritual songs, singing with grace in your hearts to the Lord. *Col. 3:16*

8. Is any merry? let him sing psalms. *James 5:13*

SOOTHSAYING   See Astrology; Fortunetelling.

SORCERY   See Occult.

SORROW   (See also Distress; Heartbreak; Sadness; Suffering.)

1. I behaved myself as though he had been my friend or brother: I bowed down heavily, as one that mourneth for his mother. *Ps. 35:14*

2. Even in laughter the heart is sorrowful; and the end of that mirth is heaviness. *Prov. 14:13*

3. A time to weep, and a time to laugh; a time to mourn, and a time to dance. *Eccl. 3:4*

4. Sorrow is better than laughter: for by the sadness of the countenance the heart is made better. *Eccl. 7:3*

5. I will turn their mourning into joy, and will comfort them, and make them rejoice from their sorrow. *Jer. 31:13*

6. Blessed are they that mourn: for they shall be comforted. *Matt. 5:4*

7. My soul is exceeding sorrowful, even unto death. *Matt. 26:38*

8. Woe unto you that laugh now! for ye shall mourn and weep. *Luke 6:25*

SOUL   (See also Heart; Immortality; Resurrection of the Dead; Spirit, Human.)

1. The Lord God formed man of the dust of the ground, and breathed into his nostrils the breath of life; and man became a living soul. *Gen. 2:7*

2. As the hart panteth after the water brooks, so panteth my soul after thee, O God. *Ps. 42:1*

3. He that keepeth the commandment keepeth his own soul. *Prov. 19:16*

4. All souls are mine; as the soul of the father, so also the soul of the son is mine: the soul that sinneth, it shall die. *Ezek. 18:4*

5. Fear not them which kill the body, but are not able to kill the soul: but rather fear him which is able to destroy both soul and body in hell. *Matt. 10:28*

6. Mary said, My soul doth magnify the Lord. *Luke 1:46*

7. Though our outward man perish, yet the inward man is renewed day by day. *2 Cor. 4:16*

SPEAKING   (See also Silence; Tongues, Gift of; Word.)

1. I am not eloquent . . . but I am slow of speech, and of a slow tongue. *Exod. 4:10*

2. How forcible are right words! *Job 6:25*

3. The words of his mouth were smoother than butter . . . softer than oil, yet were they drawn swords. *Ps. 55:21*

4. A soft answer turneth away wrath: but grievous words stir up anger. . . . A wholesome tongue is a tree of life. *Prov. 15:1,4*

5. Pleasant words are as an honeycomb, sweet to the soul, and health to the bones. *Prov. 16:24*

6. A word fitly spoken is like apples of gold in pictures of silver. *Prov. 25:11*

7. A time to keep silence, and a time to speak. *Eccl. 3:7*

8. Out of the abundance of the heart the mouth speaketh. . . . by thy words thou shalt be justified, and by thy words thou shalt be condemned. *Matt. 12:34,37*

9. Though I speak with the tongues of men and of angels, and have not charity, I am become as sounding brass, or a tinkling cymbal. *2 Cor. 13:1*

10. Seeing then that we have such hope, we use great plainness of speech. *2 Cor. 3:12*

11. Let their conversation be as it becometh the gospel of Christ. *Phil. 1:27*

12. Let your speech be alway with grace, seasoned with salt, that ye may know how ye ought to answer every man. *Col. 4:6*

SPEECH   See Language; Speaking.

SPIRIT, EVIL   See Demons; Exorcism.

SPIRIT, HOLY   See Holy Spirit.

SPIRIT, HUMAN   (See also Heart; Mind; Soul.)

1. Create in me a clean heart, O God; and renew a right spirit within me. *Ps. 51:10*

2. The spirit of a man will sustain his infirmity; but a wounded spirit who can bear? *Prov. 18:14*

3. The spirit of man is the candle of the Lord, searching all the inward parts. *Prov. 20:27*

4. Blessed are the poor in spirit: for theirs is the kingdom of heaven. *Matt. 5:3*

5. The spirit indeed is willing, but the flesh is weak. *Matt. 26:41*

6. Ye have not received the spirit of bondage again to fear; but ye have received the Spirit of adoption, whereby we cry, Abba, Father. The Spirit itself beareth witness with our spirit, that we are the children of God. *Rom. 8:15,16*

7. There is a natural body, and there is a spiritual body. And so it is written, The first man Adam was made a living soul; the last Adam was made a quickening spirit. *1 Cor. 15:44,45*

SPIRITUALISM   See Occult.

SPITE   See Bitterness; Malice; Retaliation.

SPORTS   See Competition.

SPYING   See Espionage.

STABILITY   See Constancy; Rock.

STATUS   See Priority.

STEADFASTNESS   See Constancy; Faithfulness; Loyalty.

STEALING   See Thief.

STERILITY   (See also Fertility.)

1. Isaac entreated the Lord for his wife, because she was barren: and the Lord was entreated of him, and Rebekah his wife conceived. *Gen. 25:21*

2. He turneth rivers into a wilderness, and the watersprings into dry ground; a fruitful land into barrenness. *Ps. 107:33,34*

3. The eunuch say, Behold, I am a dry tree. *Isa. 56:3*

4. Their root is dried up, they shall bear no fruit. *Hos. 9:16*

5. Rejoice, thou barren that bearest not . . . the desolate hath many more children than she which hath a husband. *Gal. 4:27*

STINGINESS   (See also Greed; Selfishness.)

1. He that withholdeth corn, the people shall curse him. *Prov. 11:26*

2. He that giveth unto the poor shall not lack: but he that hideth his eyes shall have many a curse. *Prov. 28:27*

3. There is a sore evil which I have seen under the sun, namely, riches kept for the owners thereof to their hurt. *Eccl. 5:13*

4. Ananias, with Sapphira his wife, sold a possession, And kept back part of the price. *Acts 5:1,2*

STORM   See Weather.

STORY   See Parable.

STRANGER   (See also Adoption; Exile; Guest; Hospitality.)

1. I have been a stranger in a strange land. *Exod. 2:22*

2. Love ye therefore the stranger: for ye were strangers in the land of Egypt. *Deut. 10:19*

3. The Lord preserveth the strangers. *Ps. 146:9*

4. I was a stranger, and ye took me in. *Matt. 25:35*

5. Other sheep I have, which are not of this fold: them also I must bring, and they shall hear my voice; and there shall be one fold, and one shepherd. *John 10:16*

6. Ye who sometimes were far off are made nigh by the blood of Christ. . . . therefore ye are no more strangers and foreigners, but fellow citizens with the saints, and of the household of God. *Eph. 2:13,19*

7. Be not forgetful to entertain strangers: for thereby some have entertained angels unawares. *Heb. 13:2*

STRENGTH   (See also God, the Almighty; God, Power of; Power; Weakness.)

1. The Lord is my strength and song. *Exod. 15:2*

2. Delilah said to Samson, Tell me, I pray thee, wherein thy great strength lieth. *Judg. 16:6*

3. The Lord is my strength and my shield. *Ps. 28:7*

4. Strengthen ye the weak hands, and confirm the feeble knees. *Isa. 35:3*

5. The Lord God is my strength, and he will make my feet like hinds' feet, and he will make me to walk upon mine high places. *Hab. 3:19*

6. My strength is made perfect in weakness. . . . for when I am weak, then am I strong. *2 Cor. 12:9,10*

7. He would grant you, according to the riches of his glory, to be strengthened with might by his Spirit in the inner man. *Eph. 3:16*

STRIFE   See Argument; Competition; Fighting; Hostility; War.

STRIVING   See Aggressiveness; Ambition; Competition.

STUBBORNNESS   See Defiance.

STUDY   See Reading.

STUMBLING BLOCK   See Obstacle.

STUPIDITY   See Foolishness; Ignorance.

SUBMISSION   See Obedience; Surrender.

SUBVERSION   See Betrayal; Conspiracy; Treachery.

SUCCESS   (See also Accomplishment; Victory.)

1. This book of the law shall not depart out of thy mouth; but thou shalt meditate therein day and night, that thou mayest observe to do all that is written therein: for then thou shalt make thy way prosperous, and then thou shalt have good success. *Josh. 1:8*

2. Thy wisdom and prosperity exceedeth the fame which I heard. *1 Kings 10:7*

3. If they obey and serve him, they shall spend their days in prosperity, and their years in pleasures. *Job 36:11*

4. I have not run in vain, neither labored in vain. *Phil. 2:16*

SUCCOR   See Comfort; God, Help of; Help; Relief.

SUFFERING   (See also Distress; Persecution; Sorrow; Trouble.)

1. The pains of hell gat hold upon me. *Ps. 116:3*

2. He hath borne our griefs, and carried our sorrows. . . . he was wounded for our transgressions, he was bruised for our iniquities: the chastisement of our peace was upon him; and with his stripes we are healed. *Isa. 53:4,5*

3. Why is my pain perpetual, and my wound incurable, which refuseth to be healed? *Jer. 15:18*

4. Being in agony he prayed more earnestly: and his sweat was as it were great drops of blood. *Luke 22:44*

5. The sufferings of this present time are not worthy to be compared with the glory which shall be revealed in us. . . . the whole creation groaneth and travaileth in pain. *Rom. 8:18,22*

6. Five times received I forty stripes save one. *2 Cor. 11:24*

7. If we suffer, we shall also reign with him. *2 Tim. 2:12*

8. Choosing rather to suffer affliction with the people of God, than to enjoy the pleasures of sin for a season. *Heb. 11:25*

SUICIDE   (See also Euthanasia; Murder.)

1. Thou shalt not kill. *Exod. 20:13*

2. Saul took a sword, and fell upon it. And when his armor-bearer saw that Saul was dead, he fell likewise upon his sword, and died. *1 Sam. 31:4,5*

3. Their sword shall enter into their own heart. *Ps. 37:15*

4. The devil taketh him up into the holy city, and sitteth him on a pinnacle of the temple, And saith unto him, If thou be the Son of God, cast thyself down. *Matt. 4:5,6*

5. [Judas] cast down the pieces of silver in the temple, and departed, and went and hanged himself. *Matt. 27:5*

6. In those days shall men seek death . . . and shall desire to die, and death shall flee from them. *Rev. 9:6*

SUNDAY   See Sabbath.

SUPERFICIALTY   See Hypocrisy; Shallowness.

SUPERIORITY (See also Inferiority; Priority.)

1. The heaven and the heaven of heavens is the Lord's thy God, the earth also, with all that therein is. *Deut. 10:14*

2. Thou hast made him [man] a little lower than the angels, and hast crowned him with glory and honor. Thou madest him to have dominion over the works of thy hands; thou hast put all things under his feet. *Ps. 8:5,6*

3. A truth it is, that your God is a God of gods, and a Lord of kings. *Dan. 2:47*

4. He hath put down the mighty from their seats, and exalted them of low degree. *Luke 1:52*

5. He that cometh from heaven is above all. *John 3:31*

6. He is before all things, and by him all things consist. And he is the head of the body . . . that in all things he might have pre-eminence. *Col. 1:17,18*

7. [Jesus] sat down ont he right hand of the Majesty on high; Being made so much better than the angels, as he hath by inheritance obtained a more excellent name than they. *Heb. 1:3,4*

SUPPLICATION See Prayer.

SUPPRESSION See Oppression.

SUPREMACY See Superiority.

SURRENDER (See also Defeat; Obedience; Reformation.)

1. Be ye not stiffnecked, as your fathers were, but yield yourselves unto the Lord. *2 Chron. 30:8*

2. Yielding pacifieth great offenses. *Eccl. 10:4*

3. As ye have yielded your members servants to uncleanness and to iniquity unto iniquity; even so now yield your members servants to righteousness unto holiness. *Rom. 6:19*

4. Let every soul be subject unto the higher powers. For there is no power but of God: the powers that be are ordained of God. *Rom. 13:1*

5. Submit yourselves therefore to God. *James 4:7*

6. Ye younger, submit yourselves unto the elder. Yea, all of you be subject one to another. . . . Humble yourselves therefore under the mighty hand of God, that he may exalt you in due time. *1 Peter 5:5,6*

SURROUNDINGS See Environment.

SWEARING See Blasphemy; Profanity; Vow.

SYMPATHY (See also Comfort; Pity.)

1. I am distressed for thee. *2 Sam. 1:26*

2. I have heard thy prayer, I have seen thy tears: behold, I will heal thee. *2 Kings 20:5*

3. When Job's three friends heard of all this evil that was come upon him, they came every one from his own place . . . to mourn with him and to comfort him. *Job 2:11*

4. To him that is afflicted pity should be showed from his friend. *Job 6:14*

5. Rejoice with them that do rejoice, and weep with them that weep. *Rom. 12:15*

6. Who is weak, and I am not weak? who is offended, and I burn not? *2 Cor. 11:29*

7. Be ye all of one mind, having compassion one of another, love as brethren, be pitiful. *1 Peter 3:8*

T

TACT See Diplomacy.

TALENT See Gift.

TALKING See Speaking.

TARDINESS (See also Procrastination.)

1. Why is his chariot so long in coming? Why tarry the wheels of his chariots? *Judg. 5:28*

2. The vision is yet for an appointed time . . . though it tarry, wait for it. *Hab. 2:3*

3. The people waited for Zechariah and marveled that he tarried so long in the temple. *Luke 1:21*

4. The child Jesus tarried behind in Jerusalem . . . after three days they found him in the temple. *Luke 2:43,46*

5. Lord, if thou hadst been here, my brother had not died. *John 11:21*

6. Today, after so long a time. *Heb. 4:7*

TATOOING

1. Ye shall not make any cuttings in your flesh . . . nor print any marks upon you. *Lev. 19:28*

TAXATION

1. Joseph made it a law over the land of Egypt unto this day, that Pharaoh should have the fifth part; except the land of the priests only. *Gen. 47:26*

2. He exacted the silver and the gold of the people of the land, of every one according to his taxation. *2 Kings 23:35*

3. The profit of the earth is for all. *Eccl. 5:9*

4. [Jesus] saw a man, named Matthew, sitting at the receipt of custom: and he saith unto him, Follow me. *Matt. 9:9*

5. They that received tribute money came to Peter, and said,

239

Doth not your master pay tribute? He saith, Yes. *Matt. 17:24,25*

6. Render therefore unto Caesar the things which are Caesar's; and unto God the things that are God's. *Matt. 22:21*

7. There went out a decree from Caesar Augustus, that all the world should be taxed. *Luke 2:1*

8. Render therefore to all their dues: tribute to whom tribute is due; custom to whom custom. *Rom. 13:7*

TEACHING (See also Education; Evangelism; Knowledge.)

1. Ask now the beasts, and they shall teach thee; and the fowls of the air, and they shall tell thee: or speak to the earth, and it shall teach thee: and the fishes of the sea shall declare unto thee. *Job 12:7,8*

2. Give instruction to a wise man, and he will be yet wiser: teach a just man, and he will increase in learning. *Prov. 9:9*

3. Train up a child in the way he should go: and when he is old, he will not depart from it. *Prov. 22:6*

4. Thy teachers [shall not] be removed into a corner any more, but thine eyes shall see thy teachers: And thine ears shall hear a word behind thee, saying, This is the way, walk ye in it. *Isa. 30:20,21*

5. Go ye therefore, and teach all nations . . . Teaching them to observe all things whatsoever I have commanded you. *Matt. 28:19,20*

6. [Thou] art confident that thou thyself art a guide of the blind, a light of them which are in darkness, An instructor of the foolish, a teacher of babes . . . Thou therefore which teachest another, teachest thou not thyself? *Rom. 2:19–21*

7. When . . . ye ought to be teachers, ye have need that one teach you again. *Heb. 5:12*

TEMPERANCE See Moderation; Self-Control; Sobriety.

TEMPLE (See also Body; Church.)

1. And the house which king Soloman built for the Lord, the length thereof was threescore cubits, and the breadth thereof twenty cubits, and the height thereof thirty cubits. *1 Kings 6:2*

2. Why is the house of God forsaken? *Neh. 13:11*

3. The Lord is in his holy temple. *Ps. 11:4*

4. And Jesus went into the temple of God . . . And said unto them, It is written, My house shall be called the house of prayer; but ye have made it a den of thieves. *Matt. 21:12,13*

5. I saw no temple therein [the new Jerusalem]: for the Lord God

Almighty and the Lamb are the temple of it. *Rev. 21:22*

TEMPTATION   (See also Companions, Evil; Demons; Influence; Obstacle; Seduction.)

1. If sinners entice thee, consent thou not. *Prov. 1:10*

2. Lead us not into temptation, but deliver us from evil. *Matt. 6:13*

3. Watch ye and pray, lest ye enter into temptation. The spirit truly is ready, but the flesh is weak. *Mark 14:38*

4. There hath no temptation taken you but such as is common to man: but God is faithful, who will not suffer you to be tempted above that ye are able; but will with the temptation also make a way to escape, that ye may be able to bear it. *1 Cor. 10:13*

5. In that he himself hath suffered being tempted, he is able to succor them that are tempted. *Heb. 2:18*

6. Count it all joy when ye fall into divers temptations; Knowing this, that the trying of your faith worketh patience. *James 1:2,3*

7. Blessed is the man that endureth temptation: for when he is tried, he shall receive the crown of life. . . . Let no man say when he is tempted, I am tempted of God: for God cannot be tempted with evil, neither tempteth he any man: But every man is tempted, when he is drawn away of his own lust, and enticed. *James 1:12–14*

8. Because thou hast kept the word of my patience, I also will keep thee from the hour of temptation, which shall come upon all the world, to try them that dwell upon the earth. *Rev. 3:10*

TENDERNESS   See Kindness; Meekness.

TERRORISM   (See also Cruelty; Treachery.)

1. The earth was filled with violence. *Gen. 6:11*

2. He will be a wild man; his hand will be against every man, and every man's hand against him; and he shall dwell in the presence of all his brethren. *Gen. 16:12*

3. Instruments of cruelty are in their habitations . . . in their anger they slew a man, and in their self-will they digged down a wall. *Gen. 49:5,6*

4. In the night will they come to slay thee. *Neh. 6:10*

5. He sitteth in the lurking places of the villages: in the secret places doth he murder the innocent. . . . He lieth in wait secretly as a lion in his den. *Ps. 10:8,9*

6. The people shall be oppressed, every one by another, and every one by his neighbor. *Isa. 3:5*

TEST See Temptation; Trial.

TESTAMENT See Covenant.

TESTIMONY See Scripture; Witness.

THANKFULNESS See Appreciation; Thanksgiving.

THANKSGIVING (See also Appreciation; Ingratitude.)

1. When thou hast eaten and art full, then thou shalt bless the Lord thy God for the good land which he hath given thee. *Deut. 8:10*

2. It is a good thing to give thanks unto the Lord. *Ps. 92:1*

3. Enter into his gates with thanksgiving, and into his courts with praise: be thankful unto him, and bless his name. *Ps. 100:4*

4. One of them [ten lepers], when he saw that he was healed, turned back . . . And fell down on his face at his feet, giving him thanks. *Luke 17:15,16*

5. He took bread, and gave thanks, and brake it, and gave unto them. *Luke 22:19*

6. He that eateth, eateth to the Lord, for he giveth God thanks; and he that eateth not, to the Lord he eateth not, and giveth God thanks. *Rom. 14:6*

7. Giving thanks always for all things unto God and the Father in the name of our Lord Jesus Christ. *Eph. 5:20*

THEFT See Thief.

THIEF (See also Cheating.)

1. Thou shalt not steal. *Exod. 20:15*

2. Whoso robbeth his father or his mother, and saith, It is no transgression . . . is the companion of a destroyer. *Prov. 28:24*

3. Whoso is partner with a thief hateth his own soul. *Prov. 29:24*

4. The robbers of thy people shall exalt themselves . . . but they shall fall. *Dan. 11:14*

5. Will a man rob God? Yet ye have robbed me. *Mal. 3:8*

6. With him they crucify two thieves. . . . And the scripture was fulfilled, which saith, And he was numbered with the transgressors. *Mark 15:27,28*

7. He that entereth not by the door into the sheepfold, but climbeth up some other way, the same is a thief and a robber. . . . I am the door. *John 10:1,7*

8. The thief cometh not, but for to steal, and to kill, and to destroy. *John 10:10*

9. Let him that stole steal no more: but rather let him labor. *Eph. 4:28*

THIRST   See Desire; Hunger.

THOUGHT   (See also Meditation; Prayer.)

1. Thy thoughts are very deep. *Ps. 92:5*

2. He that answereth a matter before he heareth it, it is folly and shame unto him. *Prov. 18:13*

3. As he thinketh in his heart, so is he. *Prov. 23:7*

4. My thoughts are not your thoughts. *Isa. 55:8*

5. I know the thoughts that I think toward you, saith the Lord, thoughts of peace, and not of evil. *Jer. 29:11*

6. Which of you by taking thought can add one cubit unto his stature? . . . Take therefore no thought for the morrow: for the morrow shall take thought for the things of itself. *Matt. 6:27,34*

7. Out of the heart proceed evil thoughts. *Matt. 15:19*

8. Who hath known the mind of the Lord? *Rom. 11:34*

9. Whatsoever things are true . . . honest . . . just . . . pure . . . lovely . . . of good report; if there be any virtue, and if there be any praise, think on these things. *Phil. 4:8*

TIME   (See also Eternity.)

1. My times are in thy hand. *Ps. 31:15*

2. To every thing there is a season, and a time to every purpose under the heaven. *Eccl. 3:1*

3. Time and chance happeneth to them all. For man also knoweth not his time. *Eccl. 9:11,12*

4. The signs of the times. *Matt. 16:3*

5. My time is at hand. *Matt. 26:18*

6. My time is not yet come: but your time is always ready. *John 7:6*

7. Now is the accepted time; behold, now is the day of salvation. *2 Cor. 6:2*

8. One day is with the Lord as a thousand years, and a thousand years as one day. *2 Peter 3:8*

TIREDNESS   See Weariness.

TITHE

1. Of all that thou shalt give me I will surely give the tenth unto thee. *Gen. 28:22*

2. Every one . . . from twenty years old and above, shall give an offering unto the Lord. *Exod. 30:14*

3. We made ordinances for us, to charge ourselves yearly . . . for the service of the house of our God. *Neh. 10:32*

4. Will a man rob God? Yet ye have robbed me. But ye say, Wherein have we robbed thee? In tithes and offerings. *Mal. 3:8*

5. Woe unto you, Pharisees! for ye tithe mint and rue and all manner of herbs, and pass over judgment and the love of God: these ought ye to have done, and not to leave the other undone. *Luke 11:42*

TOLERANCE **(See also Patience: Self-Control.)**

1. A wrathful man stirreth up strife: but he is slow to anger appeaseth strife. *Prov. 15:18*

2. Judge not, that ye be not judged. *Matt. 7:1*

3. Charity suffereth long . . . Beareth all things . . . endureth all things. Charity never faileth. *1 Cor. 13:4,7,8*

4. Ye suffer fools gladly, seeing ye yourselves are wise. *2 Cor. 11:19*

5. Be ye kind one to another, tenderhearted, forgiving one another, even as God for Christ's sake hath forgiven you. *Eph. 4:32*

6. Endure hardness, as a good soldier of Jesus Christ. *2 Tim. 2:3*

7. After he had patiently endured, he obtained the promise. *Heb. 6:15*

TOMB **See Burial.**

TONGUES, GIFT OF **(See also Holy Spirit; Interpretation.)**

1. They shall speak with new tongues. *Mark 16:17*

2. They were all filled with the Holy Ghost, and began to speak with other tongues. *Acts 2:4*

3. The multitude . . . were confounded, because that every man heard them speak in his own language. *Acts 2:6*

4. When Paul had laid his hands upon them, the Holy Ghost came on them; and they spake with tongues, and prophesied. *Acts 19:6*

5. To one is given by the Spirit . . . divers kinds of tongues; to another the interpretation of tongues. *1 Cor. 12:8,10*

6. He that speaketh in an unknown tongue speaketh not unto men, but unto God: for no man understandeth him. *1 Cor. 14:2*

7. If any man speak in an unknown tongue, let it be by two, or at the most by three, and that by course; and let one interpret. But if there be no interpreter, let him keep silence in the church; and let him speak to himself, and to God. *1 Cor. 14:27,28*

TORTURE **See Cruelty; Persecution.**

TRADITION **See Conservatism; Ritual.**

TRAINING **See Discipline; Education; Teaching.**

TRAIT **See Character.**

TRAITOR   (See also Betrayal; Deceit; Treachery.)
1. If ye be come to betray me to mine enemies, seeing there is no wrong in mine hands, the God of our fathers look thereon, and rebuke it. *1 Chron. 12:17*
2. Confidence in an unfaithful man in time of trouble is like a broken tooth. *Prov. 25:19*
3. Judas Iscariot . . . was the traitor. *Luke 6:16*
4. He that is not with me is against me: and he that gathereth not with me scattereth. *Luke 11:23*
5. He that eateth bread with me hath lifted up his heel against me. *John 13:18*
6. In the last days. . . . men shall be lovers of their own selves, covetous, boasters . . . trucebreakers, false accusers . . . traitors. *2 Tim. 3:1–4*

TRANQUILITY   See Peace; Silence.

TRANSFIGURATION
1. When Moses came down from mount Sinai with the two tables of testimony . . . the skin of his face shone. *Exod. 34:29*
2. [Jesus] was transfigured before them: and his face did shine as the sun, and his raiment was white as the light. *Matt. 17:2*
3. There was a cloud that overshadowed them [Jesus, Moses, and Elias]: and a voice came out of the cloud, saying, This is my beloved Son: hear him. *Mark 9:7*
4. All that sat in the council, looking steadfastly on him [Stephen], saw his face as it had been the face of an angel. *Acts 6:15*

TRANSFORMATION   See Conversion; Reform; Transfiguration.

TRANSGRESSION   See Crime; Disobedience; Mistake; Sin.

TRANSLATION   See Interpretation.

TRANSVESTITISM   See Dress; Homosexuality.

TRAVEL   See Journey.

TRAVELER   See Guest; Stranger.

TREACHERY   (See also Betrayal; Conspiracy; Deceit; Traitor.)
1. It came to pass on the seventh day, that he [Samson] told her, because she lay sore upon him: and she told the riddle to the children of her people. *Judg. 14:17*

2. She called for a man, and she caused him to shave off the seven locks of his [Samson's] head. *Judg. 16:19*

3. Mine own familiar friend, in whom I trusted, which did eat of my bread, hath lifted up his heel against me. *Ps. 41:9*

4. It was not an enemy that reproached me; then I could have borne it: neither was it he that hated me that did magnify himself against me; then I would have hid myself from him: But it was thou, a man mine equal, my guide, and mine acquaintance. *Ps. 55:12,13*

5. When thou shalt make an end to deal treacherously, they shall deal treacherously with thee. *Isa. 33:1*

6. From the prophet even unto the priest every one dealeth falsely. *Jer. 6:13*

7. All her friends have dealt treacherously with her. *Lam. 1:2*

8. I was wounded in the house of my friends. *Zech. 13:6*

9. Have we not all one father? hath not one God created us? why do we deal treacherously every man against his brother, by profaning the covenant of our fathers? *Mal. 2:10*

10. Therefore take heed to your spirit, that ye deal not treacherously. *Mal. 2:16*

TREASON See Betrayal; Traitor; Treachery.

TRESPASS See Crime; Sin.

TRIAL (See also Judgment.)

1. I charged your judges at that time, saying, hear the causes between your brethren, and judge righteously . . . Ye shall not respect persons in judgment; but ye shall hear the small as well as the great. *Deut. 1:16,17*

2. According to the sentence of the law which they shall teach thee, and according to the judgment which they shall tell thee, thou shalt do. *Deut. 17:11*

3. When he hath tried me, I shall come forth as gold. *Job 23:10*

4. In the morning the chief priests held a consultation with the elders and scribes and the whole council, and bound Jesus, and carried him away, and delivered him to Pilate. *Mark 15:1*

5. Doth our law judge any man, before it hear him, and know what he doeth? *John 7:51*

6. Sittest thou to judge me after the law, and commandest me to be smitten contrary to the law? *Acts 23:3*

7. Think it not strange concerning the fiery trial which is to try you. *1 Peter 4:12*

TRIBULATION See Suffering; Trouble.

TRIBUTE See Praise; Taxation.

TRINITY, HOLY (See also Christ; God; Holy Spirit; Unity.)

1. Go ye therefore, and teach all nations, baptizing them in the name of the Father, and of the Son, and of the Holy Ghost. *Matt. 28:19*

2. The Holy Ghost descended in a bodily shape like a dove upon him, and a voice came from heaven, which said, Thou art my beloved Son; in thee I am well pleased. *Luke 3:22*

3. The grace of the Lord Jesus Christ, and the love of God, and the communion of the Holy Ghost, be with you all. *2 Cor. 13:14*

4. The mystery of godliness: God was manifest in the flesh, justified in the Spirit. *1 Tim. 3:16*

5. There are three that bear record in heaven, the Father, the Word, and the Holy Ghost: and these three are one. *1 John 5:7*

TRIUMPH See Victory.

TROUBLE (See also Burden; Distress; Suffering; Worry.)

1. There was no peace to him that went out, nor to him that came in . . . for God did vex them with all adversity. *2 Chron. 15:5,6*

2. Man that is born of a woman is of few days, and full of trouble. *Job 14:1*

3. Many are the afflictions of the righteous: but the Lord delivereth him out of them all. *Ps. 34:19*

4. We are consumed by thine anger, and by thy wrath are we troubled. *Ps. 90:7*

5. Let not your heart be troubled: ye believe in God. *John 14:1*

6. In the world ye shall have tribulation: but be of good cheer; I have overcome the world. *John 16:33*

7. We must through much tribulation enter into the kingdom of God. *Acts 14:22*

8. We are troubled on every side, yet not distressed. . . . For our light affliction, which is but for a moment, worketh for us a far more exceeding and eternal weight of glory. *2 Cor. 4:8,17*

9. I take pleasure in infirmities, in reproaches, in necessities, in persecutions, in distresses for Christ's sake: for when I am weak, then am I strong. *2 Cor. 12:10*

TRUST (See also Belief; Constancy; Faith; Faithfulness; Loyalty.)

1. Blessed are they that put their trust in him [the Lord]. *Ps. 2:12*

2. It is better to trust in the Lord than to put confidence in man. *Ps. 118:8*

3. Trust in the Lord with all thine heart; and lean not unto thine own understanding. *Prov. 3:5*

4. Whoso trusteth in the Lord, happy is he. *Prov. 16:20*

5. Trust ye not in a friend, put ye not confidence in a guide. *Mic. 7:5*

6. I rejoice therefore that I have confidence in you in all things. *2 Cor. 7:16*

7. We have confidence in the Lord touching you, that ye both do and will do the things which we command you. *2 Thess. 3:4*

TRUTH   (See also Falsehood; Honesty; Sincerity; Witness.)

1. God is not a man, that he should lie . . . hath he said, and shall he not do it? or hath he spoken, and shall he not make it good? *Num. 23:19*

2. Thy word is true from the beginning. *Ps. 119:160*

3. Speak ye every man the truth to his neighbor. *Zech. 8:16*

4. Ye shall know the truth, and the truth shall make you free. *John 8:32*

5. I am the way, the truth, and the life. *John 14:6*

6. For this cause came I into the world, that I should bear witness unto the truth. Every one that is of the truth heareth my voice. *John 18:37*

7. Am I therefore become your enemy, because I tell you the truth? *Gal. 4:16*

8. Heaven opened, and behold a white horse; and he that sat upon him was called Faithful and True. *Rev. 19:11*

U

UBIQUITOUSNESS   See God, Omnipresence of.

UNBELIEF   See Agnosticism; Atheism; Doubt; Faithlessness.

UNCERTAINTY   See Doubt; Indecision; Instability.

UNCLEANNESS   See Impurity; Pollution; Sin.

UNDEPENDABILITY   See Unreliability.

UNDERSTANDING   (See also God, Omniscience of; Interpretation; Knowledge; Realization; Wisdom.)

1. The inspiration of the Almighty giveth them understanding. *Job 32:8*

2. O ye simple, understand wisdom: and ye fools, be ye of an understanding heart. *Prov. 8:5*

3. The heart of him that hath understanding seeketh knowledge: but the mouth of fools feedeth on foolishness. *Prov. 15:14*

4. The man that wandereth out of the way of understanding shall remain in the congregation of the dead. *Prov. 21:16*

5. Therefore speak I to them in parables: because they seeing see not; and hearing they hear not, neither do they understand. *Matt. 13:13*

6. In malice be ye children, but in understanding be men. *1 Cor. 14:20*

7. And the peace of God, which passeth all understanding, shall keep your hearts and minds through Christ Jesus. *Phil. 4:7*

8. Through faith we understand. *Heb. 11:3*

UNEMPLOYMENT   (See also Sloth.)

1. An idle soul shall suffer hunger. *Prov. 19:15*

2. Why stand ye here all the day idle? They say unto him, Because no man hath hired us. *Matt. 20:6,7*

3. If any would not work, neither should he eat. *2 Thess. 3:10*

UNFAIRNESS See Inequality; Injustice.

UNFAITHFULNESS See Adultery; Betrayal; Faithlessness.

UNGRATEFULNESS See Ingratitude.

UNHAPPINESS See Sadness.

UNITY (See also Brotherhood; Family; Fellowship; God, Family of; Reunion.)

1. All the people arose as one man. *Judg. 20:8*

2. How good and how pleasant it is for brethren to dwell together in unity! *Ps. 133:1*

3. Together shall they sing: for they shall see eye to eye. *Isa. 52:8*

4. [I pray] That they all may be one; as thou, Father, art in me, and I in thee, that they also might be one in us. *John 17:21*

5. The multitude of them that believed were of one heart and of one soul . . . they had all things common. *Acts 4:32*

6. We also are men of like passions with you. *Acts 14:15*

7. We are laborers together with God. *1 Cor. 3:9*

8. As the body is one, and hath many members, and all the members of that one body, being many, are one body: so also is Christ. *1 Cor. 12:12*

9. We all come in the unity of the faith, and of the knowledge of the Son of God. *Eph. 4:13*

10. Be likeminded, having the same love, being of one accord, of one mind. *Phil. 2:2*

UNRELIABILITY (See also Instability.)

1. He put no trust in his servants; and his angels he charged with folly. *Job 4:18*

2. He putteth no trust in his saints. *Job 15:15*

3. It is better to trust in the Lord than to put confidence in man. *Ps. 118:8*

4. I am against them that prophesy false dreams . . . and cause my people to err by their lies, and by their lightness; yet I sent them not, nor commanded them: therefore they shall not profit this people at all. *Jer. 23:32*

5. They sit before thee as my people, and they hear thy words, but they will not do them: for with their mouth they shew much love, but their heart goeth after their convetousness. *Ezek. 33:31*

6. Neither did my shepherds search for my flock, but the shepherds fed themselves, and fed not my flock. *Ezek. 34:8*

UNREST   (See also Discontent; Trouble; Worry.)

1. Why do the heathen rage? *Ps. 2:1*

2. While I suffer thy terrors I am distracted. *Ps. 88:15*

3. Thou that art full of stirs, a tumultuous city. *Isa. 22:2*

4. The wicked are like the troubled sea, when it cannot rest, whose waters cast up mire and dirt. There is no peace, saith my God, to the wicked. *Isa. 57:20,21*

5. They have no rest day nor night, who worship the beast and his image. *Rev. 14:11*

UNRIGHTEOUSNESS   See Evil; Injustice.

UNSELFISHNESS   (See also Charity; Generosity; Giving; Kindness.)

1. The liberal soul shall be made fat: and he that watereth shall be watered also himself. *Prov. 11:25*

2. They helped every one his neighbor; and every one said to his brother, Be of good courage. *Isa. 41:6*

3. When Joseph [of Arimathaea] had taken the body [of Christ], he wrapped it in a clean linen cloth, And laid it in his own new tomb. *Matt. 27:59,60*

4. Love thy neighbor as thyself. *Mark 12:31*

5. We then that are strong ought to bear the infirmities of the weak, and not to please ourselves. Let every one of us please his neighbor for his good to edification. For even Christ pleased not himself. *Rom. 15:1–3*

6. Let no man seek his own, but every man another's wealth . . . Even as I please all men in all things, not seeking mine own profit, but the profit of many, that they may be saved. *1 Cor. 10:24,33*

7. Charity . . . seeketh not her own. *1 Cor. 13:4,5*

UNTRUSTWORTHINESS   See Gossip; Unreliability.

UNWORTHINESS   (See also Humility.)

1. I am not worthy of the least of all the mercies, and of all the truth, which thou hast showed unto thy servant. *Gen. 32:10*

2. He that cometh after me is mightier than I, whose shoes I am not worthy to bear. *Matt. 3:11*

3. Lord, I am not worthy that thou shouldest come under my roof. *Matt. 8:8*

4. He that taketh not his cross, and followeth after me, is not worthy of me. *Matt. 10:38*

5. The wedding is ready, but they which were bidden were not worthy. *Matt. 22:8*

6. I have sinned against heaven, and before thee, And am no more worthy to be called thy son. *Luke 15:18,19*

7. Seeing ye put it [the word of God] from you, and judge yourselves unworthy of everlasting life, lo, we turn to the Gentiles. *Acts 13:46*

8. Whosoever shall eat of this bread, and drink this cup of the Lord, unworthily, shall be guilty of the body and blood of the Lord. *1 Cor. 11:27*

9. No man was found worthy to open and to read the book, neither to look thereon. *Rev. 5:4*

UPRIGHTNESS   See Goodness; Justice; Righteousness.

USELESSNESS   See Worthlessness.

VALOR   See Courage.
VANITY   (See also Boasting; Pride; Self-Centeredness.)
1. They have provoked me to anger with their vanities. *Deut. 32:21*
2. Every man at his best state is altogether vanity. *Ps. 39:5*
3. Men of low degree are vanity, and men of high degree are a lie: to be laid in the balance, they are altogether lighter than vanity. *Ps. 62:9*
4. I hate vain thoughts. *Ps. 119:113*
5. Most men will proclaim every one his own goodness. *Prov. 20:6*
6. He that followeth after vain persons shall have poverty. *Prov. 28:19*
7. Vanity of vanities; all is vanity. *Eccl. 1:2*
8. Thou hast said in thine heart, I will ascend into heaven, I will exalt my throne above the stars of God . . . I will be like the most High. Yet thou shalt be brought down to hell. *Isa. 14:13–15*
9. Let him that thinketh he standeth take heed lest he fall. *1 Cor. 10:12*

VEGETARIANISM   (See also Food.)
1. I have given you every herb bearing seed, which is upon the face of all the earth, and every tree, in which is the fruit of a tree yielding seed to you it shall be for meat. *Gen. 1:29*
2. For one believeth that he may eat all things: another, who is weak, eateth herbs. *Rom. 14:2*
3. The kingdom of God is not meat and drink. *Rom. 14:17*
VENERATION   See Fear of the Lord; Praise; Worship.

VENEREAL DISEASE **(See also Illness; Sex.)**

1. When any man hath a running issue out of his flesh, because of his issue he is unclean. *Lev. 15:2*

2. Put out of the camp . . . every one that hath an issue . . . Both male and female. *Num. 5:2,3*

VENGEANCE See God, Wrath of; Retaliation.

VERACITY See Truth.

VICE See Evil; Sin.

VICTIM See Christ, Crucifixion of; Martyr; Scapegoat.

VICTORY **(See also Salvation; Success.)**

1. I will sing unto the Lord, for he hath triumphed gloriously. . . . Pharaoh's chariots and . . . his chosen captains also are drowned in the Red sea. *Exod. 15:1,4*

2. The Lord shall cause thine enemies that rise up against thee to be smitten before thy face: they shall come out against thee one way, and flee before thee seven ways. *Deut. 28:7*

3. When the priests blew with the trumpets . . . the wall [of Jericho] fell down. *Josh. 6:20*

4. Samson said, With the jawbone of an ass . . . have I slain a thousand men. *Judg. 15:16*

5. David prevailed over the Philistine [Goliath] with a sling and with a stone. *1 Sam. 17:50*

6. In the world ye shall have tribulation: but be of good cheer; I have overcome the world. *John 16:33*

7. Thanks be to God, which giveth us the victory through our Lord Jesus Christ. *1 Cor. 15:57*

8. This is the victory that overcometh the world, even our faith. *1 John 5:4*

9. These shall make war with the Lamb, and the Lamb shall overcome them: for he is Lord of lords, and King of kings. *Rev. 17:14*

VIGILANCE **(See also Carefulness; Caution.)**

1. The Lord watch between me and thee, when we are absent one from another. *Gen. 31:49*

2. Set a watch, O Lord, before my mouth; keep the door of my lips. *Ps. 141:3*

3. Blessed is the man that heareth me [wisdom], watching daily at my gates, waiting at the posts of my doors. *Prov. 8:34*

4. Watch therefore: for ye know not what hour your Lord doth come. *Matt. 24:42*

5. [Christ] saith unto Peter, What, could ye not watch with me one hour? Watch and pray, that ye enter not into temptation: the spirit indeed is willing, but the flesh is weak. *Matt. 26:40,41*

6. Shepherds abiding in the field, keeping watch over their flock by night. *Luke 2:8*

7. Watching thereunto with all perseverance and supplication for all saints. *Eph. 6:18*

8. Let us watch and be sober. *1 Thess. 5:6*

9. A bishop then must be . . . vigilant. *1 Tim. 3:2*

VINE   See Wine.

VIOLENCE   See Child Abuse; Murder; Rape; Terrorism.

VIRGINITY   (See also Celibacy; Marriage; Purity.)

1. The high priest . . . shall take a virgin of his own people to be his wife. *Lev. 21:10,14*

2. A virgin shall conceive, and bear a son, and shall call his name Immanuel. *Isa. 7:14*

3. Joseph . . . took unto him his wife: And knew her not till she had brought forth her firstborn son: and he called his name JESUS. *Matt. 1:24,25*

4. For there are some eunuchs, which were so born from their mother's womb: and there are some eunuchs which were made eunuchs of men: and there be eunuchs, which have made themselves eunuchs for the kingdom of heaven's sake. He that is able to receive it, let him receive it. *Matt. 19:12*

5. In the resurrection they neither marry, nor are given in marriage, but are as the angels of God in heaven. *Matt. 22:30*

6. I say therefore to the unmarried . . . It is good for them if they abide even as I. But if they cannot contain, let them marry: for it is better to marry than to burn. *1 Cor. 7:8,9*

7. There is difference also between a wife and a virgin. The unmarried woman careth for the things of the Lord, that she may be holy both in body and in spirit: but she that is married careth for the things of the world, how she may please her husband. *1 Cor. 7:34*

8. I have espoused you to one husband, that I may present you as a chaste virgin to Christ. *2 Cor. 11:2*

VIRTUE   (See also Goodness; Modesty; Purity; Righteousness.)

1. A virtuous woman is a crown to her husband. *Prov. 12:4*

2. Who can find a virtuous woman? For her price is far above rubies. *Prov. 31:10*

3. The whole multitude sought to touch him: for there went virtue out of him. *Luke 6:19*

4. Be blameless and harmless, the sons of God, without rebuke, in the midst of a crooked and perverse nation, among whom ye shine as the lights in the world. *Phil. 2:15*

5. Whatsoever things are pure . . . lovely. . . . of good report, if there be any virtue . . . think on these things. *Phil. 4:8*

6. Follow righteousness, faith, charity, peace, with them that call on the Lord out of a pure heart. *2 Tim. 2:22*

7. Add to your faith virtue; and to virtue knowledge. *2 Peter 1:5*

VISION   See Appearance; Dream.

VISITOR   See Guest; Hospitality; Stranger.

VOCATION   (See also Ministry; Work.)

1. Many be called, but few chosen. *Matt. 20:16*

2. Lord, what wilt thou have me to do? *Acts 9:6*

3. As the Lord hath called every one, so let him walk. . . . Let every man abide in the same calling wherein he was called. *1 Cor. 7:17,20*

4. Walk worthy of the vocation wherewith ye are called. *Eph. 4:1*

5. I press toward the mark for the prize of the high calling of God in Christ Jesus. *Phil. 3:14*

6. Give diligence to make your calling and election sure: for if ye do these things, ye shall never fall. *2 Peter 1:10*

VOTING   See Election.

VOW   (See also Covenant; Perjury.)

1. Let there be now an oath betwixt us, even betwixt us and thee, and let us make a covenant with thee. *Gen. 26:28*

2. I will pay thee my vows, Which my lips have uttered, and my mouth hath spoken, when I was in trouble. *Ps. 66:13,14*

3. My [the Lord's] covenant will I not break, nor alter the thing that is gone out of my lips. Once have I sworn by my holiness that I will not lie unto David. *Ps. 89:34,35*

4. When thou vowest a vow unto God, defer not to pay it. . . . Better is it that thou shouldest not vow, than that thou shouldest vow and not pay. Suffer not thy mouth to cause thy flesh to sin; neither say thou before the angel, that it was an error. *Eccl. 5:4–6*

5. Above all things, my brethren, swear not, neither by heaven, neither by the earth, neither by any other oath: but let your yea be yea; and your nay, nay; lest ye fall into condemnation. *James 5:12*

WAGES   (See also Reward.)
1. The recompense of a man's hands shall be rendered unto him. *Prov. 12:14*
2. Every man should eat and drink, and enjoy the good of all his labor, it is the gift of God. *Eccl. 3:13*
3. He that earneth wages earneth wages to put it into a bag with holes. *Hag. 1:6*
4. I will be a swift witness against . . . those that oppress the hireling in his wages. *Mal. 3:5*
5. Be content with your wages. *Luke 3:14*
6. The wages of sin is death. *Rom. 6:23*
7. The laborer is worthy of his reward. *1 Tim. 5:18*

WAITING   See Expectation; Impatience; Patience; Procrastination; Tardiness.

WANDERING   See Aimlessness; Journey.

WANT   See Desire; Need.

WAR   (See also Army, Christian; Fighting; Hostility; Middle East Conflict; Peace; Peacemaking.)
1. The Lord is a man of war. *Exod. 15:3*
2. For the Lord your God is he that goeth with you, to fight for you against your enemies, to save you. *Deut. 20:4*
3. Thou has shed blood abundantly, and hast made great wars. *1 Chron. 22:8*
4. Scatter thou the people that delight in war. *Ps. 68:30*
5. A time of war, and a time of peace. *Eccl. 3:8*
6. Thou [the Lord] art my battle axe and weapons of war: for with thee I break in pieces the nations . . . kingdoms . . . the horse and

his rider . . . man and woman . . . captains and rulers. *Jer. 51:20–23*

7. They shall beat their swords into plowshares, and their spears into pruning hooks: nation shall not lift up a sword against nation, neither shall they learn war any more. *Mic. 4:3*

8. Ye shall hear of wars and rumors of wars. . . . nation shall rise against nation, and kingdom against kingdom. *Matt. 24:6,7*

9. We wrestle not against flesh and blood, but against principalities, against powers, against the rulers of the darkness of this world, against spiritual wickedness in high places. Wherefore take unto you the whole armor of God. . . . loins girt about with truth . . . the breastplate of righteousness . . . the shield of faith. . . . the helmet of salvation, and the sword of the Spirit. *Eph. 6:12–17*

10. There was war in heaven: Michael and his angels fought against the dragon. *Rev. 12:7*

WARNING **(See also Caution; Sign.)**

1. The judgments of the Lord are true and righteous . . . by them is thy servant warned. *Ps. 19:9,11*

2. To whom shall I speak, and give warning, that they may hear? *Jer. 6:10*

3. If thou warn the wicked, and he turn not from his wickedness . . . he shall die in his iniquity. . . . if thou warn the righteous man, that the righteous sin not, and he doth not sin, he shall surely live, because he is warned. *Ezek. 3:19,21*

4. If the watchman see the sword come, and blow not the trumpet, and the people be not warned; if the sword come, and take any person from among them, he is taken away in his iniquity; but his blood will I require at the watchman's hand. *Ezek. 33:6*

5. Being warned of God in a dream that they should not return to Herod, they departed into their own country another way. *Matt. 2:12*

6. If the trumpet give an uncertain sound, who shall prepare himself to the battle? *1 Cor. 14:8*

7. Count him not as an enemy, but admonish him as a brother. *2 Thess. 3:15*

WATCHFULNESS **See Vigilance.**

WEAKNESS **(See also Strength; Weariness.)**

1. His [the wicked's] strength shall be hunger-bitten. *Job 18:12*

2. If thou faint in the day of adversity, thy strength is small. *Prov. 24:10*

3. He giveth power to the faint; and to them that have no might he increaseth strength. *Isa. 40:29*

4. The spirit indeed is willing, but the flesh is weak. *Matt. 26:41*

5. The weakness of God is stronger than men. *1 Cor. 1:25*

6. To the weak became I as weak, that I may gain the weak: I am made all things to all men, that I might by all means save some. *1 Cor. 9:22*

7. My [God's] strength is made perfect in weakness. . . . when I am weak, then am I strong. *2 Cor. 12:9,10*

8. He was crucified through weakness, yet he liveth by the power of God. For we also are weak in him, but we shall live with him by the power of God. *2 Cor. 13:4*

WEALTH (See also Greed; Luxury; Money; Worldliness.)

1. He that trusteth in his riches shall fall. *Prov. 11:28*

2. Wealth maketh many friends. *Prov. 19:4*

3. Labour not to be rich. . . . For riches certainly make themselves wings; they fly away as an eagle toward heaven. *Prov. 23:4,5*

4. He that maketh haste to be rich shall not be innocent. . . . [he] hath an evil eye, and considereth not that poverty shall come upon him. *Prov. 28:20,22*

5. Riches and wealth . . . this is the gift of God. *Eccl. 5:19*

6. As the partridge sitteth on eggs, and hatcheth them not; so he that getteth riches, and not by right, shall leave them in the midst of his days, and at his end shall be a fool. *Jer. 17:11*

7. Lay up for yourselves treasures in heaven. . . . For where your treasure is, there will your heart be also. *Matt. 6:20,21*

8. It is easier for a camel to go through the eye of a needle, than for a rich man to enter into the kingdom of God. *Matt. 19:24*

9. A man's life consisteth not in the abundance of the things which he possesseth. *Luke 12:15*

10. Poor, yet making many rich . . . having nothing, and yet possessing all things. *2 Cor. 6:10*

11. We brought nothing into this world, and it is certain we can carry nothing out. *1 Tim. 6:7*

12. The sun is no sooner risen with a burning heat, but it withereth the grass, and the flower thereof falleth, and the grace of the fashion of it perisheth: so also shall the rich man fade away in his ways. *James 1:11*

WEARINESS   (See also Discouragement; Weakness.)
1. There [in death] the weary be at rest. *Job 3:17*
2. Wearisome nights are appointed to me. When I lie down, I say, When shall I arise, and the night be gone? And I am full of tossings to and fro unto the dawning of the day. *Job 7:3,4*
3. Withdraw thy foot from thy neighbor's house; lest he be weary of thee, and so hate thee. *Prov. 25:17*
4. The labor of the foolish wearieth every one of them, because he knoweth not how to go. *Eccl. 10:15*
5. The youths shall faint and be weary, and the young men shall utterly fall: But they that wait upon the Lord shall renew their strength . . . they shall run, and not be weary; and they shall walk, and not faint. *Isa. 40:30,31*
6. Let us not be weary in well doing: for in due season we shall reap, if we faint not. *Gal. 6:9*

WEATHER   (See also Disaster.)
1. The rain was upon the earth forty days and forty nights. *Gen. 7:12*
2. While the earth remaineth, seedtime and harvest, and cold and heat, and summer and winter, and day and night shall not cease. *Gen. 8:22*
3. Out of the south cometh the whirlwind: and cold out of the north. By the breath of God frost is given: and the breadth of the waters is straitened. Also by watering he wearieth the thick cloud: he scattereth his bright cloud. *Job 37:9–11*
4. He [the Lord] causeth the vapors to ascend from the ends of the earth; he maketh lightnings for the rain; he bringeth the wind. *Ps. 135:7*
5. Fire, and hail; snow, and vapor; stormy wind fulfilling his word. *Ps. 148:8*
6. As snow in summer, and as rain in harvest, so honor is not seemly for a fool. *Prov. 26:1*
7. A pleasant thing it is for the eyes to behold the sun. *Eccl. 11:7*
8. The Lord hath his way in the whirlwind and in the storm, and the clouds are the dust of his feet. *Nah. 1:3*
9. [Jesus] said . . . When it is evening, ye say, It will be fair weather: for the sky is red. And in the morning, It will be foul weather today: for the sky is red and lowring. *Matt. 16:2,3*

WEDDING   See Marriage.
WEEPING   See Sadness; Sorrow.

WELL-BEING   See Contentment; Health.

WICKEDNESS   See Companions, Evil; Corruption; Decadence; Depravity; Evil; Perversion; Sin.

WIDOW   (See also Orphan.)

1. I [Job] caused the widow's heart to sing for joy. *Job 29:13*

2. [If I] have caused the eyes of the widow to fail . . . let mine arm fall from my shoulder blade, and mine arm be broken from the bone. *Job 31:16,22*

3. The Lord . . . relieveth the fatherless and widow. *Ps. 146:9*

4. Plead for the widow. *Isa. 1:17*

5. How is she become as a widow! . . . She weepeth sore in the night, and her tears are on her cheeks: among all her lovers she hath none to comfort her: all her friends have dealt treacherously with her, they are become her enemies. *Lam. 1:1,2*

6. There came a certain poor widow, and she threw in two mites, which make a farthing. . . . this poor widow hath cast more in, than all they which have cast into the treasury. *Mark 12:42,43*

7. Honor widows that are widows indeed. *1 Tim. 5:3*

8. Pure religion and undefiled before God . . . is this, To visit the fatherless and widows in their affliction. *James 1:27*

WIFE   See Marriage; Mother; Woman.

WILL   See Intention.

WILLINGNESS   (See also Preparation; Zeal.)

1. Know thou the God of thy father, and serve him with a perfect heart and with a willing mind. *1 Chron. 28:9*

2. Thy people shall be willing in the day of thy power. *Ps. 110:3*

3. I heard the voice of the Lord, saying, Whom shall I send, and who will go for us? Then said I, Here am I; send me. *Isa. 6:8*

4. The spirit indeed is willing, but the flesh is weak. *Matt. 26:41*

5. My meat is to do the will of him that sent me, and to finish his work. *John 4:34*

6. They received the word with all readiness of mind, and searched the scriptures daily. *Acts 17:11*

7. Perform the doing of it. . . . For if there be first a willing mind, it is accepted according to that a man hath, and not according to that he hath not. *2 Cor. 8:11,12*

WINE   (See also Blood; Drunkenness; Eucharist.)

1. Wine is a mocker, strong drink is raging: and whosoever is deceived thereby is not wise. *Prov. 20:1*

2. Look not thou upon the wind when it is red. . . . it biteth like a serpent, and stingeth like an adder. *Prov. 23:31,32*

3. The best wine . . . goeth down sweetly, causing the lips of those that are asleep to speak. *Song of Sol. 7:9*

4. Put new wine into new bottles, and both are preserved. *Matt. 9:17*

5. I will not drink henceforth of this fruit of the vine, until that day when I drink it new with you in my Father's kingdom. *Matt. 26:29*

6. Every man at the beginning doth set forth good wine; and when men have well drunk, then that which is worse: but thou hast kept the good wine until now. *John 2:10*

7. I am the true vine . . . As the branch cannot bear fruit of itself, except it abide in the vine; no more can ye, except ye abide in me. *John 15:1,4*

8. These men are full of new wine. *Acts 2:13*

9. Drink no longer water, but use a little wine for thy stomach's sake. *1 Tim. 5:23*

WISDOM   (See also God, Omniscience of; Knowledge; Understanding.)

1. Happy is the man that findeth wisdom, and the man that getteth understanding. . . . She is more precious than rubies: and all the things thou canst desire are not to be compared unto her. *Prov. 3:13,15*

2. Wisdom is the principal thing; therefore get wisdom: and with all thy getting get understanding. *Prov. 4:7*

3. Wisdom hath builded her house, she hath hewn out her seven pillars. . . . she crieth upon the highest places of the city. . . . Forsake the foolish, and live; and go in the way of understanding. *Prov. 9:1–6*

4. The fear of the Lord is the beginning of wisdom: and the knowledge of the holy is understanding. *Prov. 9:10*

5. In much wisdom is much grief: and he that increaseth knowledge increaseth sorrow. *Eccl. 1:18*

6. Be ye therefore wise as serpents, and harmless as doves. *Matt. 10:16*

7. The wisdom of this world is foolishness with God. *1 Cor. 3:19*

8. If any of you lack wisdom, let him ask of God . . . and it shall be given him. *James 1:5*

9. The wisdom that is from above is first pure, then peaceable, gentle, and easy to be entreated, full of mercy and good fruits, without partiality, and without hypocrisy. *James 3:17*

WISH   See Desire.

WITCHCRAFT   See Occult.

WITNESS   (See also Evangelism; Honesty; Perjury; Truth.)

1. My witness is in heaven, and my record is on high. *Job 16:19*

2. A faithful witness will not lie: but a false witness will utter lies. *Prov. 14:5*

3. If he will not hear thee, then take with thee one or two more, that in the mouth of two or three witnesses every word may be established. *Matt. 19:16*

4. Go home to thy friends, and tell them how great things the Lord hath done for thee. *Mark 5:19*

5. Ye shall receive the power, after that the Holy Ghost is come upon you: and ye shall be witnesses unto me . . . unto the uttermost part of the earth. *Acts 1:8*

6. Thou shalt be his witness unto all men of what thou hast seen and heard. *Acts 22:15*

7. There are three that bear record in heaven, the Father, the Word, and the Holy Ghost: and these three are one. *1 John 5:7*

8. He that believeth on the Son of God hath the witness in himself. *1 John 5:10*

WOMAN   (See also Feminism; Man; Sex.)

1. The rib, which the Lord God had taken from man, made he a woman. . . . And Adam said, This is now bone of my bones, and flesh of my flesh: she shall be called Woman, because she was taken out of Man. *Gen. 2:22,23*

2. A gracious woman retaineth honor. *Prov. 11:16*

3. Favor is deceitful, and beauty is vain: but a woman that feareth the Lord, she shall be praised. *Prov. 31:30*

4. Blessed art thou among women. *Luke 1:28*

5. Woman, why weepest thou? whom seekest thou? . . . Sir, if thou have borne him hence, tell me where . . . and I will take him away. Jesus saith unto her, Mary. *John 20:15,16*

6. These all continued with one accord in prayer and supplication, with the women, and Mary the mother of Jesus, and with his brethren. *Acts 1:14*

7. The head of every man is Christ; and the head of the woman is the man; and the head of Christ is God. *1 Cor. 11:3*

8. A man . . . is the image and glory of God: but the woman is the glory of the man. For the man is not of the woman; but the woman of the man. Neither was the man created for the woman; but the woman for the man. *1 Cor. 11:7-9*

9. Let your women keep silence in the churches . . . they are commanded to be under obedience, as also saith the law. And if they will learn any thing, let them ask their husbands at home. *1 Cor. 14:34,35*

10. Help those women which labored with me in the gospel . . . whose names are in the book of life. *Phil. 4:3*

11. Teach the young woman to be sober, to love their husbands, to love their children, To be discreet, chaste, keepers at home, good, obedient. *Titus 2:4,5*

WOMEN'S LIBERATION   See Feminism.

WONDER   (See also Miracle; Sign.)

1. Let all the earth fear the Lord: let all the inhabitants of the world stand in awe of him. For he spake, and it was done. *Ps. 33:8,9*

2. Open thou mine eyes, that I may behold wondrous things out of thy law. *Ps. 119:18*

3. How great are his signs! and how mighty are his wonders! *Dan. 4:3*

4. They were sore amazed in themselves beyond measure, and wondered. *Mark 6:51*

5. All bare him witness, and wondered at the gracious words which proceeded out of his mouth. And they said, Is not this Joseph's son? *Luke 4:22*

WORD   (See also Book; Doctrine; God, Law of; Gospel; Inspiration; Scripture; Speaking; Writing.)

1. Man doth not live by bread only, but by every word that proceedeth out of the mouth of the Lord. *Deut. 8:3*

2. A word spoken in due season, how good is it! *Prov. 15:23*

3. Let thy words be few. For . . . a fool's voice is known by multitude of words. *Eccl. 5:2,3*

4. The words of the wise are as goads, and as nails fastened by the masters. *Eccl. 12:11*

5. In the beginning was the Word, and the Word was with God, and the Word was God. . . . And the Word was made flesh, and dwelt among us. *John 1:1,14*

6. If a man love me, he will keep my words. *John 14:23*

7. Thy word is truth. *John 17:17*

8. The word of God is quick, and powerful, and sharper than any two-edged sword . . . and is a discerner of the thoughts and intents of the heart. *Heb. 4:12*

9. Be ye doers of the word, and not hearers only. *James 1:22*

10. The grass withereth, the flower thereof falleth away: but the word of the Lord endureth for ever. And this is the word which by the gospel is preached unto you. *1 Peter 1:24,25*

WORK   (See also Performance; Vocation.)

1. Six days shalt thou labor, and do all thy work: but the seventh day . . . thou shalt not do any work. *Exod. 20:9,10*

2. In all labor there is profit. *Prov. 14:23*

3. Whatsoever thy hand findeth to do, do it with thy might. *Eccl. 9:10*

4. The laborer is worthy of his hire. *Luke 10:7*

5. I must work the works of him that sent me, while it is day: the night cometh, when no man can work. *John 9:4*

6. We are laborers together with God. *1 Cor. 3:9*

WORLD   See Creation; Earth; Environment.

WORLD, END OF   See Christ, Second Coming of; Resurrection of the Dead.

WORLDLINESS   (See also Commercialism; Covetousness; Greed; Luxury; Money; Wealth.)

1. I looked on all the works that my hands had wrought, and on the labor that I had labored to do: and, behold, all was vanity and vexation of spirit. *Eccl. 2:11*

2. Take no thought for your life, what ye shall eat, or what ye shall drink; nor yet for your body, what ye shall put on. Is not the life more than meat, and the body than raiment? . . . seek ye first the kingdom of God, and his righteousness; and all these things shall be added unto you. *Matt. 6:25,33*

3. The care of this world, and the deceitfulness of riches, choke the word, and he becometh unfruitful. *Matt. 13:22*

4. Take heed to yourselves, lest at any time your hearts be overcharged with surfeiting, and drunkenness, and cares of this life, and so that day come upon you unawares. *Luke 21:34*

5. Be not conformed to this world: but be ye transformed by the renewing of your mind. *Rom. 12:2*

6. They are the enemies . . . of Christ: Whose end is destruction, whose God is their belly, and . . . who mind earthly things. *Phil. 3:18,19*

7. Set your affection on things above, not on things on the earth. *Col. 3:2*

8. Whosoever therefore will be a friend of the world is the enemy of God. *James 4:4*

WORRY   (See also Trouble; Unrest.)

1. Fret not thyself because of evildoers. *Ps. 37:1*

2. Fret not thyself because of him who prospereth in his way. *Ps. 37:7*

3. They cried unto the Lord in their trouble, and he saved them out of their distresses. *Ps. 107:13*

4. It is in vain for you to rise up early, to sit up late, to eat the bread of sorrows: for so he giveth his beloved sleep. *Ps. 127:2*

5. Take no thought for your life, what ye shall eat, or what ye shall drink; nor yet for your body. *Matt. 6:25*

6. Take therefore no thought for the morrow: for the morrow shall take thought for the things of itself. *Matt. 6:34*

7. When they bring you unto the synagogues, and unto magistrates, and powers, take ye no thought how or what thing ye shall answer, or what ye shall say. *Luke 12:11*

8. Why are ye troubled? and why do thoughts arise in your hearts? *Luke 24:38*

9. Let not your heart be troubled: ye believe in God, believe also in me. *John 14:1*

10. Be careful for nothing; but in every thing by prayer and supplication with thanksgiving let your requests be made known unto God. And the peace of God, which passeth all understanding, shall keep your hearts and minds through Christ Jesus. *Phil. 4:6,7*

11. Casting all your care upon him; for he careth for you. *1 Peter 5:7*

WORSHIP   (See also Cults, Religious; Idolatry; Occult; Paganism; Praise; Prayer; Thanksgiving.)

1. Let my people go, that they may hold a feast unto me in the wilderness. *Exod. 5:1*

2. Give unto the Lord the glory due unto his name: bring an offering, and come before him: worship the Lord in the beauty of holiness. *1 Chron. 16:29*

3. Enter into his gates with thanksgiving, and into his courts with praise: be thankful unto him, and bless his name. *Ps. 100:4*

4. From one new moon to another, and from one sabbath to another, shall all flesh come to worship before me, saith the Lord. *Isa. 66:23*

5. Thou shalt no more worship the work of thine hands. *Mic. 5:13*

6. Thou shalt worship the Lord thy God, and him only shalt thou serve. *Luke 4:8*

7. True worshipers shall worship the Father in spirit and in truth: for the Father seeketh such to worship him. *John 4:23*

8. At the name of Jesus every knee should bow. *Phil. 2:10*

9. The four and twenty elders and the four beasts fell down and worshipped God that sat on the throne. *Rev. 19:4*

WORTHLESSNESS

1. Treasures of wickedness profit nothing. . . . the heart of the wicked is little worth. *Prov. 10:2,20*

2. They are all vanity; their works are nothing: their molten images are wind and confusion. *Isa. 41:29*

3. We have sinned. . . . we are all as an unclean thing, and all our righteousness are as filthy rags. *Isa. 64:5,6*

4. Every tree which bringeth not forth good fruit is hewn down, and cast into the fire. *Matt. 3:10*

5. Ye are the salt of the earth: but if the salt have lost his savor . . . it is thenceforth good for nothing, but to be cast out, and to be trodden under foot of men. *Matt. 5:13*

6. Though I bestow all my goods to feed the poor, and though I give my body to be burned, and have not charity, it profiteth me nothing. *1 Cor. 13:3*

WRATH   See Anger; God, Wrath of.

WRITING   (See also Book; Gospel; Reading; Scripture; Word.)

1. My tongue is the pen of a ready writer. *Ps. 45:1*

2. Have not I written to thee excellent things in counsels and knowledge, that I might make thee know the certainty of the words of truth? *Prov. 22:20,21*

3. The sin of Judah is written with a pen of iron, and with the point of a diamond. *Jer. 17:1*

4. He spread it [a roll of a book] before me; and it was written within and without: and there was written therein lamentations, and mourning, and woe. *Ezek. 2:10*

5. Write the vision, and make it plain upon tables, that he may run that readeth it. *Hab. 2:2*

6. Whatsoever things were written aforetime were written for our learning. *Rom. 15:4*

7. Ye are our epistle written in our hearts . . . written not with ink, but with the Spirit. *2 Cor. 3:2,3*

8. What thou seest, write in a book. *Rev. 1:11*

WRONGDOING   See Sin.

YEARNING   See Covetousness; Desire; Lust.
YIELDING   See Obedience; Surrender.
YOUTH   (See also Child; Immaturity.)

1. Remember not the sins of my youth. *Ps. 25:7*
2. Thy youth is renewed like the eagle's. *Ps. 103:5*
3. Thou hast the dew of thy youth. *Ps. 110:3*
4. As arrows are in the hand of a mighty man; so are children of the youth. Happy is the man that hath his quiver full of them. *Ps. 127:4,5*
5. The glory of young men is their strength. *Prov. 20:29*
6. Rejoice, O young man, in thy youth; and let thy heart cheer thee. . . . for childhood and youth are vanity. *Eccl. 11:9,10*
7. Even the youths shall faint and be weary, and the young men shall utterly fall. *Isa. 40:30*
8. It is good for a man that he bear the yoke in his youth. *Lam. 3:27*
9. Let no man despise thy youth. *1 Tim. 4:12*

ZEAL   (See also Determination; Willingness.)
1. The zeal of thine house hath eaten me up. *Ps. 69:9*
2. [He] was clad with zeal as a cloak. *Isa. 59:17*
3. His word was in mine heart as a burning fire shut up in my bones. *Jer. 20:9*
4. Ye shall search for me with all your heart. *Jer. 29:13*
5. Your zeal hath provoked very many. . . . and he which soweth bountifully shall reap also bountifully. *2 Cor. 9:2,6*
6. It is good to be zealously affected always in a good thing, and not only when I am present with you. *Gal. 4:18*
7. Whatsoever ye do, do it heartily, as to the Lord, and not unto men. *Col. 3:23*